THE RISE AND FALL
OF THE CRIMEAN SYSTEM
1855–71

THE RISE AND FALL
OF THE CRIMEAN SYSTEM
1855-71
The Story of a Peace Settlement

by

W. E. MOSSE, M.A., Ph.D.
SENIOR LECTURER IN HISTORY, UNIVERSITY OF GLASGOW

LONDON
MACMILLAN & CO LTD
NEW YORK · ST MARTIN'S PRESS
1963

MACMILLAN AND COMPANY LIMITED
St Martin's Street London WC 2
also Bombay Calcutta Madras Melbourne

THE MACMILLAN COMPANY OF CANADA LIMITED
Toronto

ST MARTIN'S PRESS INC
New York

PRINTED IN GREAT BRITAIN

... qu'on me dise le temps pendant lequel ces stipulations ont été rigoureuse-
ment observées. Au bout de quelques années les intérêts se déplacent, les
haines s'éteignent, les bons rapports s'établissent ... et les traités de cette
nature s'oublient et ne s'appliquent plus.

DUC DE MORNY, November 1855

Opinions may very much differ as to the wisdom and policy of imposing, even
after the most successful war, on a great Power like Russia conditions at once
humiliating to its dignity and very difficult to enforce in this case. ... It might
be foreseen that Russia would tolerate these conditions only so long as she was
obliged to do so and that she would seize the first opportunity to free herself
from them. The wonder is that Russia has for so long conscientiously kept
those conditions and has not, as she might easily have done, eluded them. Had
she been inclined to do so she might have built a whole fleet of ironclads and
monitors without anyone knowing much of it, or even if the thing had transpired, without risk that the Powers who signed the Treaty of 1856 would for
that undertake another war.

AUSTRIAN CORRESPONDENT OF The Times, November 1870

ACKNOWLEDGMENTS

The author wishes most gratefully to acknowledge the gracious permission of Her Majesty the Queen for access to the Royal Archives at Windsor.

He also wishes to acknowledge his indebtedness to the editors of the *English Historical Review,* the (*Cambridge*) *Historical Journal* and the *Slavonic and East European Review* for permission to reprint material first published in their respective journals.

W.E.M.

1963

CONTENTS

Introduction

The Crimean war and the settlement by which it was concluded formed the climax of Palmerston's later diplomacy. The war, in Palmerston's view, had been fought to stem the tide of Russian aggression. 'The main and real object of the war', he declared, was

> to curb the aggressive ambition of Russia. We went to war not so much to keep the Sultan and his Mussulmans in Turkey as to keep the Russians out of Turkey.[1]

The peace settlement, which followed the war, was intended to serve a similar purpose. Apart from material guarantees like the neutralization of the Black Sea and the removal of Russia from all contact with the navigable portion of the Danube and its tributaries, Palmerston sought to achieve his object above all by a policy of diplomatic 'containment'. It was his purpose to construct *'a long line of circumvallation* to confine the future extension of Russia . . . at any rate of her present circumference'. This would prevent conflict at a later date. By endeavouring 'to bar her up at all sides as well and as much as we can', he wrote, 'we are taking the best means of avoiding future collision.'[2]

The peace settlement, in Palmerston's view, had in a large measure achieved the objects of his policy. In the debate on the peace treaty, he dwelt with satisfaction on the emergence of a great defensive alliance directed against Russia. Austria, he declared, was now bound by ties of alliance with England and France. Sweden, 'long balancing between great fear on the one hand and trifling hopes on the other,' had, finally, associated herself with England, France, Austria, Prussia and Sardinia. These alliances were

> not the off-spring of a day, or the chance products of accident but the result of full deliberation and the tendency of great material and political interests.

[1] Memorandum by Palmerston enclosed in Clarendon to Cowley, private, 26 Sept. 1855, Cowley MSS in the P(ublic) R(ecord) O(ffice) in London.
[2] Ibid.

They were the more likely, therefore, to endure.[1] The Triple Treaty of 15 April 1856 moreover, by which England, France and Austria bound themselves to maintain the peace settlement, if necessary by force of arms, constituted 'a good additional Security and Bond of Union'.[2] In fact — although the terms finally imposed on Russia were not all he might have wished — Palmerston professed himself satisfied with what was, to a great extent, his handiwork. With cautious optimism, he described the recently concluded peace as

> an arrangement which effects a settlement that is satisfactory for the present, and which will probably last for many years to come, of questions full of danger to the best interests of Europe.[3]

In making this forecast, Palmerston was, of course, under no illusion as to the future direction of Russian policy. The Russians, he had told Clarendon, were clearly making peace only for the purpose of 'preparing at leisure the means of making war by and by'. Russia would be left 'a most formidable power'; in a few years' time, when she would by wise internal management have developed her immense natural resources, she would be ready once again 'to place in danger the great Interests of Europe'.[4] Moreover, Palmerston could not but see that during the peace negotiations Napoleon III, his principal ally, had shown a disconcerting lack of enthusiasm for the idea of a permanent anti-Russian coalition. Indeed it had become only too apparent that he was busily seeking a *rapprochement* with the enemy of yesterday in the interests of his Italian policy.

In fact, in the face of certain Russian 'revisionism' and of the doubtful attitude of his French ally, Palmerston himself seems presently to have developed doubts about the 'permanence' of his system. In 1871, fifteen years after the conclusion of peace, Lord Granville startled the House of Lords with some information on this point:

> General Ignatieff [he declared], told me that he remarked to Lord Palmerston — 'These are stipulations which you cannot

---

[1] Palmerston in the House of Commons, 6 May 1856, *Parl. Debates*, cxlii, c. 127.

[2] Palmerston to Clarendon, private, 1 Apr. 1856, Clarendon MSS (in the Bodleian Library, Oxford).

[3] Palmerston to the Queen, 30 Mar. 1856, *The Letters of Queen Victoria, 1837–1861*, ed. A. C. Benson and Viscount Esher (London, 1908) hereafter quoted as *QVL*, III, p. 183.

[4] Palmerston to Clarendon, private, 17 Mar. 1856, Clarendon MSS.

expect will last long,' and Lord Palmerston replied — 'They will last 10 years.' A learned civilian, a great friend of mine, told me he had heard Lord Palmerston talk on the same subject and say — 'Well, at all events they will last my life.' A noble peer ... an intimate friend of Lord Palmerston, says Lord Palmerston told him they would last seven years. Lord Palmerston certainly took occasion officially to represent to the Turkish government his opinion that within ten years from the Treaty, Russia would certainly be at war with them.[1]

Lord Russell confirmed that Palmerston 'thought the Treaty of 56 might last 7 years without war'.[2] Almost from the start, therefore, a doubt hung over the future of the Crimean system.

Moreover, the Crimean War was followed, after a few years, by a change in British opinion. During the war, Cobden and Bright had been unable to make headway against the tide of 'Palmerstonian' enthusiasm but by 1866 Clarendon, one of the architects of the Crimean system, noted that 'within the last year or two' the British public had greatly changed its mind on the subject of the Ottoman empire. 'Old Turkish proclivities' were 'rapidly evanescing'. Nor was this to be wondered at

as people know more about the united ignorance and stupidity of the Mahomedans who squat in some of the fairest regions of the world in order to prevent their being productive.[3]

Gladstone in his turn, observed four years later that

the whole policy of the Crimean War is now almost universally and very unduly depreciated, and the idea of another armed intervention on behalf of Turkey is ridiculed.[4]

Even the old Russophobia appeared to have died down. 'If a fortnight ago', the *Daily News* wrote in the autumn of 1870, England

could have been polled on the policy of the Crimean War, and a retrospective plebiscite taken, the statesmanship of that period would probably have been condemned. Wars for the preservation of the balance of power, for restricting the growth of a strong state and invigorating the infirmity of a weak one, are felt to be

[1] Granville in the House of Lords, 14 Feb. 1871, *Parl. Debates*, cciv, cc. 247 f.
[2] Russell to Granville, 22 Nov. 1870, P.R.O., G(ifts) and D(eposits) 29/79.
[3] Clarendon to Cowley, private, 24 Mar. 1866, F.O. 519/180.
[4] Gladstone to Hammond, 28 Oct. 1870, G.D. 59/58.

out of date. The anti-Russian feeling in England, dying away under the influence of new ideas of policy, was fast becoming an obsolete prejudice. . . .[1]

The position was dramatically reversed when, in 1870, the Russian government denounced the Black Sea clauses. At once, anti-Russian feeling in Britain revived 'in more than its wonted strength'.[2] The press, almost unanimously, called for an ultimatum to Russia. The virtues of the Crimean system in general and the Black Sea clauses in particular, were everywhere extolled. Both in the *Standard* and in the House of Commons, Disraeli made himself the spokesman of the new Palmerstonianism. He knew, he declared,

> that there were hon. Gentlemen on both sides of the House who think the Crimean War was a great mistake. I am not one of them. I think the Crimean War might have been prevented. . . . But when that war was declared I believe it was a just and necessary war. I believe there never was a war carried on for a nobler purpose or with purer intentions, nor one which the people generally of this country ever supported with more enthusiasm.

The terms of the settlement which followed had been criticized as inadequate, but he was not of that opinion.

> I think the Treaty was admirable, because it devised a plan for neutralizing the Black Sea, which absolutely, as far as human arrangements could control affairs, really prevented that part of the world again disturbing the general peace.[3]

Disraeli, in expressing these views, spoke for the majority of his countrymen, Whig and Tory alike. As during the Crimean War, the small band of liberals was swamped by the general flood. The Crimean policy and the Crimean system were rehabilitated almost overnight; and the neo-Palmerstonian view was strengthened still further by the Eastern crisis of 1877–8.

This also, however, was not the final verdict. The opposite view would again be vigorously expressed. Thus John Morley, in his life of Gladstone, castigated the Crimean policy:

> Three hundred thousand men had perished. Countless treasure had been flung into the abyss. The nation that had won its last

---

[1] *Daily News*, 18 Nov. 1870.
[2] Ibid.
[3] Disraeli in the House of Commons, 9 Feb. 1871, *Parl. Debates*, cciv, cc. 83 f.

victory at Waterloo did not now enhance the glory of its arms, nor the power of its diplomacy, nor the strength of any of its material interests.

Nor had the war helped Turkey.

The integrity of Turkey was so ill confirmed that even at the Congress of Paris the question of the Danubian Principalities was raised in a form that in a couple of years reduced Turkish rule over six million of her subjects to the shadow of smoke. Of the confidently promised reform of Mahometan dominion, there was never a beginning or a sign.

Instead, the Crimean War had been the prelude to general upheaval:

The vindication of the standing European order proved so ineffectual that the Crimean War was only the sanguinary prelude to a vast subversion of the whole system of European States.[1]

By the time Morley thus condemned the Crimean system, public opinion had undergone a further change. Gladstone had thundered against 'Bulgarian atrocities' and it had come to be widely accepted that in supporting Turkey against Russia, Britain had 'backed the wrong horse'. In 1907 Britain and Russia became allies; the Turks joined Britain's rival, Germany. Finally Britain accepted as a major allied war-aim the Russian 'take-over' of the Straits. Had British interests changed since Inkerman and Balaclava, or merely British policy? What had turned the 'unthinkable' into practical politics? Whatever the reasons, the British change of attitude re-opens, in retrospect, the question of Palmerstonian statesmanship and the merits of the Crimean system. Who it may be asked, showed the sounder judgment, Disraeli in his panegyrics of that system or Morley in his strictures?

The modern historian moreover — the heat of battle spent — may view the Crimean system from another aspect. That system, from its inception during the war to its final ignominious burial in 'the sepulchre of archives'[2] presents many features typical of other similar settlements; its fate was that of diplomatic arrangements imposed by a victorious coalition. Depending on

[1] John Morley, *The Life of William Ewart Gladstone* (London, 1903), I, p. 550.
[2] The expression is Lord Rosebery's.

the point of view, it could be seen as an arrangement designed to prevent a recurrence of aggression or as an attempt to perpetuate by diplomatic means an essentially temporary disturbance of the 'balance of power'. Its sanction rested on the continuation of the victorious coalition and on the 'good faith' both of the defeated power and of the victorious allies among themselves.

In fact, the Crimean 'settlement' like others of its kind gave rise to violent revisionism on the part of the defeated power. Whilst that power was still exhausted it was reduced to trying, as far as possible, to evade the provisions of the treaty. It could also explore the possibilities of separating its former opponents. Later, when both its internal and its international position had become stronger, it sought to attain its ends first by diplomatic negotiation and, finally, by means of unilateral action and the *fait accompli*. The chances of revisionism, at the same time, were improved by the progressive disintegration of the victorious coalition. The system lost much of its diplomatic (and, in the last resort, military) sanction and came to rest, essentially, on the faithful observance of treaty obligations. This proved a slender foundation. Successive *faits accomplis* were reluctantly sanctioned by the powers, the order created by the peacemakers being first modified and finally superseded. In all major features of this process, the Crimean system was typical of other similar settlements. Its detailed study, therefore, throws light on one of the recurring processes of history.

Moreover, the chequered career of the Crimean system raised more than once questions of the validity and interpretation of international engagements. Did the infraction of a general treaty in one particular invalidate the remainder? What was the nature of the obligations undertaken by a power towards its partners in a treaty of guarantee? Did treaties become obsolete and if so, in what manner and at what stage of their career? These were among the questions raised in the discussions about different aspects of the settlement. Some have an interest extending beyond the specific issues then under consideration.

Finally, the story of the Crimean system raises some general questions concerning the value and limitations of international engagements. What is the value of a unilaterally imposed peace settlement? Do treaties of guarantee serve any useful purpose? What, in general, is the relationship between original intent at the signing of a treaty and the policy or will of the given moment? Will any government, in fulfilment of treaty obligations, pursue a line of policy to which it is not otherwise inclined? Will a government in pursuance of obligations contracted years before, act in opposition to the 'national interest' of the moment? In short, is there such a thing as the much proclaimed 'faith of treaties'? Needless to say, a study of the Crimean system and its operation cannot, by itself, provide an answer to these questions. It can, however, by describing a concrete instance, give some indication of the lines along which the answer may be sought. By indicating some of the problems involved in the operation of treaties, it may help in formulating answers to the wider and more general questions.

Part I

THE BIRTH OF THE CRIMEAN SYSTEM

CHAPTER I

How Russia Made Peace[1]

Cette paix conclue aujourd'hui pourra n'être qu'une trêve, mais remise d'une année ou de deux elle trouverait le pays dans un état de faiblesse et d'épuisement tel, qu'il faudrait 50 années pour l'extraire et elle serait forcée d'observer strictement cette paix, par l'impossibilité où elle se trouverait de faire face à la guerre.

PETER VON MEYENDORFF, January 1856

Il y a sept ans, à cette table, j'ai fait un acte que je puis qualifier, puisque c'est moi qui l'ai accompli; j'ai signé le traité de Paris, et c'était une lâcheté.

ALEXANDER II, 1863

I

In 1854 — for the first time in her history — Russia had found herself confronted with that doubtful privilege of national greatness, a single-handed war against a European coalition. When Nicholas I, ignoring the prudent advice of his Minister of Foreign Affairs, had ordered his troops to re-occupy once more the Danubian Principalities, Turkey had resisted, Britain and France, after some hesitation, had come to her assistance and Austria had been converted from a close ally into a suspicious and unfriendly neutral.

The ensuing war, though fought by Russia's peasant soldiers with the heroic stoicism immortalized by Tolstoy, had yet proved unsuccessful. The administrative and military system of Nicholas I, for the apparent brilliance of which the Russian people had patiently endured the abuses pilloried by Gogol, had shown itself not only inefficient and corrupt but completely incapable of holding its own against the major nations of the West. By the end of 1854, the diplomatic edifice laboriously constructed by Nicholas had crumbled into dust; the bulk of his Black Sea squadron lay at the bottom of the sea while his soldiers slumbered in unknown graves on the battlefields of the Crimea. With the collapse of his diplomacy, the failure of his

---

[1] The bulk of this chapter first appeared as an article in the *Cambridge Historical Journal*, XI, no. 3 (1955).

armies and the breakdown of his administrative system, the
'Iron Autocrat' had lost the prestige which had made his name
terrible in Russia and in Europe. At least the educated classes in
Russia had come to curse a Tsar whose unpopular policies had
ended in abject failure. On 2 March 1855, Nicholas died of
what appeared a cold, was widely considered a 'broken heart'
and would soon be rumoured by many to be nothing less than
felo de se.

It was in these circumstances that the succession passed to
Alexander Nicolaevich, thirty-six years of age and prepared
with some care for the arduous task awaiting him. A proud man
of martial bearing, imbued with a high sense of Russia's greatness and of his own responsibility, he was unwilling to open his
reign with a national humiliation. Whilst he could hardly fail
to see that peace had become a necessity, he yet found it impossible to reconcile himself to the acceptance of 'dishonourable'
terms, such as were being canvassed by Russia's enemies. Yet
would he be able to obtain conditions which he could accept
without prejudicing the future of his empire and, perhaps, even
endangering the safety of his throne?

On the day after his father's death, Alexander assured the
members of the diplomatic corps that he would remain faithful
to the policy of the late Emperor:

> La parole de mon père m'est sacrée. . . . Comme lui, je veux la
> paix et voir se terminer les maux de la guerre; mais si les con-
> férences, qui vont s'ouvrir à Vienne n'aboutissent pas à un résultat
> honorable pour nous, alors je combattrai avec ma fidèle Russie et
> je périrai plutôt que de céder![1]

Esterhazy, the Austrian ambassador at St Petersburg, reported
that the general attitude of official Russia could be summed up
in the words 'peace on terms which are not humiliating for
Russia'. A cession of territory, the destruction of fortifications or
limitations of Russian sovereignty were considered unacceptable. It was felt that the acceptance of 'dishonourable' terms
might imperil the dynasty itself:

[1] Esterhazy to Buol, 3 Mar. 1855, cit. Vicomte de Guichen, *La Guerre de Crimée*
(1854–56) (Paris, 1936), p. 253. Guichen's system of references is defective. Cf.
also [*Diplomatic*] *Study* [*of the Crimean War*], a Russian official publication attributed
to Baron A. de Jomini of the Russian Foreign Office and reflecting the views of
Alexander Gorchakov (Engl. ed. London, 1882), II, p. 297, and S. S. Tatishchev,
Imperator Aleksandr II (St Petersburg, 1903), I, p. 144.

remué comme il l'est maintenant . . . le peuple russe . . . n'aura
guère de respect, ni d'obéissance pour un souverain qui céderait
par exemple une partie de son territoire sans y être contraint par
la force.[1]

It was in these circumstances that negotiations were opened
at Vienna on 15 March. Alexander Gorchakov, the Russian
envoy in the Austrian capital and his country's principal
spokesman at the conferences, announced that the Tsar would
consider any restriction on Russia's sovereignty in the Black
Sea as incompatible with her honour.[2] Since neither the British
nor the French government proved willing, in the last resort,
to renounce the demand for an effective limitation of Russia's
Black Sea forces, the negotiations ended in failure.[3]

The Tsar himself had laid down the limits of Russian concession. When Field-Marshal Paskievich, commander of the
Russian forces in Poland, had pleaded for a conciliatory
attitude, he replied that he had gone 'as far as was compatible
with the dignity of Russia'. Nothing would induce him to
sanction further concessions.[4] In any case, it appeared that the
allies did not desire the success of the Vienna conferences.
Austria and some of the German states would probably end
by joining Russia's enemies; Prussia might still be able to
preserve her neutrality.[5] The outcome of the siege of Sevastopol
would decide the course of the war; only a Russian victory in
the Crimea could prevent Austria from throwing in her lot with
the West.[6]

Attention therefore was focused on the defenders of Sevastopol. On the night of 23–24 May and again on 7 June, French
troops captured key positions in Totleben's great system of
fortifications.[7] Michael Gorchakov, who commanded the
Russian armies in the Crimea,[8] considered the situation desperate. 'I now think of only one thing,' he told the Tsar on 8

---

[1] Esterhazy to Buol, 15 Mar. 1855, cit. Guichen, op. cit., p. 255.
[2] Study, p. 303.
[3] For an account of the Vienna conferences cf. E. Heinrich Geffcken, Geschichte
des orientalischen Krieges 1853–1856 (Berlin, 1881), pp. 178 ff.
[4] Alexander II to Paskievich, 20 May 1855, cit. Tatishchev, op. cit., pp. 149 f.
'Na dalneischija ustupki.' Alexander declared emphatically, 'ja ni pod kakim
vidom nje soglaschus' (ibid.).
[5] The same to M. D. Gorchakov, 14 May 1855, ibid.
[6] Ibid., p. 151.
[7] Ibid., p. 153.
[8] He was a cousin of Alexander Gorchakov, the ambassador in Vienna.

June, 'how to abandon Sevastopol without losses which might rise to 20,000 men. We cannot even think of saving our ships or artillery.'[1] The Tsar would not hear of withdrawal. Sevastopol must not be voluntarily abandoned. Reinforcements would be sent, and until their arrival the fortress must hold out. Should it be overrun, the Crimean peninsula must be held at all cost.[2]

Contrary to expectation, the Russian position improved. Not only did the news from Vienna suggest that Austria might after all persist in her uneasy neutrality,[3] but on 18 June the defenders of Sevastopol beat off a determined assault.[4] This success encouraged the garrison and Gorchakov's hopes revived.[5] Three divisions of Russia's southern army joined the defenders; allied activity slackened. Austria, pressed by financial necessity, demobilized her reserves.[6]

Alexander now called for offensive action,[7] and Gorchakov, against his better judgment, and without any hope of success, obeyed. On 16 August he launched his unsuccessful attack on the Chernaya, in which the Russians suffered 8000 casualties.[8] The fate of Sevastopol seemed sealed. The Tsar, however, was undaunted. He declared that even were Sevastopol to be lost, he would consider its fall merely as the beginning of a new and decisive campaign.[9] Gorchakov, therefore, determined to hold out. If he could defend himself until the winter, the allies might raise the siege rather than face another assault of the Russian climate under the walls of the fortress.[10] The Tsar shared this opinion[11] and Nesselrode now set about trying to convince the cabinets of Europe that, contrary to widespread assertions, Russia had by

---

[1] M. D. Gorchakov to the Emperor, 8 Jun. 1855, ibid.
[2] Alexander II to M. D. Gorchakov, 16 Jun. 1855, ibid., pp. 153 f.
[3] The same to the same, 11 Jun. 1855, ibid., pp. 150 f.
[4] Ibid., p. 154.
[5] M. D. Gorchakov to the Tsar, 27 Jun. 1855, ibid. At the beginning of June he had told the Minister of War that the situation of Sevastopol was hopeless, ibid., p. 153.
[6] Ibid., p. 155.
[7] Alexander II to M. D. Gorchakov, 25 Jul. and 1 Aug. 1855, ibid., pp. 155 f.
[8] Ibid., p. 156.
[9] The same to the same, 23 Aug. 1855, ibid., p. 157. The Prince of Prussia, uncle of Alexander, visited St Petersburg towards the middle of August. On his return, he reported that the entire imperial family had shown a peaceful disposition — as had the aged Chancellor. The Tsar himself, who felt painfully the growing difficulties of the situation, 'nevertheless preserved his confidence in the outcome of the war and did not seem disposed to yield' (Guichen, op. cit., pp. 284 f.).
[10] M. D. Gorchakov to the Tsar, 26 Aug. 1855, printed in Tatishchev, op. cit., p. 158.
[11] Alexander II to M. D. Gorchakov, 2 Sept. 1855, ibid., pp. 158 f.

no means reached the end of her resources. It was England and France who were beginning to feel the strain.[1] Napoleon, perturbed by the stubborn defence of Sevastopol, was said to be ready to raise the siege and to doubt the possibility of success.[2] In fact, however, on 3 September, in a council of war held at Pélissier's headquarters, it was decided to open the bombardment of Sevastopol on the 5th and to launch a new assault on the 8th.[3] On the night of the 8th–9th the Russian forces evacuated the southern part of the city which they had defended with so much heroism and skill.

II

The news that Sevastopol had fallen, although a grievous blow to Russian pride,[4] did not greatly stir opinion at St Petersburg:

> Si l'on en juge par l'apparence, [Karnicki the Austrian chargé d'affaires reported] l'impression généralement ressentie ne serait pas aussi grande que l'on aurait dû s'y attendre après les efforts nourris, les sacrifices immenses, qui ont été faits pour la conservation de cette place et l'intérêt extraordinaire qui s'attachait à sa défense.[5]

The imperial manifesto announcing the loss to the people of Russia struck an almost defiant note.[6] On 13 September the Emperor moved to Moscow, the national capital.[7] 'Do not lose heart,' he wrote to M. D. Gorchakov, 'remember 1812 and trust in Providence. Sevastopol is not Moscow, the Crimea is not Russia. Two years after the burning of Moscow, our victorious armies stood in Paris. We are still the same Russians

---

[1] Buol to Karnicki, 4 Sept. 1855, draft, enclosing copy of Nesselrode to Gorchakov 10/22 Aug. 1855, H[aus] H[of und] S[taats] A[rchiv Vienna], P[ol]. A[rch]. R[ussland], x, fasc. 38, H[enderson] T[ranscripts] in the University Library, Cambridge.

[2] *Histoire de la Diplomatie*, ed. V. Potiemkine (Paris, s.d.), I, p. 449. There is no evidence to support the statement and no references are given.

[3] Geffcken, op. cit., p. 193.

[4] Ibid., p. 160.

[5] Karnicki to Buol, 22/10 Sept. 1855, no. 59, A-C, H.H.S.A., P.A.R., x, fasc. 37, H. T. Guichen, op. cit., p. 288, wrongly attributes this despatch to Esterhazy. Karnicki considered that public opinion had discounted in advance a blow which had been expected for some time. Pride, moreover, would restrain people from showing any dejection they might feel, and the Russian character, in any case, contained a large element of *insouciance* (ibid.).

[6] Tatishchev, op. cit., pp. 160 f.

[7] Ibid., p. 161.

and God is with us.'[1] To Gorchakov he despatched the holy
icon of St Sergei, which had accompanied the second Romanov
on all his campaigns, which had been with Peter at Poltava and
which had gone out with the Moscow militia in 1812. It was
to be kept at Crimean headquarters to be used in services at the
front. 'May the prayers of St Sergei help us,' wrote the Emperor, 'just as his blessing gave us the victory in Dmitri Donskoi's
day.'[2]

Having made these preparations for a holy war, the Tsar
called a military council to attend to the problem of strategy.
The main decision reached was to defend the Crimea at all
cost.[3] Alexander wrote to Paskievich that it was necessary
to prepare for a prolonged campaign in 1856. In spite of the
reassuring news from Vienna about the reduction of her forces,
Austria would, especially now that Sevastopol had fallen,
sooner or later join the ranks of Russia's enemies. It was better
to be prepared for the worst rather than be caught unawares.[4]
On 20 September, the Tsar left for a visit to his armies in the
south.[5]

In face of his master's determination Nesselrode, the Foreign
Minister, who secretly longed for peace, could only tell foreign
diplomats that Russia would listen to any propositions which
might be made to her:

> Quant à nous [he told Esterhazy], ce n'est pas à nous de for-
> muler maintenant des propositions quelconques; nous ne pouvons
> qu'attendre et voir venir celles qui pourront nous être faites et qui
> nous trouveront toujours prêts à les accueillir favorablement en
> tant qu'elles seront compatibles avec notre honneur.[6]

In fact, during the weeks which followed the departure of the
Tsar, diplomatic activity at St Petersburg was almost at a
standstill.[7] In the military sphere also, the fall of Sevastopol was

---

[1] Alexander II to M. D. Gorchakov, 14 Sept. 1855, ibid. Cf. the same to
Paskievich, 17 Sept. 1855, ibid., pp. 161 f.
[2] Ibid., p. 163.
[3] Ibid., pp. 163 f.
[4] Alexander II to Paskievich, 17 Sept. 1855, ibid., p. 164.
[5] Ibid., p. 165.
[6] Karnicki to Buol, 22/10 Sept. 1855, H.H.S.A., P.A.R., x, fasc. 37, H.T.
[7] At the end of October the Austrian chargé d'affaires reported to Buol 'qu'il
n'y a absolument rien de changé dans la situation. . . . Toujours la même stagnation
sur le terrain diplomatique et grande activité sur les champs de bataille' (Karnicki
to Buol, 23/11 Oct. 1855, no. 65, A–B., H.H.S.A., P.A.R., x, fasc. 37, H.T.).

followed by a period of inactivity and, before long, it became clear that the campaign of 1855 was over.[1]

If the capture of Sevastopol by the allies had little effect on the Tsar's determination, it had important repercussions in Paris. Once the great arsenal had fallen, French craving for glory was satisfied and there was little further advantage to be gained from a continuation of hostilities. War-weariness was spreading and Napoleon began to feel that unless he could offer his subjects some popular cause to revive their flagging enthusiasm, the time had come to make peace. The restoration of an autonomous Poland appeared to be an object which would justify a continuation of the war. A week after the fall of Sevastopol, therefore, Walewski, the French Foreign Minister, informed the British government that, in his master's opinion, the time had now come

> de se préparer à faire du rétablissement du royaume de Pologne, dans les conditions stipulées par le congrès de Vienne, un des objets essentiels des négociations de paix, aussitôt qu'elles deviendront possibles, en même temps qu'une des bases fondamentales de cette paix.[2]

Palmerston, however, doubted the wisdom and desirability of the proposed engagement.[3] On 22 September, therefore, Clarendon, the Foreign Secretary, informed the French government that in his opinion the two governments might agree on the principle of a restored Poland and thereafter await developments.[4] Faced with this reply, Napoleon now felt that there was little justification for continuing the war.

The Austrian government also had reached the conclusion

---

[1] After the capture of Sevastopol, Pélissier showed no eagerness to attack. 'J'attaquerai, *si vous l'ordonnez*', he replied to remonstrances from Paris, and neither Napoleon nor his Minister of War was willing to order an attack in these conditions (F. Charles-Roux, *Alexandre II, Gortchakoff et Napoléon III* (Paris, 1913), p. 39). Cowley, the British ambassador in Paris, reported that Pélissier had declared that 'to attack the Russian position on Mackenzie Heights is more difficult than to take Sevastopol' (Cowley to Clarendon, private, 17 Oct. 1855, Clarendon MSS.)

[2] Cit. Geffcken, op. cit., p. 196. For a detailed account of Napoleon's various plans for Poland cf. G. B. Henderson, *Crimean War Diplomacy* (Glasgow, 1947), pp. 15 ff. 'Napoleon zeigte die grösste Beharrlichkeit in Bezug auf Polen, und es verging während des Krieges kaum ein Monat, in dem er sich nicht über diesen Gegenstand aussprach' (ibid., p. 23).

[3] Palmerston to Clarendon, private, 16 Sept. 1855, Clarendon MSS.

[4] Guichen, op. cit., p. 294. Cf. Persigny's despatch of 18 Sept. in A. Stern, *Geschichte Europas* (Berlin, 1920), II, p. 555.

that the moment had come for a further attempt to end hostilities. In August, Buol, the Foreign Minister, had told a diplomat that once a decision had been reached in the Crimea, efforts for peace must be renewed to avoid the outbreak of general hostilities in the spring.[1] After the fall of Sevastopol, he had explained to Bourqueney, the French minister in Vienna, the terms of peace which he now considered reasonable and was willing to recommend at St Petersburg.[2] Napoleon was delighted at this Austrian initiative, and on 17 October, 'after due deliberation, the emperor and his Council . . . agreed that the Buol-Bourqueney affair ought to be followed up'.[3] Bourqueney, who had come to Paris was told, after his return to Vienna, to resume conversations with Buol.

Direct contact, at the same time, was being established between St Petersburg and Paris. The Russian government did, indeed, decline the proffered mediation of the Saxon minister Beust[4] but when Seebach, Nesselrode's son-in-law, who looked after Russia's interests in Paris,[5] reported that he had been approached confidentially by Walewski, the Chancellor saw no obstacle to a direct exchange of views.[6] Walewski, Seebach reported, was 'personally well-inclined', but Napoleon was 'dominated by his fear of England' and determined to maintain his alliance with that country. Russia, Walewski had said, must now make practical and precise proposals which took into account the situation created by the fall of Sevastopol. These proposals must be such as to enable the French government to overcome British reluctance to the re-opening of negotiations; they must include either the limitation of Russian naval forces in the Black Sea by Russo-Turkish agreement or the neutralization of that sea. Should the Russian government be willing to settle with France on this basis, it must do so without delay to forestall Austrian intervention.[7]

In fact there was little time to lose, for on 14 November Buol and Bourqueney had initialled in Vienna a memorandum em-

---

[1] Stockhausen to Lenthe, 13 Sept. 1855, no.70, Staatsarchiv Hannover 9, Türkei no. 27, H.T.

[2] Elliott to Clarendon, 3 Oct. 1855, F.O. 7/458 unnumbered.

[3] Cowley to Clarendon, private, 13 Oct. 1855, Clarendon MSS.

[4] Tatishchev, op. cit., p. 177.

[5] He was the Saxon minister in Paris.

[6] Nesselrode to Beust, 22 Nov. 1855, ibid.

[7] *Study*, pp. 343 ff.

bodying the terms which, on behalf of England and France, the Austrian government would present at St Petersburg. Russia was to accept the neutralization of the Black Sea; a Russo-Turkish convention, to be annexed to the treaty of peace, would lay down the number of light vessels the two powers might retain in the Black Sea. Furthermore, the Austrian government had 'developed' the stipulation dealing with the Danubian Principalities to include a rectification of frontiers designed to cut off Russia from contact with the navigable portions of the Danube. To the four points already accepted by the Russian government as a basis of negotiation[1] had been added a fifth reserving the right of the belligerents to put forward at a future conference further conditions 'dans un intérêt européen'. Austria was to present these terms at St Petersburg, and in case of their rejection, to break off diplomatic relations.[2] The British government, which had merely been informed of the progress of the Austro-French conversations, was offended at the manner in which agreement had been reached, dissatisfied with the terms proposed, and determined to secure alterations. Discussions were therefore opened between Paris and London to overcome British objections. Not until 5 December was agreement reached on the amendments to be transmitted to Vienna.

Nesselrode, meanwhile, had received Walewski's offer to open direct negotiations. He knew that an ultimatum was being prepared in Vienna and that there was little time to lose.[3] He longed for peace,[4] but the Tsar, in spite of a pressing letter from the King of Prussia,[5] was still in a warlike mood:

> He had become impregnated with the sentiment of our military honour during his sojourn in the midst of his armies. He was little disposed to make terms with our adversaries at the moment when they were about to experience for the first time the real difficulties of war. The recollections of 1812 electrified our patriotic enthusiasm.[6]

---

[1] For their history cf. Henderson, op. cit., pp. 98 ff.

[2] Memorandum signed by Count Buol and M. de Bourqueney. Copy in Clarendon to the Queen, 19 Nov. 1855, R[oyal] A[rchives], G 40/81.

[3] Werther to Manteuffel, telegram, 26 Nov. 1855, P[reussisches] G[eheimes] S[taats] A[rchiv], A[usw.] A[mt] I A Bq. Türkei 44, vol. 29, H.T.

[4] Cf. Guichen, op. cit., p. 285.

[5] Ibid., p. 298.

[6] Study, p. 347.

The very desire for peace shown by Napoleon and his entour-age[1] seemed to prove that the chances of war were not ex-hausted.[2] It appeared, moreover, to be indicative of internal difficulties in France. In a highly significant letter to M. D. Gorchakov, Alexander declared that he saw no hope of an early end to hostilities. Peace would come about only through the outbreak of disorder in France caused by a bad harvest and by the growing discontent of the lower classes:

> Former revolutions always began in this way and it may well be that a general revolution is not far off. This I regard as the most probable conclusion to the present war; neither from Napoleon nor from England do I expect a sincere desire for peace on terms compatible with our views and as long as I live, I will accept no others.[3]

The Tsar, therefore, continued to occupy himself with mili-tary preparations. He helped to draw up a plan of campaign for 1856, more particularly, gave orders for defensive prepara-tions at Nicolaev.[4] M. D. Gorchakov was urged to adopt aggres-sive measures.[5] Finally, after a visit to the Crimea itself, the Tsar returned to his capital imbued with the martial senti-ments of his military entourage.[6] Seebach was informed that Russia rejected any limitation of her naval forces. She would, however, agree to an arrangement under which all flags of war

---

[1] Whilst Nesselrode had been negotiating with Paris through Seebach, Gor-chakov had started a private correspondence with Morny, one of Napoleon's inti-mates. The early part of the correspondence has been lost, the rest is printed in [*Extrait des Mémoires du Duc de*] *Morny* [*Une Ambassade en Russie*] (Paris, 1892), pp. 7 ff. The official Russian publication claims that the initiative came from the French side (*Study*, p. 345). The correspondence was at first general in terms; not till the end of November did serious discussion begin about the most suitable method for implementing the third point (*Morny*, op. cit., pp. 26 ff.).

Morny offered to meet Gorchakov in Dresden, but the correspondence had only just become serious when it was terminated on orders from St Petersburg. In view of the concurrent negotiations between Nesselrode and Walewski conducted through Seebach, the episode of the Gorchakov-Morny correspondence is in itself of small importance. It bulks large in the histories of the period on account of Gorchakov's later prominence as Foreign Minister. Gorchakov himself was to see to it that his exchanges with Morny received the fullest publicity (*Study*, pp. 345 f.). The correspondence between Nesselrode and Seebach, on the other hand, has never been published.

[2] Alexander II to M. D. Gorchakov, 24 Oct. 1855, Tatishchev, op. cit., pp. 174 f.

[3] Ibid.

[4] Tatishchev, op. cit., p. 186.

[5] Alexander II to M. D. Gorchakov, 18 Oct. 1855, printed ibid., p. 167.

[6] *Study*, p. 347; Karnicki to Buol, telegram, 1 Dec. 1855, H.H.S.A., P.A.R., x, fasc. 38, H.T.

would be excluded from the Black Sea except for such vessels as the two riverain powers might wish to maintain there. Their number would be determined by direct negotiation between Russia and the Porte.[1] This suggestion was to be communicated to Vienna as well as Paris, to forestall unacceptable Austrian proposals.[2] Finally, Gorchakov was instructed to curtail his private correspondence with Morny lest it give Napoleon an exaggerated idea of Russia's need for peace.[3]

Gorchakov made his communication on 6 December; Buol replied that he would bring the proposal to the attention of the allies.[4] Walewski in reply to the Russian overture also said that he would inform his allies.[5] Some days later he added that as Austria was about to submit proposals to Russia, which had been concerted with the governments of England and France, he was unable to continue direct negotiations.[6] In Paris, as in Vienna, the Russian initiative had come several weeks too late.

Events, meanwhile, had moved rapidly in the Western camp. On 5 December, England and France had reached agreement on the amendments to be proposed in Vienna. Ten days later, these were accepted by Austria.[7] On 16 December, Esterhazy left for St Petersburg with the terms agreed on by the three powers. At the same time Seebach, about to visit St Petersburg, was received by Napoleon. The Emperor declared that Russia must be mad if she did not now make peace: in 1856, allied superiority would be overwhelming. If the present proposals were rejected there would be no further approaches. The Russian cabinet must bear in mind that British ministers had to consider Parliament and public opinion. They might have heard rumours of Anglo-French dissensions, but these were of small importance; the ultimatum was his as well as England's and hopes of separating him from his ally were vain. Peace could be obtained only by unconditional acceptance.[8]

---

[1] *Study*, p. 350.
[2] Ibid., p. 351.
[3] Ibid., p. 347.
[4] Geffcken, op. cit., p. 205.
[5] Hatzfeldt to Manteuffel, private, 20 Dec. 1855, P.G.S.A., A.A., I A Bq. Türkei 44, vol. 29, H.T.
[6] Ibid.
[7] Geffcken, op. cit., p. 200. For the amendments proposed by the British government cf. ibid., pp. 201 ff.
[8] Hatzfeldt to Manteuffel, private 20 Dec. 1885, P.G.S.A., A.A., I A Bq. Türkei 44, vol. 29, H.T.; Geffcken, op. cit. p. 206.

III

Whilst awaiting the Austrian ultimatum, the Tsar and Nesselrode learnt from a German source[1] that on 21 November Sweden had signed an agreement with the Western powers, and shortly afterwards the Swedish minister at St Petersburg officially communicated its contents. Sweden undertook not to cede any of her territory to Russia or to permit its occupation by Russian troops. Any demands of this nature she would communicate at once to the cabinets of London and Paris, who would support her in resisting them.[2] The news of this agreement, which came as a complete surprise, created a strong impression in St Petersburg.[3] The treaty which seemed purely defensive, was suspected of containing secret clauses of an aggressive nature.[4] Its psychological effect was considerable. 'It was a precedent of extreme importance in existing circumstances. It shook the position, already tottering, of the neutral states, and gave a moral support of much value to our adversaries, at a moment when the war, by being prolonged, threatened to assume a general character.'[5]

A worse shock was to follow. The King of Prussia, Russia's last remaining friend, addressed to his nephew a pressing appeal to make peace:

> Je frémis, mon bon et cher Alexandre, [he wrote] en me pénétrant de la responsabilité qui pèse sur nous deux; sur moi, si je ne réussissais pas de donner à une lettre que je vous adresse à l'occasion des propositions qui me sont étrangères, l'accent de la persuasion que la situation réclame; sur vous, cher et bon Alexandre, si vous fermez les yeux sur les dangers, qui se préparent contre la stabilité de tout Gouvernement légitime en Europe.[6]

Refusal to make peace now would produce the gravest consequences:

---

[1] *Study*, p. 336.

[2] For the text of the treaty see Guichen, op. cit., p. 346.

[3] Esterhazy to Buol, 29 Dec. 1855, ibid., pp. 312 f.

[4] In fact, the treaty was accompanied by an exchange of notes establishing the conditions in which it was to be converted into an offensive alliance against Russia. A joint plan of campaign was already under discussion between Marshal Canrobert and the Crown Prince of Sweden (Stern, op. cit., p. 124; A. Debidour, *Histoire diplomatique de l'Europe* (Paris, 1891), II, p. 142).

[5] *Study*, p. 338.

[6] Printed without date in Geffcken, op. cit., pp. 208 f.

...je... vous supplie, mon cher neveu, d'aller aussi loin que possible dans vos concessions, en pesant mûrement les conséquences qui pourraient se rattacher pour les véritables intérêts de la Russie, de la Prusse elle-même, et de l'Europe entière à une prolongation indéfinie de cette horrible guerre. Les passions subversives une fois déchaînées, qui pourrait calculer les suites d'un débordement universel?[1]

Prussia, it now appeared, might be forced to join the enemies of Russia.

The threatening storm found Alexander still determined to reject conditions which he considered dishonourable. On 23 December he told M. D. Gorchakov that he expected to receive from Vienna new terms which had been concerted between the Austrian cabinet and Russia's enemies. He did not yet know what these would be, but information from different sources indicated that nothing good could be expected. Their rejection would lead to a rupture of diplomatic relations with Austria. This might in the end produce a final break, although Austria's continued reduction of her forces did not suggest that she was preparing for war. The conclusion was inescapable that by the spring Russia's condition would be critical. They must prepare for the worst, but now, as always, he put his trust in the Almighty. His conscience was clear: everything possible had been done to indicate Russia's readiness to enter further negotiations:

We have reached the utmost limit [the Tsar dramatically declared] of what is possible and compatible with Russia's honour. I will never accept humiliating terms and am certain that every true Russian shares my feelings. It only remains for us — crossing ourselves — to march straight ahead and by our united efforts to defend our native land and our national honour.[2]

The Tsar in fact, was preparing to lead his people in a war *à outrance* against the foreign invader.

Two days later Alexander learnt, unofficially, the terms of the Austrian ultimatum.[3] On 28 December, Esterhazy made his official communication. In doing this, he drew Nesselrode's attention to the many previous opportunities for making peace

[1] Ibid.
[2] Alexander II to M. D. Gorchakov, 23 Dec. 1855 (Tatishchev, op. cit., p. 179).
[3] Geffcken, op. cit., p. 208.

which Russia had missed, adding that the note he was about to submit was the result of 'a supreme effort'. The Four Points[1] still remained the basis of his proposals but they had now been 'developed' to facilitate final agreement. The terms must be accepted unconditionally. He had not come to St Petersburg 'en *négociateur*, mais simplement comme *porteur* d'un travail du Cabinet de Vienne'. Any counter-proposals would make agreement impossible.[2] Werther, the Prussian Minister, had received instructions to second Esterhazy's efforts[3] and undertook to do so to the best of his ability.[4] On 30 December Seebach arrived with a message from Napoleon urging acceptance of the Austrian terms. During several conversations with the Tsar he pleaded the cause of peace. He added, however, that he had found Walewski somewhat less emphatic than the Emperor about the need for unconditional acceptance.[5]

It was in these circumstances that the Tsar decided to consult his late father's most trusted advisers. The Council met at 8 p.m. on Monday, 1 Jan. 1856, in his private study in the Winter Palace. After reading aloud the text of the Austrian communication, Alexander invited the councillors to express their opinion. The most important speech was made by Kiselev, Minister of State Domains, who drew attention to the difficulties facing Russia. Never before in her history had her fleet been destroyed by two great naval powers; her resources were inferior to those of her adversaries; she had no prospect of finding allies and lacked the means for an effective continuation of the war. The neutral powers were inclining to the side of her enemies; it would be imprudent to run the risks of another campaign which would raise the demands of the allies and make peace more difficult to obtain. Moreover, whilst the great mass of the Russian people was penetrated with a profound sense of its duty, there were elements which might begin to waver. Russia must not place herself in a position where she might have to accept conditions which it was still possible to

---

[1] For the Four Points see A. J. P. Taylor, *The Struggle for Mastery in Europe, 1848–1918*. (Oxford 1954), pp. 654 ff.

[2] Esterhazy to Buol, 29 Dec. 1855, no. 76 (Guichen, op. cit., pp. 311 ff.).

[3] Ibid., and the same to the same, telegram, 30 Dec. 1855, H.H.S.A., P.A.R., x, fasc. 37, H.T.

[4] Guichen, op. cit., p. 313, n. 40.

[5] Esterhazy to Buol, telegram, 30 Dec. 1855, H.H.S.A., P.A.R., x, fasc. 37, H.T., and the same to the same, 12 Jan. 1856, no. 2 D, ibid., fasc. 39, H.T.

avert. The shortage of arms and supplies would become increasingly grave. In these circumstances they should, without rejecting the Austrian terms, propose amendments based on the principle of Russia's territorial integrity and on a juster method for neutralizing the Black Sea. If the allies desired peace, they would accept amendments, if not, then God's Will be done.

Adjutant-General Orlov supported Kiselev's proposal; his colleague Vorontsov went further and declared that even were the allies to reject the Russian amendments, it would still be necessary to accept their terms rather than face the hazards of a further campaign. Constantine Nicolaevich, the Tsar's younger brother, asked what would happen in 1857 even if it proved possible to fight another campaign in 1856. Dolgorukov, the Minister of War, favoured peace if it could be obtained with decency.

Nesselrode then read a draft despatch to Gorchakov accepting the Austrian proposals but rejecting the cession of territory and the fifth point (additional conditions in a European interest) and introducing some minor alterations in the words of the text.[1] The Tsar afterwards told M. D. Gorchakov that unconditional acceptance was impossible: the counter-propositions reached the extreme limit of concession.[2] On 5 January a despatch embodying the Russian reply was sent to Vienna.[3] Two days later Seebach left for Paris to persuade the French government to accept Russia's modifications.[4]

IV

Nesselrode dreaded the prospect of Austria joining Russia's enemies. He feared that even a simple diplomatic rupture might have fatal consequences ('des conséquences funestes') and had urged Alexander Gorchakov to spare no pains to keep up at least a semblance of peaceful relations.[5] When an anxious inquiry addressed to Esterhazy about Austria's

[1] A. P. Sablotski-Desjatovski, *Graf P. D. Kiselev* (St Petersburg, 1883), pp. 3 ff.; Tatishchev, op. cit., pp. 182 ff. For the Russian amendments cf. Geffcken, op. cit., pp. 211 f.

[2] Alexander II to M. D. Gorchakov, 6 Jan. 1856, Tatishchev, op. cit., p. 184.

[3] Esterhazy to Buol. Telegram, 7 Jan. 1856, H.H.S.A., P.A.R., x, fasc. 39, H.T.

[4] The same to the same, telegram, 7 Jan. 1856 and no. 2 D, 12 Jan. 1855, ibid.

[5] Nesselrode to Gorchakov, 11/23 Dec. 1855, no. 479 réservée, quoted in Gorchakov to Nesselrode, 22 Dec./3 Jan. 1855/6 W[ürtembergisches] S[taats] A[rchiv] (Stuttgart), cccxiv, no. 49.

C

readiness to accept modifications produced a negative reply,[1] Nesselrode tried to convince the Tsar of the need for unconditional acceptance.[2] Orlov and Kiselev seconded his efforts.[3] They had however, to contend with contrary influences in the Tsar's entourage.[4]

On 7 January Nesselrode informed Esterhazy that the Russian reply had been despatched and was of a conciliatory nature. The Austrian envoy then read a communication from Buol stating that any counter-proposal or reservation would be considered a refusal and would be followed by a rupture of diplomatic relations.[5]

On 11 January, Buol received the Russian reply. The following day he informed Gorchakov that since it did not contain an acceptance, relations would be severed on the 18th.[6] In communicating this news to Esterhazy, Buol instructed the ambassador to read to Nesselrode sections of a secret despatch[7] designed to dispel Russian apprehensions about the fifth point. As regards the rectification of the frontier, the Russian government must understand that Austria would be supported by her allies.[8]

Gorchakov had different ideas. He was convinced that Napoleon was already casting his eyes on Italy, was irritated against Austria and desired a reconciliation with Russia. He would eagerly seize an opportunity of negotiating over the head of the Austrian government.[9] Gorchakov therefore urged Nesselrode 'to reject the ultimatum of Austria and to address Napoleon in a direct manner with propositions which would satisfy France, but would exclude from the programme the clause added by Count Buol as to the territorial concession in Bessarabia, which was purely an Austrian interest.'[10]

---

[1] Esterhazy to Buol, telegram, 3 Jan. 1856, ibid.
[2] The same to the same, 12 Jan. 1856, no. 2 A-G, ibid.
[3] The same to the same, 20 Jan. 1856, no. 7 A-F, ibid.
[4] The same to the same, 12 Jan. 1856, no. 2 A-G, ibid.   [5] Ibid.
[6] Buol to Esterhazy, telegram, 12 Jan. 1856, ibid.
[7] This despatch is the same to the same, 16 Dec. 1855, ibid., fasc. 38, no. 2, confidential.
[8] The same to the same, telegram, 12 Jan. 1856, ibid., fasc. 39.
[9] *Study*, p. 360.
[10] Ibid. Some mystery surrounds the form of Gorchakov's advice; the *Study* asserts that it was telegraphed; Geffcken, op. cit., p. 215, maintains that Gorchakov sent a telegram asking Nesselrode to await the arrival of a despatch due on 17 Jan. before making a decision. It is impossible to establish which is the correct account. It is therefore uncertain whether, before the decisive Council of 15 Jan., Nesselrode had before him Gorchakov's actual proposals or merely a telegram asking him

On 11 January the Russian counter-proposals were received in Paris. Walewski's language was firm. He expected to secure the support of the German Confederation for the Austrian ultimatum and hoped that this would induce the Tsar to yield.[1] Napoleon, however, informed Queen Victoria that he would prefer to continue the negotiations rather than make new sacrifices for a purely Austrian interest and a question which did not strengthen Turkey. French opinion would reproach him for wasting blood and treasure 'pour obtenir quelques landes de la Bessarabie!!!'.[2] The Queen replied that they should at least await the rupture of Austro-Russian relations before continuing the negotiations.[3] Had the Tsar but known it, the adoption of Gorchakov's advice would probably have strengthened his hand.

On 12 January Nesselrode had communicated to Esterhazy the terms of the Russian reply. The ambassador then told him that unless there was an unconditional acceptance, relations would be broken off six days later.[4] The following day a telegram reporting Buol's observations to Gorchakov dispelled the last illusions.[5] The Tsar still hesitated, but Nesselrode was determined on peace.[6] On 15 January the King of Prussia telegraphed to Werther that Prussia supported the Austrian proposals. He should urge their acceptance to avoid the risk of a diplomatic rupture between the two countries.[7]

That day the Tsar once again assembled his advisers in the Winter Palace. To those present at the previous meeting was added Meyendorff, the most experienced diplomat of the previous reign. The Tsar explained (in French) that the situation must now be reconsidered, bearing in mind that unless the ultimatum was accepted, Esterhazy would leave on the 18th.

to await their arrival. Geffcken summarizes the telegram, Jomini the despatch, but since both use a defective system of references, it is impossible to establish the truth. The point is of some importance, since Gorchakov and his partisans later blamed Nesselrode for not having submitted the despatch to the Council and even accused him of having concealed it from the Tsar (*Study*, p. 360).

[1] Lüttichau to Beust, III, 13 Jan. 1856, Sächsisches, Haupt Staats Archiv, Ausw. Min. Repos. 29, no. 9, Paris 1856, H.T.

[2] Napoleon to Victoria, 14 Jan. 1856, *QVL.*, III, pp. 162 f.

[3] Victoria to Napoleon, 15 Jan. 1856, ibid., p. 164.

[4] Esterhazy to Buol, 12 Jan. 1856, no. 4, H.H.S.A., P.A.R., x, fasc. 39, H.T.

[5] The same to the same, 29 Jan. 1856, no. 7 A-F, ibid.

[6] The same to the same, 12 Jan. 1856, no. 2 E, ibid.

[7] Guichen, op. cit., p. 351. It is not possible to establish whether this communication was made to Nesselrode before or after the Council of 15 Jan. 1856.

Nesselrode then read a memorandum prepared by his Ministry. Russia's resistance, it claimed, remained unbroken, her resources were not exhausted. The struggle could be continued, but experience had shown the disadvantages of a defensive war waged on a wide front flanked by two seas, the control of which gave Russia's adversaries an incontestable preponderance. A victory, moreover, would offer only a temporary respite; a defeat might affect Russia's vital interests.

The situation was aggravated by the threatened rupture with Austria. An allied council in Paris had decided that in the coming campaign the bulk of the French forces would operate on the Danube and in Bessarabia. Hostilities would be carried to the vicinity of the Austrian border, and, certain of being supported, Austria might yet join the fighting. Her attitude would affect that of the remaining neutrals, already shaken by Sweden's treaty with the allies. The King of Prussia might be unable to resist the pressure to which he would be subjected. The number of Russia's adversaries, therefore, was likely to increase; she might in the end find herself opposed to the whole of Europe. The allies, moreover, might establish an effective blockade of Russia through their control of the Baltic and Black Seas supplemented by agreements with Austria and the Scandinavian states and, perhaps, those of Germany as well. Such a blockade would strangle Russia and prejudice her political and economic future.

In the long run, therefore, Russia's position would become untenable; sooner or later she must accept terms of peace. The British attitude left no doubt about the fact that these terms would become increasingly severe. If the present proposals were accepted, Russia would confound the plans of her enemies; after the conclusion of peace she would be able to dissolve a coalition composed of antagonistic elements. France was sympathetic to Russia; Napoleon had more than exhausted the advantages to be derived from the war and felt the need to make peace. Russian diplomacy must assist his efforts to emancipate himself from the British alliance. If the present terms were refused, Napoleon would be driven once again into the arms of England; if they were accepted, his *amour propre* would be flattered and he would become the arbiter of the coming peace. France and Russia would then be able to give a new direction to their policies.

The terms proposed by Austria were painful, but Russia had resigned herself to most of them months ago. Many details were left to be determined in conference and Russia might find support. Should the negotiations end in failure, Russia would have given Europe proof of her pacific sentiments. She would have thrown upon the allies the responsibility for continuing the war and would have given the neutral states an excuse for keeping out of it. For all these reasons the Austrian terms should be accepted at once and without reservation.[1]

Vorontsov, who spoke next, declared in a voice charged with emotion that, however painful the terms, nothing could be gained by a continuance of the present unequal struggle. Resistance would lead to a more humiliating peace: the Crimea, the Caucasus, even Finland and Poland might in the end be endangered. Since the struggle must end at some point, peace should be concluded whilst resistance still remained possible.

Orlov added that though the terms under discussion would be criticized by the ignorant and the ill-intentioned, the bulk of the people would welcome the conclusion of peace. The decision in any case, must be made by the government alone. There was no need to fear public criticism which in Russia counted for little.

Kiselev warned that a continuation of the war threatened dangers as yet hardly suspected. Russia's new provinces had been acquired less than fifty years before; they were not completely fused with the older lands. Volhynia and Podolia swarmed with hostile agents; Finland was ready to return to Swedish rule; the Poles would rise as one man whenever allied military operations made this possible. The possibility of defending these countries in the face of superior forces was doubtful; once lost, they could never be regained. Compared to perils like these, the sacrifices now demanded were insignificant; rather than face such risks, the ultimatum must be accepted.

Meyendorff observed that a continuation of the struggle would inevitably lead to bankruptcy. The war had already cost three hundred million roubles in extraordinary expenditure; revenue had fallen short of anticipation; the productive capacity of the empire was impaired. If the conflict continued Russia might at the end find herself in a position similar to that of

[1] Memorandum by Nesselrode, 15 Jan. 1856 (Tatishchev, op. cit., pp. 185f).

Austria after the Congress of Vienna when, exhausted by the struggle against France, she had been forced to adopt a policy of peace at any price. Sweden after the wars of Charles XII had sunk to the rank of a third-rate power; Russia might share her fate if she now decided to fight on. If, on the other hand, she accepted a peace which in no way impeded the development of her resources, she might 'in a few years' be as strong as she had been before the war. She might then accomplish what could not be achieved at present. A peace now need only be a truce; postponed by a year or two, it would leave the empire in a state of exhaustion from which it might take fifty years to recover. During that time, important European questions might be decided without or against Russia. For these reasons he voted for immediate and unconditional acceptance. The Tsar gave signs of approval.

After Dolgorukov had drawn a vivid picture of Russia's military weakness, the incompetent Bludov, with tears in his eyes, concluded a speech against acceptance with the words of Choiseul: 'Puisque nous ne savons pas faire la guerre, faisons la paix!'[1]

The Tsar's official advisers had thus declared with virtual unanimity for peace, but different views were held by many who did not share official responsibility:

> The national feeling was wounded by the very idea of a humiliating peace. Russia was not conquered, she had still a numerous army gloriously tried; she had her recollections, her patriotism, her perseverance, the difficulties which her immense territory and her severe climate opposed to invasion; she might await the enemy at home, repeat the examples of 1812, leave him to exhaust himself in ineffective efforts, fatigue him by dint of patience, and await the favourable moment for crushing him.[2]

Grand-duke Constantine made himself the spokesman of these views, and a 'passionate discussion' between him and his brother took place in the apartments of the dowager Empress

---

[1] Tatishchev, whose account (op. cit., pp. 186 f.) is based on the official minutes of the meeting, follows the earlier version of Jomini (*Study*, pp. 366 ff.). An independent account by Meyendorff, written shortly after the meeting, appears in *Peter von Meyendorff, Ein russischer Diplomat an den Höfen von Wien und Berlin*, herausg. Otto Hoetzsch (Berlin, 1923), III, pp. 214 ff. Meyendorff's report suggests that certain statements were excluded from the official minutes and others toned down.

[2] *Study*, pp. 369 f.

immediately after the meeting of the council. The Tsar's mind, however, was made up: Prussia threatened to join the allies; the losses in men had been tremendous; there were difficulties in recruiting; last, but not least, the finances were exhausted.[1] The Grand-duke's arguments, in consequence, were unable to shake his determination.

At 2 p.m. the following day, Esterhazy received from Nessel-rode a note announcing Russia's acceptance.[2] Gorchakov received the news at lunch; it affected him so much that he had to retire to bed, but by 7 p.m. he was able to inform Buol of the decision.[3] At 9 p.m. the King of Prussia sent the news by tele-graph to Queen Victoria.[4] The following day, Napoleon announced it officially at a meeting of the allied war council in Paris.[5] The turning point had been reached.

The Tsar's motives in finally accepting terms which he considered dishonourable and which, some weeks earlier, he would have rejected with scorn, are declared by the official account to have been humanitarian.[6] There is reason to believe that other considerations influenced his decision. In October, Manteuffel had learnt from a private source that if the war continued there was a danger of disturbances in Russia. A section of the nobility was disgruntled and there were intrigues against the Tsar.[7] In November, Werther had referred to his difficult position

> placé entre le parti russe, composé de l'armée et des *masses fanatiques*, d'une part, de l'autre la haute société et les classes aisées et intelligentes, lasses de la guerre et dont l'irritation faisait craindre *une révolution de palais*.[8]

A highly placed Russian, who claimed to express the views of the Tsar himself, explained that Russia was greatly weakened. He feared, moreover, an internal movement ('un mouvement intérieur') which would be of the utmost gravity. Peace was an absolute necessity.[9] There existed in Russia a public opinion which even the autocratic Tsars ignored at their peril.[10]

[1] Werther to Manteuffel, 27 Jan. 1856, Guichen, op. cit., p. 351.
[2] Esterhazy to Buol, telegram, 16 Jan. 1856, H.H.S.A., P.A.R., x, fasc. 39, H.T.
[3] Geffcken, op. cit., p. 216.
[4] Ibid.   [5] Ibid., p. 217.   [6] *Study*, p. 271.
[7] Cit. Guichen, op. cit., p. 299.   [8] Ibid., p. 303.
[9] Cit. Guichen, op. cit., p. 354, from a letter in a private German archive.
[10] Pozzo di Borgo once said to a diplomat in Paris: 'Nous avons aussi notre Constitution et une responsabilité malheureusement non ministérielle, Article unique: —' and he made the gesture of strangling (Geffcken, op. cit., p. 211, n. 1).

V

On 25 February the plenipotentiaries of the belligerents met in Paris to convert the preliminaries into a treaty of peace. Apart from a Russian attempt to exchange Kars[1] for the territory to be ceded in Bessarabia, the negotiations were uneventful.[2] On 30 March peace was signed in Paris.

The terms finally accepted by Alexander II were hard. Two of the conditions in particular deeply hurt Russian pride. The first of these, introduced at the instance of Austria, provided for a 'rectification' of the frontier between Russia and Turkey (or, more directly, the vassal principality of Moldavia), designed to remove the Russian empire from all contact with the navigable portion of the Danube and its tributaries. This 'rectification' involving as it did, the first Russian cession of territory after an unlucky war, was a blow to national self-respect. Still more humiliating, however, was the compulsory neutralization of the Black Sea imposed, more particularly, at the instance of Great Britain. By Art. XI of the Treaty of Paris the waters and ports of the Black Sea, whilst open to the mercantile marine of every nation, were 'formally and in perpetuity interdicted to the Flag of War, either of the Powers possessing its coasts or of any other Power'.[3] Moreover, since the neutralization of the Black Sea made the maintenance or establishment of naval installations upon its coasts 'alike unnecessary and purposeless', the Tsar and Sultan engaged 'not to establish or maintain upon the Coast any Military-Maritime Arsenal' (Art. XIII).[4] These

---

[1] On 28 Nov. the Turkish fortress of Kars in Asia Minor had fallen into Russian hands.

[2] For a detailed study of the congress cf. H. Temperley, 'The Treaty of Paris of 1856 and its Execution', *The Journal of Modern History*, IV, no. 3, pp. 387 ff.

[3] For the terms of the Treaty of Paris see *The Great European Treaties of the Nineteenth Century*, ed. Sir A. Oakes and R. B. Mowat, (2nd impr., Oxford, 1921), pp. 176 ff. Russia and Turkey, the two riverain powers were, however, permitted to maintain in the Black Sea a number of light vessels 'necessary for the service of their Coasts'. Their number and size was laid down in a separate Russo-Turkish convention, annexed to the treaty. This was to have 'the same force and validity as if it formed an integral part thereof'. It was to be neither modified nor annulled without the assent of all the signatories (Art. XIV). In addition, to ensure the proper execution of regulations to be established by common consent for the navigation of the river Danube, each contracting power was given the right 'to station, at all times, two Light Vessels at the Mouths of the Danube' (Art. XIX).

[4] This stipulation worked — as indeed it was intended to — one-sidedly against Russia. The Sultan, in future as in the past, would be able to maintain such installations as he wished on the shores of the Bosphorus and the Sea of Marmora, unaffected by the neutralization.

stipulations, restricting as they did 'in perpetuity' the sovereign rights of a great power over its coasts and territorial waters were, in their severity, without precedent in the annals of European diplomacy.[1]

They were, accordingly, resented in Russia. Alexander II, whilst accepting the inevitable under pressure from his advisers, never reconciled himself to the sacrifice. He had repeatedly informed Michael Gorchakov that he considered such terms dishonourable and would on no account accept them. His attitude never changed. According to the later recollections of Alexander Gorchakov, he told a meeting of his council in 1863:

> Il y a sept ans, à cette table, j'ai fait un acte que je puis qualifier, puisque c'est moi qui l'ai accompli; j'ai signé le traité de Paris, et c'était une lâcheté!

When those present protested, the Tsar, striking the table with his fist, added: 'Oui, c'était une lâcheté et *certes je ne la ferai plus*.'[2] Indeed for the next fifteen years following the signing of the treaty, it would be the principal object of Alexander's diplomacy to free Russia from its shackles.[3]

---

[1] The nearest precedent had occurred in 1713 when Art. IX of the Treaty of Utrecht obliged the French government, within a period of six months, to raze the fortifications and fill in the harbour of Dunkirk. She also had to promise never to restore them. The stipulation, re-affirmed more than once in subsequent treaties, was cancelled in 1783. The restrictions now imposed on Russia were far more sweeping in character. The nearest parallel is to be found in the limitations on German sovereignty imposed by the Treaty of Versailles.

[2] S. Goriainov, *Le Bosphore et les Dardanelles* (Paris, 1910), p. 147.

[3] 'Toute la politique extérieure d'Alexandre II, pendant les premières quinze années de son règne, ne poursuivait qu'un seul but, celui de s'affranchir de cet asservissement' (ibid.).

CHAPTER II

The Triple Treaty of 15 April 1856[1]

Foreseeing that the Russian government would try to challenge the Treaty of Paris at the earliest opportunity, the victorious allies, in the meantime, had made arrangements to secure the maintenance of the settlement. The British and Austrian governments in particular, although for slightly different reasons, tried to safeguard their gains by means of an agreement designed to perpetuate the Crimean coalition. The 'treaty of guarantee' entered into by England, Austria and France, became an essential part of the Crimean system.

I

The idea of perpetuating, by means of a diplomatic engagement, the Crimean association of England, France and Austria, went back at least to the spring of 1855. It appears to have originated, during the abortive Vienna conferences, in the fertile brain of Lord John Russell, the first British plenipotentiary. Russell then told Clarendon, the Foreign Secretary, that he had 'been always anxious to get Buol to agree to a defensive Treaty with France and us, separate from Russia. This did not suit his ideas, but an escapade of Gorchakov's, retracting and quibbling on the guarantee, has reconciled him to it.'

Russell had thereupon invited Drouyn de Lhuys, French Foreign Minister and first plenipotentiary, to draw up a 'project of Treaty'. This, in due course, was submitted to the Austrian Emperor. Francis-Joseph gave his approval, explaining that 'he thought it necessary to provide for the future and that the present war should not end by a mere Treaty of Peace. He thought Russia would long bear ill-will to Austria for the part she had taken, and he wished to be united in a Treaty with the Maritime Powers, with a view to a permanent political system.'[2]

[1] The bulk of this chapter first appeared as an article in the *English Historical Review*, (April 1952).

[2] Russell to Clarendon, private, 23 Apr. 1855, Clarendon MSS.

In spite of this approval, however, the failure of the Vienna conferences put an end to the discussions.

The idea of a tripartite treaty, nonetheless, had by this time struck firm roots in Vienna. Among its warmest advocates was Bourqueney, the French minister. Throughout the course of the Eastern question, he told Cowley[1] he had had one constant preoccupation. Supposing that peace was concluded on the terms most advantageous to the allies, Russia would, thereafter, have but one object in view: to get rid of the restrictions imposed upon her at the earliest possible moment. He had, therefore, asked himself, if it would not be a wise measure to make Austria, if possible, a party to a treaty, obliging her to take up arms if, after the conclusion of peace, Russia should violate its terms in the future. Austria was so much nearer the seat of action than either France or England, that the value of her co-operation could hardly be overrated. It was on this account that he had attached so much value to Buol's suggestion to Russell and Drouyn which contained the *casus belli* for the future and made Austria a joint guarantor with England and France against eventual Russian aggression upon Turkey.[2]

When, after the fall of Sevastopol, discussions about the possibility of new negotiations with Russia were resumed between Vienna and Paris, the Austrian government once more raised the question of a tripartite treaty. Napoleon, although satisfied with the terms to be offered to Russia, 'showed extreme repugnance to the idea of a Treaty of Guarantee' such as Buol desired. Two considerations, above all, accounted for his reluctance. Napoleon, in the first place, did not believe in the future of Turkey and showed 'rooted scorn for the Turks and everything belonging to them'. He had declared more than once that the Emperor Nicholas had been right and that Turkey was 'dying a lingering death'.[3] Moreover, the plans now germinating in his mind required a close understanding with Russia rather than Austria. He had, in fact, reached the paradoxical conclusion that great benefit would accrue to Europe if England and France could bring Russia into their alliance. With Russia on their side, he considered, Germany would be paralysed and

---

[1] The British ambassador in Paris.
[2] Cowley to Clarendon, private, 13 Oct. 1855, ibid.
[3] The same to the same, private, 30 Oct. 1855, ibid.

they would be able to dictate their own terms to Austria with regard to Italy.[1] If England, France and Russia were agreed, they would be able between them to settle all important questions.[2] Napoleon's triple alliance, therefore, wore a very different look from that proposed by Buol. However, in spite of his aversion to the Austrian proposal, he 'finally adopted it'[3] as part of the price to be paid for bringing about peace through the intermediary of Austria.

In consequence, the memorandum, initialled by Buol and Bourqueney in Vienna on 14 November which laid down the course of procedure for opening negotiations with Russia, declared among other things that

> Les stipulations de la paix seraient complétées par un traité d'alliance entre l'Autriche, la France et la Grande Bretagne, garantissant l'intégrité et l'indépendance de l'Empire Ottoman, et rétablissant comme *casus belli* toute infraction portée par la Russie aux stipulations de la dite paix.[4]

Napoleon gave the memorandum his official blessing. The British government, after securing a number of amendments, did likewise. The principle of a 'triple guarantee' had thus been firmly written into the Crimean settlement.

II

When, towards the end of March it was becoming clear that the negotiations in Paris would end in the conclusion of peace, Buol took the initiative in reminding Napoleon and Clarendon of the Triple Treaty provided for in the memorandum of 14 November. His own government, he announced, was ready to discuss the details.[5]

The Austrian reminder displeased Napoleon;[6] Clarendon's first reaction, on the other hand, was to pat Buol on the back

[1] The same to the same, private, 23 May 1856, ibid.
[2] Brunnow to Nesselrode, 24 Apr. 1856 (O.S.), quoted in Tatishchev, op. cit., I, 202.
[3] Cowley to Clarendon, private, 30 Oct. 1855, Clarendon MSS.
[4] Memorandum signed by Count Buol and M. de Bourqueney, copy enclosed in Clarendon to the Queen, 19 Nov. 1855, R.A. G 40/81.
[5] Clarendon to Palmerston, private, 24 Mar. 1856, Palmerston MSS (at Broadlands).
[6] Buol told Clarendon of Napoleon's opinion that it was all 'sufficiently provided for by the Treaty itself' and that a separate treaty would 'give unnecessary offence to Russia', (ibid.).

and to assure him that England 'attached great importance to the Treaty'.[1] However, on hearing of Napoleon's reluctance, the Foreign Secretary also had second thoughts. He reported to Palmerston that Napoleon wished to avoid the tripartite treaty, arguing that the general treaty of peace contained 'sufficient guarantees against Russia'. Buol was ready to sign if the British government wished it. 'Shall we', Clarendon now asked, 'have this Treaty or not?' If there was to be a treaty, he must 'put some pressure upon the Emperor'.[2]

Palmerston's decision was not for a moment in doubt. 'Such a Treaty', he told the Queen, 'to which Prussia might possibly be induced afterwards to accede, would be an Engagement of great value in more ways than one.'[3] Clarendon therefore was urged to pursue the negotiation. 'As to the Triple Treaty between England, Austria and France for maintaining the Integrity and Independence of the Turkish Empire', he was told, 'it would be very unadvisable to give that up and no good reason could be assigned for doing so.' Prussia might perhaps 'be persuaded to accede to it afterwards and Sardinia would probably join in it, and that would tend still further to remove bad Feeling between her and Austria'.[4]

Clarendon therefore set to work on Napoleon, explaining that 'the Treaty was part of our bond, & that we must have it'.[5] On 7 April he was able to inform Palmerston that the Emperor had withdrawn his objections.[6] Two days later, Cowley, Hübner, and Bourqueney, the second plenipotentiaries of the three powers, met to prepare a draft of the proposed engagement.[7]

The draft which emerged from their deliberations consisted of three public and two secret articles. By the first public article, England, France, and Austria were to guarantee 'solidairement entre Elles' the independence and integrity of the Ottoman Empire. In the following article, the contracting powers declared that they would consider as the *casus belli* any infraction of the terms of the treaty of peace. The third article laid down the procedure of ratification. By the first of the secret

---

[1] Ibid.
[2] Clarendon to Palmerston, 31 Mar. 1856, Palmerston MSS.
[3] Palmerston to the Queen, 1 Apr. 1856, R.A. G 47/1.
[4] Palmerston to Clarendon, 1 Apr. 1856, Clarendon MSS.
[5] Clarendon to Palmerston, 12 Apr. 1856, Clarendon MSS, draft.
[6] Palmerston to the Queen, 8 Apr. 1856, R.A. A 25/47.
[7] Comte de Hübner, *Neuf Ans de Souvenirs* (Paris, 1904), I, 415 f.

articles the three powers undertook, in the event of an infraction of the general treaty, to seek without delay an understanding with the Porte 'sur les mesures devenues nécessaires'. They would also agree amongst themselves on the employment of their naval and military forces. The second secret article, adopted at the instance of Cowley and Hübner,[1] provided for immediate consultation among the contracting parties, should Russian military or naval concentrations appear to threaten the integrity and independence of Turkey.[2]

The draft was at once transmitted to the Foreign Office in London, and was accepted by the cabinet with some verbal alterations 'for the sake of greater precision'.[3] On 13 April, Palmerston authorized Clarendon to sign the agreement 'subject to the alterations suggested'.[4]

In the meantime, the full delegations of the three powers had met at the Quai d'Orsay to consider the draft treaty. Walewski had announced that Napoleon would not agree to the second secret article, 'and he supported this decision by a variety of vague and foolish arguments, the real upshot of which was that the secret article would become public, and the Russians would take offence'. Buol was 'very firm' and appeared 'indifferent about offending or pleasing Russia'. Clarendon and Cowley 'insisted upon the utility of recording the dangers that were likely to occur'. They asserted 'that it was for the interest of peace for the three Powers to concert together as to the means of preventing what would lead to war, rather than to wait until the *casus belli* had actually arisen.' This, they maintained, was all the more important as the proposed triple treaty 'was not likely to be acted upon soon but that 10 or 20 years hence, the secret article as proposed would be at once a guide to our Successors in office, and an obligation upon them'.[5]

---

[1] Ibid., I, 416 f.

[2] 'La concentration de troupes Russes considérables', the article declared, 'sur l'une ou l'autre frontière de la Turquie ainsi qu'un accroissement notable des forces navales de la Russie dans les eaux tributaires de la mer Noire, appelleront sans retard les délibérations des Hautes Parties Contractantes' (Palmerston to Clarendon, 13 Apr. 1856, F.O. 27/1167, no. 42).

[3] Palmerston to Clarendon, 13 Apr. 1856, F.O. 27/1167, no. 42.

[4] Ibid.

[5] This was odd doctrine on the part of a British Foreign Secretary. Clarendon must have been well aware that no secret article of a treaty could constitute any obligation upon his successors in office. It is in any case curious that Clarendon and Cowley should, with the approval of Palmerston, have made themselves the advocates of the inclusion of secret articles in the proposed triple treaty.

Walewski, however, remained adamant. He 'could say nothing except that the Emperor had forbidden him to accept the Article'. Clarendon, in reply, observed that the British plenipotentiaries could not agree to the treaty without it until they had consulted their government. He did not positively refuse, he later explained to Palmerston, because the Emperor 'might have closed with that, as he would be glad to be rid of the Treaty altogether'. In the end, a new draft was settled to which Walewski thought the Emperor would agree.[1] There was now to be only one secret article stipulating that if the *casus foederis* arose, the contracting parties would 'entre Elles et avec la Sublime Porte' determine without delay 'l'emploi de leurs forces navales et militaires'.[2] Such a treaty, Clarendon considered, would be satisfactory, and England ought to sign it.[3]

Palmerston, who received the new draft on 13 April after he had informed Clarendon of the cabinet's approval of the original one, regretted the weakening of the treaty. He now told the Foreign Secretary, that the British government 'would much prefer retaining the Second Secret Article of the Original Draft'. It was possible, he added rather hopefully, 'that some modification of the second secret article might remove the objection felt to it by the Emperor of the French, such as that any such concentration of military forces on any part of the frontier adjoining to Turkey, or any *creation* of a naval force in the Russian waters communicating with the Black Sea, would be the subject of deliberation between the Contracting Parties and the Porte.' However, if Napoleon would not consent to this, Clarendon was to sign the modified treaty subject to some verbal amendments.[4]

Clarendon felt that no time should be lost in getting the treaty signed, and on 15 April this was done at the Quai d'Orsay after a session of 'three mortal hours', caused by mistakes in the copies, which had to be written all over again.[5] The treaty as finally signed differed from the revised draft approved by Palmerston in that it contained no secret clauses at all. The

---

[1] Clarendon to Palmerston, private, 12 Apr. 1856, Palmerston MSS.
[2] Amended draft, copy in Palmerston to Clarendon, 13 Apr. 1856, F.O. 27/1167, no. 43.
[3] Clarendon to Palmerston, 12 Apr. 1856, Palmerston MSS.
[4] Palmerston to Clarendon, 13 Apr. 1856, F.O. 27/1167, no. 43.
[5] Clarendon to Palmerston ,15 Apr. 1856, Palmerston MSS.

remaining secret article had finally been incorporated in the second article of the treaty itself.[1]

In form, the new agreement strengthened the obligations of the contracting powers to co-operate in the defence of Turkey. They had, indeed, already undertaken this obligation by the terms of Art. VII of the Treaty of Paris, but whereas the general treaty by its very nature could not envisage military sanctions, any infraction of its terms was now a *casus belli*.[2] As a logical consequence, the new treaty provided for joint military consultations should the *casus foederis* arise, a stipulation which had found no place in the terms of the general treaty. Finally the new treaty appeared to create a special obligation on the part of each of the contracting powers towards its two partners, to co-operate in the achievement of their joint defensive purpose.[3]

The real significance of the Triple Treaty, however, lay in its character as a political demonstration. It has been described by Geffcken with much justification as a 'Sonderbund des Misstrauens gegen Russlands guten Glauben'[4] and it was as such that it was later to be understood by the public. Buol and Hübner considered that it would 'oppose a firm barrier to the adversaries of the new European system'[5] and Palmerston saw in it 'a good additional Security and Bond of Union'.[6] Both Austria and England, in fact, welcomed the Triple Treaty as the

---

[1] The treaty, as finally signed on 15 Apr. 1856 consisted of a preamble, three articles and a conclusion. The articles were as follows:

I. 'Les Hautes Parties Contractantes garantissent solidairement entre Elles l'indépendance et l'intégrité de l'Empire Ottoman, consacrées par le traité conclu à Paris, le trente Mars mil huit cent cinquante six.'

II. 'Toute infraction aux stipulations du dit Traité sera considérée par les Puissances signataires du présent traité comme *casus belli*. Elles s'entendront avec la Sublime Porte sur les mesures devenues nécessaires et détermineront sans retard entre elles l'emploi de leurs forces militaires et navales.'

III. 'Le présent Traité sera ratifié, et les Ratifications en seront échangées dans l'espace de quinze jours, ou plus tôt si faire se peut.'

(B[ritish and] F[oreign] S[tate] P[apers] *1855–56*, XLVI., pp. 25 f.)

[2] For a discussion of the obligations undertaken with regard to the defence of Turkey by the signatories of the treaty of 30 March 1856, cf. H. Temperley, loc. cit. pp. 523 ff.

[3] For an analysis of the technical differences between a collective and an individual guarantee cf. R. B. Mowat, *Select Treaties* (London 1915), pp. xix f. and xxxvi, and Temperley, loc. cit., p. 527. For an interesting discussion of the interpretation subsequently given by the British government to its obligations under the treaty of 15 Apr. 1856, cf. Geffcken, op. cit., pp. 290 ff., and Temperley, loc. cit., pp. 528 ff.

[4] Geffcken, op. cit., p. 289.

[5] Buol and Hübner to the Emperor, 16 Apr. 1856, quoted in Temperley, loc. cit., p. 528.

[6] Palmerston to Clarendon, private, 1 Apr. 1856, Clarendon MSS.

cornerstone of a defensive alliance directed against Russia. It could not, for that very reason, commend itself to Napoleon, who would soon express the opinion that in signing it, the allied powers had 'acted disloyally' towards Russia. Russia, he argued, had a right to resent an act which proved that the allies had no faith in the engagement which she had just contracted.[1]

III

Napoleon and Walewski in fact, had felt uneasy from the start about the effect which the knowledge that a separate treaty was being negotiated by the three powers would have on the unsuspecting Russian plenipotentiaries and on the future of Franco-Russian relations. They had therefore asked their partners that the talks might be conducted in secret, and the British and Austrian representatives had agreed to the request.[2]

The respite, however, which Napoleon and Walewski had gained as a result of this expedient, was not of long duration. On 25 April, Clarendon, who had meanwhile returned to London, wrote to Cowley that he assumed Walewski would not object to the publication of the Triple Treaty.[3] Cowley replied that France did not intend to ratify the treaty until the last moment[4] and that Walewski had shown himself 'very averse' to its being published. Cowley had, however, informed him that the British government could not help themselves and that a treaty of that nature '*must* be laid before Parliament'.[5] Walewski had then begged Cowley for at least a few days' delay, 'in order that this Treaty might not see the light at the same time as the Treaty of Peace.'[6] This request the British

---

[1] Cowley to Clarendon, private, 26 Jun. 1856, Clarendon MSS.

[2] Ibid. Clarendon was later to agree with Napoleon 'that we shd have done better if we had informed Russia that it was our intention to enter into such a treaty in virtue of engagements previously contracted' (ibid.).

[3] Clarendon to Cowley, private, 25 Apr. 1856, Cowley MSS (in the Public Record Office). 'I conclude', Clarendon wrote, 'that Walewski will not object to the publicn of the Tripartite Treaty?' (ibid.).

[4] Article III of the treaty of 15 Apr. laid down that the exchange of ratifications was to be completed within fifteen days of signature at the latest (cf. *B.F.S.P. 1855–1856*, XLVI., pp. 25 f.).

[5] He had no idea, Cowley rather ingenuously added, whether he was right in this or not, but had thought it better to say as much to Walewski (Cowley to Clarendon, private, 27 Apr. 1856, Clarendon MSS).

[6] Cowley to Clarendon, private, 27 Apr. 1856, Clarendon MSS. The ratifications of the general treaty of peace were to be completed by 30 Apr. at the latest, and their completion would of course be followed by the publication of the general treaty.

D

government refused. The ministers, Clarendon informed Cowley, had no option about presenting the Triple Treaty. It had to be done, and indeed he was sorry that he had not laid it on the table of the House already.[1] Walewski in the meantime had grudgingly ratified the treaty, but was still anxious that its publication should be held up. He now asked Cowley to enquire on his behalf whether publication could not be delayed 'until after Whitsuntide'.[2] Clarendon replied by telegraph that the British ministers were '*obliged* to lay the Triple Treaty on the Table'. They could not have justified themselves before Parliament if it had suddenly appeared in *The Daily News* 'as the other Treaty did'.[3]

On the evening of 2 May Clarendon in fact presented the Triple Treaty to Parliament. In doing so, he 'made no flourish of trumpets' but merely said that it had been signed 'in pursuance of an agreement come to by the three powers at Vienna'. He should not, he wrote to Cowley, 'attach any particular importance to it.'[4] Palmerston did not share this view. On 6 May, in the debate on the treaty of peace, he dwelt with satisfaction on the treaty of 15 April. 'With regard to the triple alliance of England, France, and Austria to secure the faithful performance of this treaty', he told Parliament, 'I must say that I think the ability displayed by my noble Friend (Lord Clarendon), and by his able associate (Lord Cowley), in the negotiation in Paris cannot be overrated.' Their names would go down to posterity as the names of men who had taken an active part in accomplishing 'one of the most important settlements during many ages of history'.[5]

The circumstances surrounding the publication of the Triple Treaty have been shrouded in a good deal of mystery. The negotiations for its conclusion were carried on in close secrecy, and its seemingly casual publication by the British government merely added to the mystery surrounding its origins. As a result an impression grew up that the treaty of 15 April was in fact

---

[1] Clarendon to Cowley, private, 29 Apr. 1856, Cowley MSS.

[2] Clarendon to Cowley, private, 1 May 1856, Clarendon MSS.

[3] Clarendon to Cowley, private, 2 May 1856, Cowley MSS. The complete text of the treaty of 30 Mar. 1856 had appeared prematurely in an English translation on 23 Apr. in the second edition of the *Daily News*. On the following day, the same paper had also published the French text (*Daily News*, 23 and 24 Apr. 1856).

[4] Clarendon to Cowley, private, 2 May 1856, Cowley MSS.

[5] *Parl. Debates*, cxlii (1856), c. 127.

intended to be secret, and was divulged in some unaccountable way by the British ministers. On 19 May Vitzthum, the Saxon minister in London, spoke of it as a document 'which was not originally intended to see the light', and he even referred to it as 'the Secret Treaty of 15 April'.[1] A similar impression was later to arise among historians. Charles-Roux claimed that Napoleon revealed the existence of the treaty to the Russians 'bien qu'il dût rester secret'.[2] Temperley in his turn asserted 'that the text of the alliance treaty was meant to be secret and only transpired by accident'.[3] Indeed the Triple Treaty became known among historians as the Secret Treaty of 15 April 1856.

In fact, however, the treaty in its final form was never intended to be secret. At the beginning of the negotiations Napoleon and Walewski obtained a promise that these should be concealed from the Russian plenipotentiaries.[4] That undertaking came to an end with the signature of the treaty on 15 April. Thereafter it would be natural not to reveal its terms until the completion of the ratifications.[5] After 30 April however, there no longer existed any valid reason for keeping the treaty secret.

Walewski, for reasons which he explained to Cowley, would have preferred to delay the publication of the Triple Treaty until a later date, but the British ministers were opposed to such a course. For this opposition they gave to the French several different reasons. It is impossible to say how far they were sincere. Certainly both Palmerston and Clarendon when pressing for an early publication of the treaty, were influenced by political considerations. Geffcken suggests, and Palmerston's speech in the House of Commons on 6 May supports the view, that the ministers intended to use the treaty of 15 April to make the general treaty, which was certain to

---

[1] C. F. Vitzthum von Eckstaedt, *St. Petersburg and London, 1852–1864* (London, 1887), I, p. 200.

[2] F. Charles-Roux op. cit., p. 106.

[3] Temperley, loc. cit., p. 528.

[4] Cowley to Clarendon, private, 26 Jun. 1856, Clarendon MSS.

[5] Agreement had been reached among the plenipotentiaries that the terms of the general treaty of peace should not be published till after the exchange of ratifications (Clarendon to Palmerston, private 27 Mar. 1856, Palmerston MSS). Cowley, it appears, considered that this provision applied also to the Triple Treaty. 'As far as we are concerned', he later told Napoleon who had criticized the concealment of the treaty from the Russians, 'the Treaty had been published as soon as it was ratified' (Cowley to Clarendon, private, 26 Jun. 1856, Clarendon MSS).

encounter criticism, more palatable to Parliament and the public.[1] Furthermore, a diplomat of Palmerston's experience and perspicacity could not fail to appreciate the effect which publication of the Triple Treaty would have on the unwelcome Franco-Russian *rapprochement*. Clarendon's sarcastic enquiry about the manner in which Walewski had 'explained it or apologized for it to his Russian friends'[2] suggests that this idea was prominent in the minds of the British ministers.

IV

If it was indeed the object of Palmerston and Clarendon, when insisting on the early publication of the Triple Treaty, to disturb the increasingly friendly relations between France and Russia, their policy was not without success. When it became clear that the treaty would be laid before the British Parliament at an early date, Napoleon decided that before this happened, he must communicate its contents to the Russian plenipotentiaries. Walewski was charged with this unpleasant duty, and on 30 April Orlov was able to inform his government of the contents of the treaty.[3] In acknowledging Walewski's communication, the Russian envoy remarked 'que le cabinet français aurait eu meilleure grâce de l'en instruire quinze jours plutôt, mais qu'il savait que l'Angleterre et l'Autriche avaient mis cette combinaison en avant afin de compromettre la France aux yeux de la Russie et de rompre la cordialité qui commençait déjà à inquiéter les Cours de Vienne et de Londres'.[4] Three days later, in a conversation with Orlov, Napoleon himself laid the blame for the delay in informing the Russians of the treaty on his Foreign Minister. When he understood from Walewski, he explained, that its text had not yet been communicated to the Russian plenipotentiaries, he expressed his displeasure because this proceeding had an air of duplicity of which he was incapable. He strongly begged Orlov to assure the Emperor Alexander of this fact.[5]

---

[1] Geffcken, op. cit., p. 289.
[2] Clarendon to Cowley, private, 23 Apr. 1856, Cowley MSS.
[3] S. Goriainov, 'Les Étapes de l'Alliance Franco-Russe', in *Revue de Paris* (Paris, 1912), 1 (Jan.-Feb. 1912), p. 12.
[4] Orlov to Nesselrode, 18/30 Apr. 1856, 1856 Paris II. réc. 658, no. 86, quoted in Goriainov, loc. cit., p. 12.
[5] Orlov to Nesselrode, 22 Apr./3 May 1856, quoted in Tatishchev, op. cit., I, p. 202.

In spite of Napoleon's explanation, however, Orlov could not hide his irritation at the conclusion by France, behind his back, of an agreement directed against Russia. On 7 May, Hübner gleefully reported to Buol, that the Triple Treaty 'a produit sur le Cte Orloff une impression pénible et . . . a détruit des illusions auxquelles il semble s'être livré'.[1] A few days later Cowley in his turn noted that Orlov's attitude towards France had undergone a complete change. Walewski had 'fallen very low in his opinion', and his general tone in speaking of France left Cowley with the impression that he would 'warn his Emperor against founding his policy on a too intimate alliance with this country'.[2]

Orlov, in his reports to St Petersburg, tried to make the best of an unfortunate situation. The idea of this triple alliance, he explained, was not a new one. Buol, in fact, had found it as a tradition in the archives of the Vienna Chancery, for a similar alliance had been concluded in 1814 before the Congress of Vienna. The idea, which had arisen in the minds of Metternich and Talleyrand, had originally been a fruitful one, but in trying to follow an antiquated policy, Buol should have remembered how unstable the combination had proved. He should also have remembered how the Emperor Alexander I had been able to defeat the narrow calculations of his enemies by the magnanimous but contemptuous way in which he had ignored the treaty when it had finally come to his knowledge. Orlov felt certain that this example of wise statesmanship would be followed by the Emperor Alexander II in the present case.[3]

Alexander II, however, felt little inclination at first to follow his uncle's example. 'Cette conduite de la France envers nous', he noted on the margin of Orlov's first report about the Triple Treaty, 'n'est pas loyale et doit nous servir à mesurer le degré de confiance que Napoléon peut nous inspirer.'[4] The imperial cabinet, the Austrian envoy in St Petersburg reported to Buol, had been 'fort désappointé d'apprendre l'existence de cette transaction qui était en dehors de son attente et de toutes ses prévisions'. Public opinion had been hurt by this mark of distrust of Russia's intentions and the hopes of a French alliance

[1] Hübner to Buol, 7 May 1856, H.H.S.A., P.A. Frankreich, ix, fasc. 51, no. 36, Litt.B.
[2] Cowley to Clarendon, private, 16 May 1856, Clarendon MSS.
[3] Orlov to Nesselrode, 18/30 Ap. 1856, quoted in Tatishchev, op. cit., p. 201.
[4] Goriainov, loc. cit., p. 12.

had considerably declined. 'L'opinion générale s'en est émue et en a été blessée, parce qu'elle n'y entrevoit que l'arrière pensée d'un vote de défiance dirigé contre la Russie, au moment où cette puissance venait de donner les preuves les plus évidentes de ses intentions bienveillantes pour la conservation de l'Empire Ottoman. Pour ceux surtout qui désiraient voir naître une alliance intime entre la Russie et la France, le traité du 15 Avril a été un vrai mécompte.'[1] The *rapprochement* between Russia and France, it might appear, had received a serious check.

V

During the weeks which followed the publication of the Triple Treaty, European diplomacy was conducted largely under the shadow of that event. The Tsar — to show that he did not stand alone — towards the end of May paid a demonstrative visit to his nephew in Berlin. His gesture was regarded, throughout Europe, as a reply to the Triple Treaty.[2] Orlov in Paris gave vent to Russian feelings. He did not, Cowley recorded with satisfaction 'go away in such good humour as he was in after the signature of peace'.[3]

To counteract this Russian irritation, Napoleon — his eyes already fixed on his future Italian policy — left no stone unturned to 'play down' the unhappy event. He told Orlov of his regret at having been forced to sign the treaty. It no longer had any purpose or justification and contained nothing but commonplaces.[4] Brunnow in his turn was treated to an assurance that the signing of the treaty was due solely to the insistence of Clarendon and Buol.[5] The Empress Eugénie confided to Orlov that Napoleon had refused categorically to enter any engagement obliging him to go to war. She knew from Walewski

---

[1] Esterhazy to Buol, 24 May 1856, H.H.S.A., Pol. A.R., x, fasc. 39, no. 34, A-C. Only a few Russians seem to have formed a different estimate of the Triple Treaty. 'Quoiqu'il soit qualifié généralement ici', Esterhazy recorded, 'pour me servir de l'épithète le plus modéré, de mauvais procédé, il n'en est pas moins vrai que j'ai même entendu des Russes éclairés faire l'apologie de cette transaction qui, dans l'intérêt bien entendu de la Russie, formait une digue aux rêves et aux utopies des panslavistes, ainsi qu'aux velléités d'une alliance inconsidérée avec la France.'

[2] Ch. Friese, *Russland und Preussen vom Krimkrieg bis zum Polnischen Aufstand* (Berlin, 1931), p. 112.

[3] Cowley to Clarendon, private, 1 Jun. 1856, Clarendon MSS.

[4] Orlov to Nesselrode, 22 Apr./3 May 1856, quoted in Tatishchev, op. cit., i, p. 202.

[5] Brunnow to Nesselrode, 11/23 May 1856, quoted in Goriainov, loc. cit., p. 13.

que les Anglais et les Autrichiens voulaient à toute force entrer dans les détails des casus belli, mais Napoléon a rejeté péremptoirement et trés décidément cette exigence, en disant: 'Je ne signerai qu'une formule générale, car c'est à moi seul que je réserve de décider dans l'application ce qui constitue un casus belli ou non.'[1]

Napoleon's attempt to put the 'blame' for the conclusion of the treaty on England and Austria led to serious strain in the Crimean alliance. Clarendon, in informing Cowley that the treaty had been laid before Parliament, added that he had avoided any explanation as to its origins, though he could have pointed out 'that the project of this tripartite Treaty was contained in a mem-m settled between Austria & France of wch we had disputed the binding force upon us & that the idea had not originated with us'. He had no wish to say anything of the kind, but if Walewski insisted on telling the Russians that it was 'an *English* plan to annoy them & shew distrust of their good faith', he would certainly 'state the facts & in public too'. Cowley should hint to Walewski that the Foreign Secretary had been prudent '& that he shd be equally so. . . '.[2] Walewski, however, was not prudent. In fact, Cowley soon reported his suspicion that 'in order to cover himself', he had thrown the onus as far as he could on the British government. To counter this, the ambassador had told Fould, the most pro-British of Napoleon's ministers, that the treaty was in fact 'the joint concoction' of Walewski and the Austrian government. It was the great argument which had been made use of towards England to induce her to come into the Austro-French views; 'at which Fould seemed greatly astonished . . .'.[3] Clarendon replied that he had 'felt certain that Walewski wd endeavour to lay the tripartite Treaty upon us . . .'. This however, must not be allowed to pass. He was delighted at what Cowley had told Fould and had himself let Brunnow 'behind the curtain too'.[4] If necessary, the memorandum of 14 November might be shown. Brunnow knew of its existence and said he had searched for it in vain among the published papers.[5] Before long, Cowley had to

---

[1] Ibid.   [2] Clarendon to Cowley, private, 2 May 1856, Cowley MSS.
[3] Cowley to Clarendon, private, 15 May 1856, Clarendon MSS.
[4] Brunnow at this time was visiting London, where he had represented Russia before the war.
[5] Clarendon to Cowley, private, 16 May 1856, Cowley MSS.

report that Napoleon also laid the responsibility for the treaty entirely upon England.[1] Clarendon countered by instructing Cowley to

> tell Brunnow or Orloff exactly how the thing passed about the Tripartite Treaty & that we made no point whatever about it beyond declaring ourselves ready & therefore willing to sign the Treaty that had been arranged & proposed to us by France & Austria in Octr last.[2]

It must remain doubtful whether Orlov and Brunnow accepted this explanation at its face value, but they may well have reflected on the curious fact that of the two western allies each was trying to throw the responsibility for the treaty upon the other.

Indeed, Napoleon, faced with Russian coolness, blamed the British government for having placed him in an awkward situation. On 26 June he complained to Cowley that he had been seduced into signing the Triple Treaty. Since they had heard of this treaty, the Russians had completely changed their attitude towards him; a thousand small things showed this. The allies had acted dishonestly towards Russia in not informing her before the signature of the treaty of peace of their intention to sign the Triple Treaty. Russia was entitled to feel offended at an act which demonstrated the mistrust felt towards her by the allies. He himself felt humiliated by what he had done. Cowley agreed that it would have been better to have announced to Russia beforehand the intention of signing the treaty. However, it had been at the instance of France that this had not been done. He was glad the treaty had been signed as every act of the Russian government was a demonstration of its bad faith. Indeed he considered that before many years were out, the allies would have to apply the treaty. Napoleon replied that this might be so but that his government had been 'très bête' in wishing to conceal it.[3]

Clearly, the publication of the Triple Treaty at the instance of the British government, had subjected Anglo-French relations to a serious strain. The divergence of views between the two principal allies on this point did not augur well for the future of the Crimean settlement.

---

[1] Cowley to Clarendon, private, 18 May 1856, Clarendon MSS.
[2] Clarendon to Cowley, private, 19 May 1856, Cowley MSS.
[3] Cowley to Clarendon, private, 26 Jun. 1856, Clarendon MSS.

VI

Palmerston, in the meantime, was happily pursuing his dream of expanding the 'triple entente' into a league of states grouped together to prevent future Russian encroachments. In this, he was encouraged by news received from Berlin. The King of Prussia, indeed, had at first 'expressed surprise at this Treaty, and thought at one moment that it was in contradiction with that concluded on the 30th of March'. However, on further examination, he was 'not disposed to find fault with it'. There were, moreover, in Berlin people who were 'grieved at Prussia's isolation on this point'.[1] On receiving this information, Clarendon at once instructed Cowley to ask Walewski 'whether it might not be worth while to sound the Prussian Government as to its disposition to accede to the Treaty'. Prussia would probably decline doing so 'but she could not then say that she had not been communicated with or had a choice on the subject'.[2]

Walewski placed the British proposal before the Emperor Napoleon, whom he found 'decidedly opposed to it'. On being questioned by Orlov about the object of the treaty, Walewski told Cowley, the Emperor had assured the Russian plenipotentiary 'that it was not intended to imply want of confidence in the arrangements lately made with Russia — that it was the complement of engagements entered into with Austria during the War, and would not have been thought of unless such previous engagements had existed'. How then, Walewski asked, could the French government now invite Prussia to accede to a treaty of which it had spoken in this manner?[3] Cowley agreed that in the circumstances it was 'next to impossible that the French Government should take any prominent part in the matter'.[4] Clarendon concurred in this view.[5]

He was equally sceptical about Palmerston's proposal to invite the Austrian government to accede to the treaty concluded on 21 November 1855 between the Western allies and

---

[1] Bloomfield to Clarendon, 17 May 1856, no. 190, confidential, copy in Clarendon to Cowley, 26 May 1856, F.O. 146/624, no. 439.

[2] Clarendon to Cowley, 26 May 1856, F.O. 146/624, no. 439.

[3] Cowley to Clarendon, 29 May 1856, F.O. 27/1127, no. 551.

[4] Ibid.

[5] 'I only made the useless (as I think it) suggestion to please Palmerston', Clarendon confided to his faithful subordinate (Clarendon to Cowley, private, 30 May 1856, Cowley MSS).

Sweden.[1] He did not think that such an invitation would be of any use to England and France, and considered that it 'certainly wd now be a just cause of irritation to Russia'. Furthermore, Austria would refuse and then take credit with Russia for having rejected a proposal which could not but be offensive to her. France would make known at St Petersburg that she had 'endeavoured in vain to check our rancorous hostility to Russia & the thing wd not be done & we shd pass for having exhibited a spite wch we don't feel . . .'.[2] In spite of these misgivings, however, an attempt was made to sound the Austrian government. Buol, as Clarendon had foreseen, declined the invitation. 'In return to my observation as to the necessity of a little combined action on the part of the Allies,' Seymour was obliged to report, 'Count Buol made some answer which I do not feel competent to report. He appeared to me to be intimating that there were hesitations and difficulties in Paris, which it belonged more especially to Her Majesty's Government to remove.'[3]

Equally unsuccessful were attempts undertaken by the British government to strengthen the structure of 15 April by restoring normal diplomatic relations between Austria and Sardinia. 'Sardinia,' Palmerston wrote, 'is closely allied with England & France. It is for the Interest of Europe that Austria should also be closely allied with England & France, but how can those Four States be on that Footing of Cordial Intimacy while there remains unadjusted a deeply irritating grievance which a measure of one of the Four occasions to another of the Four.'[4] Palmerston was trying to square the circle. 'As regards any impression which my observations made upon him', Seymour reported after one of the many conversations in which he dutifully attempted to wrest concessions from Buol with regard to Italian affairs, 'the attempt as I knew beforehand might as well not have been made.' ' "We start from different points," Buol invariably replied, "our principles are opposed." '[5] Palmerston's attempts to reconcile Austria and Sardinia in the interest of his Eastern policy was doomed to failure. His

---

[1] This was the treaty by which England and France had guaranteed the territorial integrity of the Swedish monarchy; cf. Geffcken, op. cit., p. 198.
[2] Clarendon to Cowley, private, 30 May 1856, Cowley MSS.
[3] Seymour to Clarendon, 19 Jul. 1856, F.O. 7/488, no. 519, confidential.
[4] Palmerston Memorandum, 13 Sept. 1856, F.O. 96/25.
[5] Seymour to Clarendon, 10 Jul. 1856, F.O. 7/488, no. 501, confidential.

endeavours to extend the scope of the triple alliance were equally unsuccessful.

Nor were relations between Austria and France developing in the direction of greater cordiality. Already during the congress Buol had noted with regret the tendency of the French representatives to side with Austria's rivals Russia and Sardinia. During the months which followed therefore, he left no stone unturned to improve relations with France. For a moment, things looked hopeful. During June, following a temporary coolness between France and Russia, Napoleon showed some apparent eagerness to improve relations with Austria. The respective Ministers were raised to ambassadorial rank. The British envoy in Vienna commented sourly on 'a friendship now considered so well established, cordial and proof against all fluctuations'.[1]

It was a short-lived delusion. Before long, the Austrian government was forced to recognize that not only was there profound disagreement on the Italian question but that, in the East also, Austria and France were drifting apart. One bone of contention between them was the future of the Danubian Principalities, which Napoleon wished to unite. Such a union, in the opinion of Buol, would favour only Russia. In supporting it, Britain and France 'would patronize a system which Austria would feel obliged to resist to the utmost of her ability'.[2] It was a scheme 'injurious to the interests of Austria, to the rights of Turkey and . . . certain to promote the ambitious views of Russia'.[3] 'Pour la France', Buol reproachfully remarked to a French diplomat, 'c'est une politique chevaleresque et de sentiment, c'est une question de vie ou de mort pour notre Empire.'[4] Moreover, Buol blamed the French government for its Russian leanings. 'Il y a vraiment de l'aveuglement', he lamented

à ne vouloir pas reconnaître que malgré les désastres de Sévastopol, la Russie n'a rien changé à sa politique, si ce n'est qu'elle demande aujourd'hui à la diplomatie ce qu'elle n'a pu obtenir par les armes.[5]

[1] Seymour to Clarendon, 28 May 1856, F.O. 7/486, no. 367.
[2] The same to the same, 11 Jun. 1856, ibid., no. 404, secret and confidential.
[3] The same to the same, 18 Jun. 1856, ibid., no. 416.
[4] de Heukern to Walewski, 1 Jul. 1856, A[rchives des] A[ffaires] E[trangères] in Paris, Autriche 464, unnumbered.
[5] Ibid.

Clearly there was little basis for an Austro-French understanding in the East.

Indeed the triple alliance on which Buol had staked his career and Palmerston pinned his hopes, was not in a healthy condition. Already, new issues were beginning to divide the members of the victorious coalition. The moment was fast approaching when Russian diplomacy could, with some hope of success, begin its first modest offensive against the Crimean system.

Part 2

TESTING TIME

It is impossible to frame a form of words which cannot be broken through and evaded; you must, therefore, trust to stipulations being kept with frankness and good faith, according to their obvious meaning. If you hold that your enemy is so faithless, that he is so slippery an antagonist, as to observe no treaty, clearly you can have no peace, no treaty, and you must have won to extermination.

SIDNEY HERBERT in the House of Commons, 6 May 1856

If a treaty be found to be injurious to the interests of a country and some means of violating it are obvious, I do not know of what country in Europe we could predicate a strict observance of that treaty.

LORD JOHN RUSSELL in the House of Lords, 5 May 1856

The treaty of 15 April had been an attempt to perpetuate the military and diplomatic grouping which had forced Russia to her knees in the Crimean war. The solidity of the coalition was put to its first test when the Russian government, taking advantage of ambiguities in the Treaty of Paris, tried to reduce the extent of its losses. The Tsar and Gorchakov, at this stage, had to rely on the weapons of the weak: chicanery and the exploitation of divisions among the victors. Although Russia was unlikely by these methods to achieve a major diplomatic triumph, she had little to lose by the attempt. Hers, in fact, was essentially a first limited offensive, a probing action designed to test the solidity of the victorious coalition and, perhaps, regain a little lost territory. Palmerston, recognizing the character of the Russian action, was resolved to resist it with every means at his disposal. The future peace of Europe, he argued, might well depend on the firmness of the powers in meeting the first signs of Russian encroachment. If Russia was allowed 'either by Fraud or by Force to break her Bonds, and to avoid a full & faithful Execution of her Engagements', it would be vain to suppose that after she had 'recovered from the Exhaustion which drove her to accept our Conditions', she would look upon the treaty as anything but waste paper. She would reasonably conclude 'that if a powerful alliance before which She had succumbed, were either afraid or unwilling to hold her to her engagements while the Ink that recorded them was scarcely dry', she might well 'reckon upon being allowed to do what she liked at a later Time when the alliance was loosened and Russia should have repaired her losses and have reorganized her means'.[1] Russian encroachments, therefore, must be opposed at the very beginning, to avoid more serious disputes at a later date. 'Principio desta', Palmerston exclaimed (taking slight liberties with his Ovid), was a good maxim in politics as well as in medicine.[2] Russia's first limited offensive, therefore, became the occasion of a diplomatic tussle between Palmerston and Gorchakov, the new Russian Minister of Foreign Affairs.

[1] Palmerston to Clarendon, private, 7 Aug. 1856, Clarendon MSS.
[2] The same to the same, private, 25 Aug. 1856, Clarendon MSS.

CHAPTER III

England, Russia and the Questions of Serpents Island and Bolgrad[1]

I

On 25 May 1856, Gorchakov addressed a despatch to Brunnow, Russia's representative in Paris. Russia, he declared, had for a long time been in possession of Serpents Island, situated some 90 nautical miles off the delta of the Danube. She had maintained there a lighthouse, 'indispensable pour signaler ce récif aux navigateurs se rendant à Odessa et à Ackerman.' Owing to the late war, she had been forced to abandon the lighthouse, but as the resumption of commercial relations was bound to increase navigation, she must now reestablish it. The Russian government had therefore given orders to this effect. Brunnow was to communicate these facts to both Walewski and Cowley,[2] 'en leur demandant de vouloir bien donner par le télégraphe à leurs Amiraux les ordres nécessaires pour que les postes qui pourraient se trouver sur l'île des Serpents soient retirés et qu'il ne soit opposé aucune entrave au rétablissement du phare tel qu'il existait avant la guerre.'[3]

On 8 June, Brunnow accordingly asked Cowley whether any British or French troops were stationed on Serpents Island. Cowley replied that he did not think the island had ever been occupied by the allies, and Brunnow then observed that the Russians had established a lighthouse there before the recent war and were now about to restore it. Cowley in reporting this conversation to Clarendon, advised that enquiries should be made about the possible strategic importance of the island

---

[1] The bulk of this chapter first appeared in two articles in the *Slavonic Review*, xxix, no. 71 (1950) and the *Cambridge Historical Journal*, x, no. 1 (1950).

[2] Russia had as yet no diplomatic representative in London, and Gorchakov therefore decided to make this communication to the British government through its ambassador in Paris.

[3] Gorchakov to Brunnow, Varsovie 13/25 mai 1856, copy in A.A.E. Roumanie, 1856–57, vol. 4.

and about the rights of Russia to proceed to its re-occupation.[1]

A week later, Cowley learnt the opinion of the French government. Walewski had discovered that the island was only 3,000 metres in circumference, that it had no roadstead and could offer no shelter to shipping. The lighthouse was of service to steamers plying between Odessa, the Bosphorus and the mouths of the Danube, and was more likely to be looked after efficiently by the Russians than by the Turks. On the grounds of utility therefore, he felt 'inclined to pronounce in favour of Russia'. The question of right, however, appeared to him to be entirely against that power, 'unless she could produce some title of which he was ignorant.' When Cowley threw out the suggestion that both island and lighthouse might be handed over to the International Danube Commission set up by the Treaty of Paris, Walewski raised no objection.[2]

Cowley's report brought Palmerston on the scene. The Russian pretension to Serpents island, he declared, could not for one moment be tolerated. It was quite immaterial to enquire to whom it had heretofore belonged. It had most probably been occupied by Russia 'because it lay to the North of the Boundary Line between Russia and Turkey, and as the Delta of the Danube belong to Russia, this Island off the Delta naturally belonged to Russia also'. Now that the boundary line between Russia and Turkey was removed far to the north, the island was necessarily included within the Turkish limits. From a military point of view it was 'quite wrong' that Russia should have possession of an island commanding the approaches to the Danube. Walewski had said that it was small and in itself valueless; so much the more obvious was it that the Russians wanted to get it 'for Purposes of obstruction and Military Command'. The island was Turkish territory by the Treaty of Paris and Turkish territory it must remain. The duty of maintaining the lighthouse might be laid on the International Danube Commission, but the territorial sovereignty remained with Turkey. Walewski must be told that the British fleet would see to it that that sovereignty was respected.[3]

An official despatch embodying Palmerston's views was at

---

[1] Cowley to Clarendon, 8 Jun. 1856, F.O. 27/1128, no. 597.
[2] Cowley to Clarendon, 15 Jun. 1856, F.O. 27/1128, no. 635.
[3] Palmerston Memorandum, 17 Jun. 1856, Clarendon MSS.

once transmitted to Paris. Her Majesty's government, Clarendon declared, was not prepared to tolerate the pretension of
Russia to keep Serpents Island. The object of the recent treaty
had been to free the navigation of the Danube from the interference of Russia, 'that Power having invariably made use of its
control in order to impede instead of assist the navigation of
that river.' To leave or rather to hand over to Russia an island
off the mouths of the Danube would therefore be 'an act of folly'
which the British government would not allow to be committed
so long as British warships remained in the Black Sea. The island
was Turkish territory by the Treaty of Paris and Turkish territory it must remain. The British and French fleets must see to it
that this sovereignty was respected.[1]

On 4 July, as a precautionary measure, Clarendon advised
the Turkish government to place a small force on the island.[2]
A week later he learnt from Constantinople that a few seamen
sent by the Turkish Admiralty were in fact in occupation and
looking after the light.[3] Palmerston, however, did not feel reassured. Lyons, the British Commander in Chief, he urged,
should be ordered to station a vessel of war off the island to
support the Turkish occupation. Moreover, the Porte should
be advised to reinforce its garrison.[4] Clarendon agreed and
gave instructions for the Admiralty and Stratford, the ambassador at Constantinople to be written to as suggested by
Palmerston.[5] On 21 July, a telegram was accordingly sent to
Stratford.[6] It was already too late.

II

That very day, a message from Stratford was received at the
Foreign Office. The Russians, he reported, had sent to occupy
Serpents Island. Surprised to find the Turks already in occupa-
tion, they had left 'a detachment of ten men with an officer or
two'. Such was the information which he had obtained from the
Turkish Admiralty, and he had no reason to doubt its accuracy.[7]

[1] Clarendon to Cowley, 18 Jun. 1856, F.O. 146/625, no. 539.
[2] Clarendon to Stratford, telegram, 4 Jul. 1856, F.O. 78/1164, no. 758.
[3] Stratford to Clarendon, 26 Jun. 1856, F.O. 78/1182, no. 791.
[4] Palmerston Memorandum, 20 Jul. 1856, F.O. 96/25.
[5] Ibid.
[6] Clarendon to Stratford, telegram, 21 Jul. 1856, F.O. 78/1164, no. 817, draft.
[7] Stratford to Clarendon, telegram, 19 Jul. 1856, F.O. 78/1184, no. 901.

E

In the face of this new development, Palmerston at once proposed that Lyons should be ordered 'to dislodge the Russian Detachment which after Conclusion of Peace has by force taken Possession of an Island which belongs to Turkey'.[1] The cabinet, however, rejected the suggestion and on July 23 Lyons was instructed instead merely to station a ship off the island to support the Turkish occupation.[2]

The next step now lay with Lord Lyons. On July 27 the Admiral, flying his flag in the Bosphorus, wrote a memorandum for the use of Captain Hillyar, commanding the frigate H.M.S. *Gladiator*. Hillyar was to proceed at once to Serpents Island and on his arrival there 'quietly to make it manifest' that he recognized on the island no authority other than that of the Turks. Should the Sultan's officer find it necessary to remonstrate against usurpation of authority from any quarter, Hillyar, upon request, would join in such remonstrance. Should there be persistence in the usurpation of authority, he was to return to the Bosphorus for further instructions, taking care 'to let it be known by the offending party as well as by the Sultan's Officer', that he was about to do so. Should he, on the other hand, find the Turkish authorities in 'indisputed & undisturbed occupation of the Island', he was to remain for two days and then to rejoin the Admiral's flag in the Bosphorus.[3]

In pursuance of these instructions, Hillyar left the Bosphorus on the morning of July 28 and on the following day the *Gladiator* dropped anchor off Serpents Island. He found the Turkish flag flying and the island occupied by a Turkish garrison of 50 men under the command of a captain. He also discovered a Russian naval lieutenant in command of seven unarmed seamen, all of whom occupied a room in the lighthouse. According to the Turkish captain, the Russians had not usurped the slightest authority, or attempted to interfere with him in any way. Indeed he looked upon them in the light of guests, as he was obliged to supply them with meat and other necessaries. As his accommodation was limited, he would be glad to be relieved of their presence.

---

[1] Palmerston Memorandum, 22 Jul. 1856, Clarendon MSS.
[2] Admiralty to Lyons, telegram, 23 Jul. 1856, copy in Hammond to Secretary of Admiralty, 22 Jul. 1856, P.R.O. Adm[iralty] 1/5678.
[3] Lyons to Hillyar, 27 Jul. 1856, copy in Admiralty to Foreign Office, 14 Aug. 1856, F.O. 78/1238.

The Russian officer, Hillyar discovered, was confined to his bed with a severe attack of fever, and was immediately given every attention by the surgeon of the *Gladiator*. He declined an offer from Hillyar to convey him and his party to Odessa, saying that his orders were to stay on Serpents Island until sent for. Hillyar then told him that the British government recognized only the authority of the Sultan, to whom the island belonged. The lieutenant rejoined that he had never assumed the least authority or attempted to interfere with the Sultan's officer. His sole duty was to look after some gear and oil which had been sent by a small steamer from Nicolaev for the use of the lighthouse, and landed four days ago. These fittings and stores the Turkish officer had refused to make use of as he had himself eight workmen employed on repairing the light in readiness for a new set of lamps which had been ordered from England. A temporary and very indifferent light, Hillyar learnt, had been operated by the Turks since the beginning of July.

Having collected this information, Hillyar sailed to the Sulina mouth of the Danube where under the terms of Art. XIX of the Treaty of Paris, a British gunboat was stationed. Having asked the captain of this vessel to keep an eye on the island, he then turned back to pay it another visit. Finding the Turks in undisputed authority, he left to rejoin Lord Lyons. On the afternoon of August 2, the *Gladiator*, her mission successfully accomplished, dropped anchor in the Bosphorus.[1]

In the meantime, however, the British cabinet had decided that the Russians must be ejected. If there was a Russian detachment on the island, the First Lord of the Admiralty had telegraphed to Lyons on July 29, that detachment must be removed.[2] On 3 August, therefore, Lyons instructed Hillyar to return once more to the island. Should he find the Russian detachment still living in the lighthouse, he was to offer once again to convey it to Odessa or any other Russian port in the neighbourhood. Should the offer be again refused, he was to proceed to Odessa to inform the Russian governor there that the limited space on the island and the heat of the weather made it desirable that the Turkish detachment should be

---

[1] Hillyar to Lyons, 2 Aug. 1856, copy in Admiralty to Foreign Office, 15 Aug. 1856, F.O. 78/1238.

[2] Lyons to Admiralty, 4 Aug. 1856, no. 42, copy in Admiralty to Foreign Office, 15 Aug. 1856, F.O. 78/1238, confidential.

immediately relieved of the presence of the Russians. He was to offer, for this purpose, the services of the *Gladiator* and should these be declined he was to inform Lyons of the fact as speedily as possible.[1]

By issuing these instructions, the sailor-diplomat in the Bosphorus was taking it upon himself to disobey the orders of the Admiralty. In forwarding to London a copy of his instruction to Hillyar, he defended his action by explaining that he was in possession of information not available to his superiors when the removal of the Russians was ordered. The Russian party, he pointed out, consisted of only one lieutenant and seven seamen, all of them unarmed. The Turks were in full possession of the island with their colours flying, and they were looking after the light. In view of these facts, Lyons expressed the hope that his instructions to Hillyar might 'appear to their Lordships sufficient to meet this case in its present stage'.[2]

Hillyar, meanwhile, had returned to Serpents Island on the afternoon of 5 August. On landing, he had found matters in the state in which he had left them five days earlier. The Russian lieutenant again refused to evacuate the Russian party to Odessa, stating that he 'could not leave without instructions from a superior officer'. On 6 August, the *Gladiator* reached Odessa. Hillyar explained to the military governor of the town the purpose of his visit, and on being asked to do so, he left a written communication, requesting in the name of Lord Lyons the speedy removal of the Russian detachment and offering the services of the *Gladiator* for the purpose. The Governor promised to transmit the request to Count Stroganov, Governor-General of New Russia and Bessarabia and to notify Hillyar of the reply.

The following day, the Captain of the port received a communication, instructing him to inform Hillyar 'that the Governor-General would take the necessary steps with respect to the Russians on Serpent's Island and that there was no occasion for the *Gladiator* to remain any longer'. Hillyar, however, was not to be shaken off, and now addressed to the Governor-General a request to inform him in writing of the measures he intended to

---

[1] Lyons to Hillyar, 3 Aug. 1856, copy in Admiralty to Foreign Office, 15 Aug. 1856, F.O. 78/1238.
[2] Lyons to Admiralty, 4 Aug. 1856, no. 4, confidential, copy in Admiralty to Foreign Office, 15 Aug. 1856, F.O. 78/1238.

take and of the date on which the Russian party was likely to be sent for.[1]

Stroganov replied on 8 August that he had addressed himself to General Lüders, Commander-in-Chief of the Second Army 'pour demander ses ordres à ce sujet'. He would inform Hillyar 'des dispositions de Son Excellence dès qu'elles seront communiquées'.[2]

In the meantime, on 7 August, the Russian authorities in Odessa had applied to St Petersburg for instructions. The Russian government had decided to reject the British demand and to refer the dispute to the collective decision of the powers who had signed the treaty of peace. Gorchakov informed Morny, the French ambassador, on 8 August, that instructions in this sense had been sent to the authorities at Odessa. 'Remercier le commandant anglais pour sa proposition et la décliner,' they had been told, 'disant que nos hommes resteront dans l'île des Serpents jusqu'à ce qu'il soit décidé par la conférence de Paris à qui appartient cette île.'[3]

Not till the evening of 10 August did Hillyar receive his reply from Stroganov. 'Son Excellence', the Count then wrote on behalf of General Lüders, 'm'a chargé de vous prier d'agréer ses remerciments pour l'offre de transporter ces marins à bord du Gladiator ... offre dont il ne saurait profiter, vu que nos matelôts et leur officier ont l'ordre de rester dans l'île des Serpents jusqu'à ce que la Conférence de Paris ait pris une décision au sujet de cette Ile.'[4] After acknowledging the receipt of this communication, Hillyar left Odessa and arrived off Serpents Island the following morning. He found, awaiting him, a British gunboat, which he at once despatched to the Bosphorus with a report for Lord Lyons.[5]

That very morning, there had arrived off the island on the side opposite to where the *Gladiator* had cast anchor, a small Russian steamer. When Hillyar landed on the island, he was met near

[1] Hillyar to Stroganov, 7 Aug. 1856, copy in Admiralty to Foreign Office, 30 Aug. 1856, F.O. 78/1239.
[2] Stroganov to Hillyar, 27 Jul./8 Aug. 1856, copy in Admiralty to Foreign Office, 30 Aug. 1856, F.O. 78/1239.
[3] Morny to Walewski, 8 Aug. 1856, A.A.E. Russie 212, no. 1.
[4] Stroganov to Hillyar, 29 Jul./10 Aug. 1856, copy in Admiralty to Foreign Office, 30 Aug. 1856, F.O. 78/1239.
[5] Hillyar to Lyons, 11 Aug. 1856, copy in Admiralty to Foreign Office, 30 Aug. 1856, F.O. 78/1239.

the lighthouse by 'Mr. Botteanoff who styles himself "conseiller d'Etat et Gentilhomme de la Cour" ', accompanied by four Russian officers in full uniform. Not recognizing Hillyar's nationality, and having mistaken the *Gladiator* for a Turkish vessel, Botteanoff explained that he had come 'to make his arrangements to take possession of the place which had been given up to the Russians by the Conferences'. He appeared 'quite astonished' when he learnt that Hillyar was the captain of a British frigate, and had arrived only that morning from Odessa, where he had been to request the removal of the Russians from the island. He showed Hillyar a part of his instructions from General Lüders, 'to the effect "that he was to inform the Turkish Commandant that the Island would shortly be given up to Russia", which he then said was the object of his mission.' It emerged that Botteanoff had received his instructions, forwarded by telegraph from St Petersburg, on 8 August, the second day after Hillyar's arrival at Odessa. Botteanoff had been detained for three days on the passage, owing to strong contrary winds.[1]

Hillyar at once gave Botteanoff to understand that the Russians would not be allowed to assume the slightest authority on the island, and that the Russian officer and party already there were looked upon by the Turks merely as visitors until the Royal Navy should receive further instructions about them. Botteanoff, 'having remained on the Island some hours, minutely inspecting all the buildings,' left for the Sulina mouth of the Danube, as he was 'desirous of communicating with a Superior Turkish Officer'. Once again, however, the state-counsellor lost his race with the Royal Navy, for Lieutenant Hudson in H.M.S. *Clinker* had reached Sulina before him, 'in time to put the Turkish Commandant on his Guard.' As a result, 'Monsieur Botteanoff failed in his object of obtaining permission to land at Serpents' Island several things for the Light House which he was most anxious to do.'[2] Whilst Hillyar

[1] 'It therefore appears to me quite evident,' Hillyar observed, 'that the reason Count [*sic*] Strogonoff detained the Gladiator so long before he gave his answer, was to allow Mr. Botteanoff full time to reach Serpents' Island before me, that he might make his claims and endeavour to gain the Turkish Commandant over to his views' (Hillyar to Lyons, 11 Aug. 1856, copy in Admiralty to Foreign Office, 30 Aug. 1856, F.O. 78/1239).

[2] Hillyar to Lyons, 14 Aug. 1856, copy in Admiralty to Foreign Office, 30 Aug. 1856, F.O. 78/1239.

remained to watch the island, Hudson after his return from Sulina proceeded to the Bosphorus with a report for Lord Lyons about the activities of state-counsellor Botteanoff.

III

On 14 August, the Foreign Office received from the Admiralty copies of Hillyar's report on his first visit to Serpents Island and of Lyons's instructions for his second mission.[1] The failure of Lyons to remove the Russian detachment angered Palmerston, who gave vent to his feelings in three energetic letters to the faithful Clarendon. 'In cases of this kind,' he declared, 'quick Action and a Fait accompli carry the Day & save a great Deal of Trouble afterwards.' If there was only one sick lieutenant with several unarmed men, that was only one more reason for their removal, as it could be done 'without Resistance or Collision'. Had there been fifty or a hundred armed men, who could not have been removed without a fight, he would have better understood 'the Hesitation as to a Proceeding which might bring about a Conflict'. It was all very well to say that the Turks considered the Russians as guests and that the Russian party did not dispute the rightful occupation by the Turks. The Russian government was no partner to this language and would maintain that the presence of a Russian officer and men constituted 'a joint occupation continued by the assent of the allies, and an admission by them of a joint or doubtful Right'. The British government should now tell Lyons to remove the detachment and take it to Odessa, 'taking care of the sick Lieutenant & giving him medical assistance.' They should inform the Russian and French governments that they had done so, saying that this measure merely restored matters 'to the State in which they were when after the conclusion of the Treaty the Russian Detachment landed on the Island which was then in Possession of the Turks', and that if the Russians had arguments to bring forward in favour of their claims, those arguments would be just as open to consideration as if their detachment had remained on the island.[2] Clarendon agreed. He told the Queen,

---

[1] Admiralty to Foreign Office, 15 Aug. 1856, with enclosures, F.O. 78/1238.

[2] Palmerston to Clarendon, private, 15 Aug. 1856, three letters, Clarendon MSS. The incident, Palmerston considered, had been managed 'with the usual cunning of the Muscovite'. The Russians had committed 'an act of aggression after the Signature & Ratification of Peace, in a Sea on which we are strong & they are weak

who was staying at Osborne, that since the Russians seemed determined not to quit Serpents Island, and since Lord Lyons had not carried out his instructions to remove them, he must 'again be required to do so'.[1]

Palmerston's views on Serpents Island, however, were not shared by Granville, the Lord Privy Seal and a former Foreign Secretary, who during the critical weeks was on his way to Russia as special ambassador to attend the coronation of Alexander II. 'Of course we are masters of the Fate of the Island of Serpents,' Granville told his friend and colleague Clarendon, 'and we can keep possession of the Black Sea as long as we have a fair pretence for saying that the Russians have not carried out their engagements.' 'I should doubt our having right on our side, as no mention was made of it at Paris.'[2] Granville on reaching St Petersburg, had discovered that his views were shared by the British minister Lord Wodehouse. 'He thinks,' Wodehouse wrote to Clarendon the day after Granville's arrival, 'and I am inclined to agree with him, that our right to eject the Russians from Serpents' Island may be doubtful: and as Gortchacoff has expressed himself ready to submit the question to the decision of the powers who signed the Treaty of Paris we might leave them in occupation "pendente lite".'[3]

The arguments put forward by Granville and Wodehouse were not without their effect upon the Queen, who still felt a lingering distrust of Palmerston's adventurous policies and who attached great weight to the opinions of the Lord Privy Seal. 'As Ld. Lyons has not complied with the order to remove the Russians from S.I.,' she told Clarendon, 'he who is not wont in general to shrink from doing what he thinks right & as Lords Granville & Woodehouse [sic] doubt our right to do so, the Queen is very doubtful whether it will be politic to renew the

they throw down the gauntlet to us by this act, and in order to provide for either Case namely our submitting or resisting they send only an unarmed Boats [sic] Crew, so that if we submit it shall be clear to all Mankind that we submit not from any local Difficulty but simply from Fear of Russia; while on the other Hand if we resist & remove the Detachment, the Fact of its consisting of half a dozen unarmed Men saves the Honour of the Detachment and of the Russian Govt because Resistance by such a Detachment is impossible'. In fact, the Russian government appeared to have shaped their course in this matter 'as if purposely to try our mettle and to see whether we are afraid of them or not' (ibid.).

[1] Clarendon to the Queen, 15 Aug. 1856, R.A. G 48/63.
[2] Granville to Clarendon, private, 1 Aug. 1856, Clarendon MSS.
[3] Wodehouse to Clarendon, private, 9 Aug. 1856, Clarendon MSS.

order to Ld. Lyons. We ought not to put ourselves in the wrong where we have been complaining of wrong.'[1]

The expression of the Queen's opinion produced a complete *volte face* on the part of Palmerston. 'I am ready,' he had written on 15 August, 'to take upon myself the whole Responsibility of removing these Russians from Serpents Island, but I cannot take on myself the Humiliation of allowing them to remain there.'[2] Yet by 17 August he had drafted a despatch to Wodehouse stating that the Russian detachment was not now to be removed from the island.[3] Clarendon, in submitting this draft to the Queen explained that the Russians were not to be ejected as they did not interfere with the Turkish garrison. Instead, the British government would represent the circumstances to the Russian government and 'earnestly . . . recommend' the withdrawal of the detachment.[4] On 18 August, a telegram was sent to Lyons. As the Turks were in full and undisputed possession of Serpents Island, the Admiral was told, it was unnecessary at present to remove the Russian lieutenant and seven unarmed men. This however was not to be considered as an admission of any claim to the island on the part of Russia. Lyons must prevent any further Russian landing on the island. The Russian government was being informed of this instruction. Medical aid should be afforded to the sick lieutenant and he and his men should be given a passage to Odessa 'whenever they desire to go there'.[5] In this way, the moral scruples of the Queen backed by Lyons' sense of proportion, by the misgivings of Granville and Wodehouse and by the moderation of Clarendon had carried the day against Palmerston's diplomacy of direct action. As a result, the question of Serpents Island was left to be settled by diplomatic negotiation.

IV

On 18 August, Wodehouse was informed by telegraph of the British decision. He was to communicate it to the Russian government and 'earnestly recommend the withdrawal of the detachment from the Island'. A copy of the instructions to

---

[1] The Queen to Clarendon, 16 Aug. 1856, R.A. G 48/65, draft.
[2] Palmerston to Clarendon, 15 Aug. 1856, Clarendon MSS.
[3] Clarendon to Wodehouse, 18 Aug. 1856, F.O. 96/25, draft.
[4] Clarendon to the Queen, 17 Aug. 1856, R.A. G 48/66.
[5] Text in Wodehouse to Clarendon, 19 Aug. 1856, F.O. 65/472, no. 113.

Lyons was also transmitted to him.[1] Wodehouse at once approached his French colleague with a view to joint representations, but learnt that the French government preferred that the island should go to Russia because the Russians would keep the lighthouse in proper order, whilst the Turks were likely to neglect it. Morny considered, moreover, that 'the only practical mode of coming to a conclusion would be to reassemble the Congress at Paris'.[2] In the face of this attitude, Wodehouse communicated to Gorchakov by letter the instructions which had been given to Lyons, adding a strong recommendation that the detachment be withdrawn.[3] Gorchakov, however, refused to give up his position. He replied that, having on the orders of his Emperor referred the question to the conference in Paris, 'je dois persévérer à contester le droit que s'arrogerait une Puissance pour décider à elle seule ce qui évidemment est du ressort collectif de tous les Gouvernements qui ont signé le traité de Paris.'[4]

Gorchakov's position was made clear in a despatch to Brunnow. The island, he declared, had been in undisputed Russian occupation since 1833. He had never doubted Russia's right to re-occupy it in order to provide for the maintenance of the lighthouse. Brunnow had been charged with enquiring of Walewski and Cowley if there were British or French troops on the island and had been informed that it was never occupied by the allies. No suspicion, Gorchakov ingenuously asserted, had ever crossed his mind, that the Russian right to occupy the island might become a matter of dispute. The island, had no strategic or military value and was 'sans aucune importance pour nous'. It was the action of the British government which had forced Russia 'de donner à cet incident une gravité que son objet ne pourrait jamais acquérir de lui-même'. The British challenge made it necessary for Russia '. . . de prouver qu'un état de Ier ordre ne saurait accepter la loi arbitraire d'un état quelconque'. Russia therefore could only repeat to the British cabinet 'qu'il n'est point dans le vrai en prétendant substituer sa volonté isolée à celle des ses co-signataires du traité de Paris'. He believed that Walewski favoured the neutralization of the island, and Brunnow was authorized if the conference re-assembled, to agree

[1] Ibid.
[2] Wodehouse to Clarendon, 21 Aug. 1856, F.O. 65/472, no. 117, confidential.
[3] Copy in Wodehouse to Clarendon, 21 Aug. 1856, F.O. 65/472, no. 120.
[4] Copy in Wodehouse to Clarendon, 28 Aug. 1856, F.O. 65/472, no. 128.

to this and to the maintenance of the lighthouse by the International Danubian Commission.[1]

In fact, ever since the beginning of August, Gorchakov had been aware of the fact that on the question of Serpents Island there existed a difference of opinion between the British and French governments. On 1 August, before the arrival of Morny at St Petersburg, Baudin, the French chargé d'affaires, had reported to Walewski that whereas the British and Austrian ministers had pronounced themselves 'très fortement' against the Russian claim, he himself in a conversation with Gorchakov had not entered into a detailed discussion of the question as he had no instructions.[2] Morny himself, before leaving Paris, had been informed by Walewski that the island was 'un rocher de peu d'importance', and that Admiral Hamelin had expressed the opinion that the lighthouse would be better maintained by a regular government like the Russian. 'Pénétré de ces idées,' Morny reported to his chief on 17 August, 'je n'ai pas dû en arrivant ici, me montrer bien rigoureux auprès du Prince Gortchakoff sur la question de l'évacuation de l'île des Serpents et . . . je me suis trouvé parfaitement satisfait d'en référer à la conférence de Paris.' There was even 'assez de loyauté et de bon vouloir' in Russia's proposal to submit the dispute to the conference, 'attendu qu'aucun article du traité du 30 mars ne lui retire formellement la possession de l'îlot et qu'on ne peut faire valoir pour la lui contester que de pures considérations, et je me suis vu d'autant plus fondé à adhérer à ce mode d'accomodement que je n'ai pas douté, en définitive, qu'une fois passé à la Conférence, la question ne fût résolue contre la Russie.'[3] A difference of opinion thus existed between the governments of England and France. 'La divergence me parait profonde entre Paris et Londres,' Morny observed, 'sur cette misérable question de l'île des Serpents. Autant que je puisse me le rappeler, vous m'avez fait envisager la question comme devant être soumise à une délibération, tandis que le Cabinet anglais déclare ici en termes formels qu'il n'y a pas incertitude dans son esprit et que son escadre ne quittera la mer noire qu'après que l'îlot aura été abandonné aux Turcs.'[4]

[1] Gorchakov to Brunnow, 11/23 Aug. 1856, A.A.E. Russie 212.
[2] Baudin to Walewski, 1 Aug./20 Jul. 1856, A.A.E. Russie 212, no. 5.
[3] Morny to Walewski, 17/5 Aug. 1856, A.A.E. Russie 212, no. 4.
[4] Ibid.

This division of opinion among the allies was grist to Gorchakov's mill. 'If I appreciate the present state of affairs rightly,' Wodehouse told Clarendon, 'the policy of the Russian Government consists in throwing all kinds of petty difficulties and delays in the way of the execution of the late Treaty, not so much with the hope of ultimately evading the fulfilment of its conditions, but with the view to raise questions which may cause dissensions between the Allied Powers, and especially between England and France, and thus ultimately to break up the Western Alliance.'[1] He did not believe, Granville added in his turn, that there had been 'any set intention to evade the main conditions of the peace', but the Russians had 'tried to avail themselves of every loophole to get a petty advantage', and, 'like the man in the street who is desired by the Policeman to move on,' they thought it 'consistent with their dignity to do so as slowly and sulkily as possible'. They might also have been influenced by 'a wish to flourish in the eyes of some of their savage neighbours, and they have had hope of dividing England & France, & I am not quite sure that they have not a little succeeded in the latter attempt'.[2] Morny, whose close relations with Gorchakov gave him a special insight into the working of Russian diplomacy, confirmed the estimate of his British colleagues. 'Toutes les fois', he reported to Walewski, 'que sur une même question l'ambassade d'Angleterre tiendra un autre langage que moi, on sera naturellement enclin à se figurer qu'il existe des semences de désunion entre la France et l'Angleterre et je n'ai pas besoin de vous dire, qu'on ne verrait sans plaisir se développer ces germes imaginaires.'[3]

The French government, in the meantime, was shifting to a position unfavourable to Gorchakov's claims. On 11 August, Walewski told Morny, that though the Emperor Napoleon had not yet reached a final decision, he was inclined to favour the British view. 'Nous ne saurions toutefois nous dissimuler,' he explained 'que les objections faites à l'argument que le cabinet de St. Pétersbourg tire du silence du traité nous paraissent sérieuses et que l'opinion qui consiste à regarder le rocher comme une sorte d'annexe du territoire cédé par la Russie s'appuie sur des

[1] Wodehouse to Clarendon, 3 Sept. 1856, F.O. 65/472, no. 138, confidential.
[2] Granville to Clarendon, private, 15 Aug. 1856, Clarendon MSS.
[3] Morny to Walewski, 17/5 Aug. 1856, A.A.E. Russie 212, no. 4.

données historiques qui méritent considération.'[1] However, just as the French government appeared to be coming closer to the British point of view, a new issue, that of Bolgrad, offered Gorchakov a further opportunity to develop his offensive.

V

The dispute about Bolgrad had arisen out of the execution of Art. XX of the Treaty of Paris. Under the terms of this article the new Russo-Moldavian frontier in Bessarabia, designed to remove Russia from all contact with the navigable portions of the Danube, was to pass to the south of a place called Bolgrad.[2] When in June the delimitation commission had assembled to lay out the new frontier on the ground itself, the allied commissioners had received an unpleasant shock. From an 'unpublished Russian Survey' in the possession of the Russian delegation it emerged that Bolgrad, to the south of which the new frontier was to be drawn, was situated not, as had previously been supposed, some distance to the north of Lake Yalpuck [which had water-communications with the lower Danube], but near the shore of the lake itself.[3] As a result of this discovery, a difference of opinion had arisen between the Russian and Turkish commissioners. The Russians had argued that a line passing south of Bolgrad must necessarily cut the lake and that part of the lake to its *thalweg* must therefore belong to Russia. The Turks on the other hand had insisted that they should have at least sufficient space for a road between the town and the lake, so as to allow free land-communications at all seasons between Moldavia and the territory to the east of the lake ceded to her under the Treaty of Paris.[4]

On 8 June, the commissioners during a preliminary reconnaissance of the ground, had reached the town of Bolgrad. 'Bolgrad', the French commissioner, Col. Besson, reported to his government, 'est situé sur une position qui paraît très saine, et qui n'est pas à moins de 50 m au dessus du lac Yalpuck. La ville compte actuellement 824 maisons habitées par 8214 individus. Les rues sont larges, bien alignées et horizontales: elles sont fort propres ainsi que les maisons qui les bordent. L'église

---

[1] Walewski to Morny, 11 Aug. 1856, A.A.E. Russie 212, no. 9, draft.
[2] For Art. XX of the Treaty of 30 Mar. 1856, cf. Oakes and Mowat, loc. cit.
[3] Stanton to Stratford, 31 May 1856, F.O. 195/532, no. 3.
[4] Stanton to Clarendon, 7 Jun. 1856, F.O. 78/1196, no. 2.

et le jardin publique sont très remarquables pour le pays. Il s'y tient chaque semaine une foire ou grand marché fréquenté principalement par des colons Bulgares. Le gouvernement Russe peut être fier de la création de Bolgrad, et, à cause de l'influence de cette ville sur les Bulgares de la rive droite du Danube, il doit faire de grands efforts pour la conserver.'[1]

The allied commissioners, however, in the course of their reconnaissance of the Bolgrad district not only found a relatively clean and well-constructed market town, but also discovered that a village situated three miles to the north of the lake had until recently been known as Bolgrad. 'Divers faits établissent,' they declared in a note addressed to their Russian colleagues, 'que le village appelé actuellement Tabak, situé sur les bords de la rivière Yalpuck . . . s'appelait récemment encore Bolgrad, et doit être considéré aujourd'hui comme le Bolgrad primitif.' The map sent to the French commissioner by his government 'comme le meilleur document officiel connu à Paris' proved 'que l'on n'a pus [sic] entendre au Congrès de Paris par Bolgrad que l'ancien Bolgrad (Tabak), qui se trouve sur les bords de la rivière Yalpuck . . .'. The new town of Bolgrad, the commissioners concluded, 'établi depuis 1828, qui ne se trouve pas sur les cartes officielles sus-mentionnées, . . . ne coincide pas avec le Bolgrad mentionné dans l'art. 20.'[2]

To this assertion, the Russian commissioners replied in a long and confusing note. They attempted to show — with arguments which could have convinced no one but themselves — that the village marked on the map of the French commissioner as Bolgrad (Tabak), had always been known as Tabak, and that the name of Bolgrad had been reserved exclusively for the new town on the lake, established between 1820 and 1828 by inhabitants of the older settlement of Tabak. The name of Bolgrad had appeared by the side of that of Tabak on the special map of the Russian general staff of 1820[3] presented to the commis-

[1] Besson to Walewski, 17 Jun. 1856, A.A.E. Roumanie, 1856–57, IV, no. 8.

[2] Note Verbale des Commissaires de l'Autriche, de la France, de la Grande Bretagne, et de la Porte Ottomane, communiquée à Messieurs les Commissaires de la Russie concernant la question de Bolgrad. Le 11 Juin 1856, copy in Stanton to Clarendon 15 Jun. 1856, F.O. 78/1196, no. 3.

[3] It was a copy of this out-of-date map which had been made use of at the Paris congress when laying down the frontier. This map, of course, had not shown the town of new Bolgrad on the lake, which was not yet in existence, but merely the locality of Bolgrad (Tabak), situated some distance to the north of the lake.

sion, because at the time it was drawn the move from Tabak to Bolgrad was still in progress and the new town on the lake had not yet been established. That new town was the only Bolgrad which had ever existed and was therefore the town indicated by Art. XX. In accordance with international custom, the new frontier west of the town must run along the *thalweg* of the lake.[1] Faced with these opposing views as to the Bolgrad intended by the congress, the commissioners had decided to refer for instructions to their respective governments.[2]

In the meantime, the British government had reacted to the first telegraphic enquiry from its commissioner, Stanton, despatched after the Russian commissioners' map had shown that Bolgrad might be situated on the shore of Lake Yalpuck itself. 'A space', Palmerston and Clarendon [who did not yet know of the existence of two Bolgrads], had ruled, 'should be left for a road between Bolgrad and Lake Yalpuck.' Cowley had been instructed to communicate this view to Walewski with a warning that the proceedings of Russia must be 'narrowly watched' and that 'all attempts at encroachment should be firmly resisted'.[3]

Walewski agreed. Space, he declared, must be left for a road between Bolgrad and the lake, and the lake itself, as intended by the treaty, must be completely Moldavian.[4] Walewski, at the same time, instructed Besson to appeal to the good faith of the the Russian commissioners, and to remind them that the plenipotentiaries in Paris had intended that the frontier should run to the north of Lake Yalpuck. The proposal for the construction of a road between the town and the lake seemed to carry out the intentions of the congress, and Besson should support it.[5]

When the British government learnt of the existence of two Bolgrads, new instructions were at once sent to Stanton. Only one town called Bolgrad, he was told, had been marked on the map which was laid before the congress, and when it had been

---

[1] Note Verbale des Commissaires de la Russie, communiquée à Messieurs les Commissaires de l'Autriche, de la France, de la Grande Bretagne, et de la Porte Ottomane concernant la question de Bolgrad, 1/13 Juin 1856, copy in Stanton to Clarendon, 15 Jun. 1856, F.O. 78/1196, no. 3.

[2] Protocol no. 4. of the delimitation commission, copy in Stanton to Clarendon, 15 Jun. 1856, F.O. 78/1196, no. 3.

[3] Clarendon to Cowley, 11 Jun. 1856, F.O. 146/625, no. 512.

[4] Cowley to Clarendon, 15 Jun. 1856, F.O. 27/1128, no. 633.

[5] Walewski to Besson, 14 Jun. 1856, A.A.E. Roumanie, 1856–57, IV, no. 4, draft.

determined to allow the frontier to be carried south of Bolgrad, 'it was evident to the Members of the Congress . . . that ample room was left between Bolgrad and Lake Yalpuck, which Lake was to belong exclusively to Moldavia.' It had also been 'the undisguised and unquestioned determination of the Congress' that the Russian frontier should be removed from the Danube and that no inland water-communication whatever with that river should be possessed by Russia. Stanton was to 'keep these objects steadily in view' and to 'consent to no arrangement by which the Spirit of the Treaty and the policy of the Four Contracting Powers in this most important matter . . .' would be nullified by Russia.[1] A copy of this instruction was sent to Cowley for transmission to Walewski, but when it reached Paris the French minister had already left the capital for his summer vacation, and diplomatic activity was virtually at a standstill.

On 18 July, a despatch to Wodehouse, foreshadowed a shift in British policy. It was not till lately, Clarendon stated, that the British government had become aware of the existence of two Bolgrads. Only one had been shown on the map used by the congress, and between it and Lake Yalpuck there appeared to be sufficient space. Otherwise, it would not have been stipulated that the frontier should be drawn to the south of Bolgrad. It had been the clear and unmistakable object of the congress, an object accepted by the Russian plenipotentiaries also, that Russia should be debarred from communication with the Danube and with the navigable portion of the Pruth. From this principle it was impossible to depart, and Her Majesty's government must consider 'that an attempt, founded upon an error in a map, to gain an advantage that was not intended, would be inconsistent with the honour and dignity of Russia'. If the commissioners were to find upon examination that the stipulations of the treaty could not be executed 'by drawing the Frontier Line south of the new Bolgrad', it appeared only reasonable that it should be drawn 'south of the old Bolgrad'.[2]

The change in British policy foreshadowed by Clarendon had been a slow one. As late as 5 August, he still told Stanton to 'insist upon the boundary being drawn so as to leave between the Northern extremities of the different lakes and the boundary

[1] Clarendon to Stanton, 1 Jul. 1856, F.O. 78/1196, no. 2, draft.
[2] Clarendon to Wodehouse, 18 Jul. 1856, F.O. 181/301, no. 104.

line sufficient space for free communication by land and without the intervention of any Russian territory between the Western and Eastern district of Southern Bessarabia ceded by the Treaty to Moldavia.'[1] It was not till 8 August that Palmerston and Clarendon informed the British commissioner that 'the only just way of settling the question as to Bolgrad would be to hold the Russians to the Bolgrad which was shown to the congress at Paris, and that the second Bolgrad should go for nothing'.[2] Not until 12 August did they finally tell him that 'the Bessarabian frontier should be traced to the north of the present town of Bolgrad', as 'the only satisfactory mode of fulfilling the intentions of the Congress'.[3] Stanton's new instructions had, as a matter of course, been transmitted to Paris, accompanied by a request that Besson might receive similar orders.[4]

However, in the meantime, Napoleon and Walewski also had taken up their position. On 1 August, instructions had been sent to Besson. 'Sans doute,' he had been told, 'si l'on s'en tenait à la lettre du traité de Paris . . . on serait fondé à prétendre qu'il s'agit du village indiqué sur cette carte sous la désignation de Bolgrad (Tabak) et nullement de la ville de Bolgrad.' The imperial government, however, had decided to regard the matter from a point of view 'selon lui plus équitable'. They had referred themselves to the motives which had induced the Russian plenipotentiaries to ask during the congress that the line should be drawn to the south of Bolgrad. Orlov and Brunnow had asked for and the congress had agreed to give them the *chef-lieu* of the Bulgarian Colonies, and the matter was thus 'une question de bonne foi'. Besson, therefore, was authorized to adopt the views of his Russian colleagues 'quant à la désignation de Bolgrad'. The Russian proposal, however, to draw the frontier along the *thalweg* of Lake Yalpuck was totally inadmissible, and the French government sincerely hoped that the Russian commissioners would desist themselves from this pretension. If they did this, Besson should work out with his colleagues details of a line of frontier which would follow a road to be constructed between new Bolgrad and the lake.[5]

[1] Clarendon to Stanton, 5 Aug. 1856, F.O. 78/1196, no. 3, draft.
[2] Clarendon to Stanton, 8 Aug. 1856, F.O. 78/1196, no. 5, draft.
[3] Clarendon to Stanton, 12 Aug. 1856, F.O. 78/1196, no. 6, draft.
[4] Clarendon to Cowley, 12 Aug. 1856, F.O. 146/631, nos. 792 and 793.
[5] Walewski to Besson, 1 Aug. 1856, A.A.E. Roumanie, 1856–57, IV, no. 5, draft.

F

On 5 August, Walewski returned to Paris and on the following day agreed with Cowley about the need for an uninterrupted
communication between Moldavia and the newly ceded territory. Walewski expressed himself 'so far willing to meet the
wishes of Russia as to leave Southern Bolgrad to her; with the
proviso that the town shall be cut off entirely from Lake
Yalpuck by a road, the said road to belong exclusively to
Moldavia'. Cowley replied, that though he spoke without
official authority, he did not expect that Clarendon would
object to such an arrangement.[1] The next day, Walewski in a
despatch to Morny, developed his views on the question of
Bolgrad. His despatch followed the lines of his instruction to
Besson. Orlov's demand at the congress for the capital of the
Bulgarian colonies, he concluded, 'nous décide donc à admettre
que s'il y a pu y avoir erreur ou malentendu quant à la position
topographique de Bolgrad, il n'y en a point eu en ce qui
regarde la localité même que les Plénipotentiaires ont entendu
désigner.'[2]

Five days later, Clarendon finally told Cowley that the
British government no longer accepted the solution based on a
Moldavian road. They now considered that the Russians should
'take Northern Bolgrad as the Bolgrad of the Treaty, that being
the town pointed out to the Congress, and referred to by the
words of the Treaty'. The attempt to substitute the southern
settlement for the northern was 'an act unworthy of a great
Power like Russia', to which England and France could not
submit 'without exposing themselves and their negotiators to
derision'.[3] On 14 August, Cowley informed Walewski of the
change in British policy, and handed him a copy of the new
instructions sent to Stanton two days before.[4] The divergence
between the British and French views was thus officially
established.

Much fruitless recrimination followed, each side insisting
that it had correctly interpreted the intentions of the congress
and blaming the other for having announced its policy without
consulting its allies. On the whole, Walewski had the better
of the argument pointing out that when adopting the solution of

[1] Cowley to Clarendon, 7 Aug. 1856, F.O. 27/1131, no. 898.
[2] Walewski to Morny, 7 Aug. 1856, A.A.E. Russie 212, no. 2, draft.
[3] Clarendon to Cowley, 12 Aug. 1856, F.O. 146/631, no. 793.
[4] Cowley to Clarendon, 14 Aug. 1856, F.O. 27/1132, no. 934.

the Moldavian road, the French government had had reason to suppose that it would find itself in agreement with the British.[1]

Gorchakov, in the meantime, had readily yielded to the persuasions of Morny, and had abandoned his claim to a frontier along the *thalweg* of Lake Yalpuck. On 21 August, Morny reported to Walewski Gorchakov's conditional acceptance of the French proposal.[2] Two days later, Gorchakov told Brunnow that the Russian commissioners had believed that the frontier along the *thalweg* offered the only possible solution of the local difficulty. However, since this proposal was not 'dans le sens littéral du traité', the commissioners had now been instructed 'de se désister de cette prétention et de chercher à se placer sur le tracé du traité au moyen d'une ligne tirée entre le lac et Bolgrad.'[3] Gorchakov had thus skilfully aligned Russia's policy with that of France in a question in which he knew differences to exist between France and her British ally. He had placed himself in a strong position and might entertain a hope, if not of material gain, at least of an increase in Franco-British tension.

VI

It was in these circumstances that Palmerston decided on a determined attempt to secure agreement — on his own terms — between the governments of England and France. On 31 August, he invited the French chargé d'affaires to urge his government to adopt the British view for the sake of the alliance. He 'took the opportunity to talk to him about Serpents Island & Bolgrad & to beg him to tell Walewsky that we could not give way about either & that we greatly wished he would support us at Petersburgh & prevent a Difference arising between England and France — which would be a great Delight to the Russians'.[4] Walewski, however, rejected the appeal. Ever since the beginning of the dispute, his efforts had been directed towards finding a compromise solution acceptable to both the British and Russian governments. He therefore told Howard, the British chargé d'affaires, that since the French government had now adopted

[1] Walewski to Malaret, 16 Aug. 1856, A.A.E. Angleterre 705, no. 81, draft.
[2] Morny to Walewski, 21 Aug. 1856, A.A.E. Russie 212, no. 5.
[3] Gorchakov to Brunnow, 11/23 Aug. 1856, copy in A.A.E. Russie 212.
[4] Palmerston to Clarendon, private, 1 Sept. 1856, Clarendon MSS.

the British view on Serpents Island, he hoped that England, in return, would accept the French solution for Bolgrad. In this way, all difficulties about the execution of the treaty would be at once removed.[1] This, however, was not what Palmerston had hoped for. In his view, Walewski in arguing for mutual concessions was 'putting these matters upon an entirely erroneous basis'. The real question at issue was whether a treaty which the allies had purchased from Russia by immense exertions should be faithfully executed, or whether Russia should be allowed 'by Chicane, by false Statements & by unfounded Pretensions' to evade in very important points the faithful execution of that treaty. This was not a matter in which the British government could consult 'the personal wishes of Ct. Walewsky' or defer to the opinion of the French government. The British government were 'responsible to Parliament & to the British Nation for their Conduct in these matters', and they must 'look to their own Responsibilities and fulfill their Duty', whatever course the French government chose to pursue.[2]

Walewski, impressed by the firmness of the British attitude, now urged the Russian government to make concessions. On 6 September, the Russian minister in London, in conversation with the French chargé d'affaires, had suggested that his government might be willing to abandon its claims to both Serpents Island and Bolgrad 's'il était certain en agissant ainsi, que personne ne se méprendrait sur les motifs de sa conduite, et que l'on saurait bien en Europe qu'il ne cède point devant l'attitude hostile de l'Angleterre'.[3] Walewski at once asked Morny for explanations. The language of the Russian minister in London, he wrote, 'porterait à penser que le Cabinet de Saint Pétersbourg dans un esprit de conciliation n'est pas éloigné de faire abandon de ses prétentions tant en ce qui concerne la possession de Bolgrad que celle de l'île des Serpens.' Morny would be able to discover whether the views put forward were in fact, those of the Russian government. 'Ces dispositions', Walewski added, 'hâteraient, sans nul doute, la solution des différents points qui ont donné naissance au désaccord regrettable qui s'est

[1] Howard to Clarendon, 1 Sept, 1856, F.O. 27/1133, no. 66.
[2] Palmerston Memorandum, 2 Sept. 1856, Clarendon MSS.
[3] Malaret to Walewski, 7 Sept. 1856, A.A.E. Angleterre 705, no. 182.

élevé entre les puissances signataires de la paix.'¹ The Russian diplomat, however, who had merely expressed a personal opinion, was promptly disavowed by his government. On 9 September Brunnow officially informed Walewski 'que rien n'a modifié les dispositions du cabinet de Pétersbourg en ce qui concerne Bolgrad et l'île des Serpens'.²

On the following day Palmerston addressed a pressing personal appeal to Walewski. The Russian pretension to Serpents Island, he argued, was 'purement et simplement une tentative d'agression contre la Turquie'. The claim to new Bolgrad was 'une supercherie [sic] . . . un tour de passe-passe qui est déshonorant pour la Russie, et qui rendrait ridicules ceux qui en seraient les dupes'. Austria and Turkey 'comme de raison' were entirely on the side of England, but France seemed disposed to change sides and to associate herself with Russia. 'Si cet état des choses continue,' Palmerston declared, 'le Traité ne s'exécutera pas, et lorsque le Parlement se réunit nous aurons à expliquer le pourquoi. Réfléchissez un peu, je vous en prie, sur l'effet que cela doit nécessairement produire sur cette alliance entre nos deux pays, si honorable pour tous les deux et si utile aux intérêts de toute l'Europe. Il ne dépend que de vous de mettre fin à tous ces embarras. . . . Conseillez aux Russes de se contenter de la Bolgrad du Congrès et de retirer de l'île des Serpens [sic] leurs sept matelots et leur lieutenant malade, et comme vous avez eu une grande part à la conclusion de la paix, vous aurez aussi la satisfaction de savoir que vous avez contribué efficacement à en amener la fidèle et honorable exécution.'³

Faced with Palmerston's message, Walewski decided, to address to the Russian government a further appeal for concessions. The French government, he informed Morny in a despatch of 17 September, adhered to its original opinion about the future of Bolgrad. 'Nous ne saurions néanmoins', he added, 'nous dissimuler qu'il y a peu de chance de modifier les dispositions des cabinets qui en pensent autrement et que l'espoir que nous avons eu un moment de les rallier à notre manière de voir s'affaiblit de jour en jour. Soutenu dans cette attitude par l'Autriche et la Porte, pressé d'ailleurs par l'opinion du pays, le

---

¹ Walewski to Morny, 8 Sept. 1856, A.A.E. Russie 212, no. 25, draft.
² Walewski to Malaret, 9 Sept. 1856, A.A.E. Angleterre 705, no. 96, draft.
³ Palmerston to Walewski, private, 10 Sept. 1856, printed in Hon. Evelyn Ashley, *The Life of Lord Palmerston* (London, 1876), ii, pp. 117 ff.

cabinet de Londres notamment persiste à ne reconnaître que l'ancien Bolgrad pour point de (illegible) dans le tracé de la nouvelle frontière.' In these circumstances, Morny, without going back on his instructions about Bolgrad, should draw Gorchakov's attention 'sur des difficultés qui ont si vivement frappé le ministre de Russie à Londres et conseiller au Cabinet de St. Pétersbourg de peser mûrement dans sa sagesse les inconvénients qui peuvent résulter d'une aussi complète opposition des prétentions respectives.'[1] But before this despatch reached its destination, Walewski received from Morny a telegraphic reply to his first appeal. Faced with Morny's urgent request to make 'table rase de toutes ces petites questions relatives aux détails de l'exécution du Traité de Paris', Gorchakov on 18 September agreed to give up Russia's claim to Serpents Island provided she was allowed to retain new Bolgrad, separated from Lake Yalpuck by a Moldavian road as suggested by France.[2]

Walewski therefore, in reply to Palmerston's private appeal, observed that the British government must either accept the compromise solution of giving up new Bolgrad in exchange for Serpents Island, or agree to both matters being submitted to the decision of the powers in conference.[3] Palmerston's reply showed growing irritation. He would not continue, he wrote, 'une discussion sans effet' nor repeat arguments 'qui n'ont pas eu de succès'. He was 'bien fâché' that Walewski should decline 'le rôle de pacificateur que j'ai pris la liberté de vous proposer', but since he seemed to prefer to let events decide about the future, 'nous ne pouvons qu'accepter cette alternative, quoique avec bien des regrets, dont la responsabilité ne pèsera pas sur nous.'[4]

It was at this point, when deadlock appeared to have been reached, that Persigny, the French ambassador in London, Walewski's personal rival and a great admirer of Palmerston, entered the lists. On 23 September, he addressed to Walewski a despatch, which he asked him to lay before the Emperor. Any concession by the British government on Bolgrad, Persigny

---

[1] Walewski to Morny, 17 Sept. 1856, A.A.E. Russie 212, no. 26, draft.
[2] Morny to Walewski, telegram, 18 Sept. 1856, A.A.E. Russie 212.
[3] Walewski to Palmerston, private, 20 Sept. 1856, copy in Windsor MSS, G 49/13.
[4] Palmerston to Walewski, private, 24 Sept. 1856, quoted in Ashley op. cit., II, p. 122.

argued, would jeopardize the position of Palmerston's administration. Had the British government accepted any of Walewski's compromise proposals, 'j'aurais été effrayé pour le cabinet Anglais et pour la paix elle-même, que la chute de Lord Palmerston compromettrait sérieusement.' It would be 'mille fois préférable de nous rallier à l'opinion anglaise . . . que de persévérer dans une opinion qui, sans intérêt réel . . . trouble sérieusement la situation politique de nos alliés, et peut, de proche en proche, compromettre la paix elle-même.'[1] Hard on the heels of this plea, Walewski received from St Petersburg the reply to his second appeal. 'Question de Bolgrad', Morny telegraphed, 'est ici la pierre de touche de notre fermeté et de notre sincèrité. Ne précipitez rien avant d'avoir reçu ce que je vous écris aujourd'hui.'[2]

In this situation there was now nothing for Walewski to do except to refer the matter to the Emperor who was staying at Biarritz.[3]

Napoleon was embarrassed by the Anglo-Russian dispute, which threatened to upset his plans for the future organization of Europe. His chief interest on the morrow of the Congress of Paris lay not in the East but in the re-organization of the Italian peninsula. To achieve his aims he needed the support both of his principal ally, and of his recent enemy. When Morny had set out on his mission to Russia, he had been instructed to work for improved relations between England and Russia, and to cooperate on all matters with both Gorchakov and Granville.[4] Apart from the wider question of the future of Anglo-Russian relations, Napoleon had no interest whatever in either Serpents Island or Bolgrad. Indeed, the future of the Ottoman Empire, about which Palmerston cared so much, was, to him, a matter of little concern. Even whilst French armies were still fighting in the Crimea, Cowley had lamented the Emperor's 'great insouciance respecting the East in general'.[5] Soon, he would himself explain to Prince Albert that he 'could not muster up any sympathy for such a sorry set as the Turks'.[6] Napoleon therefore

[1] Persigny to Walewski, 23 Sept. 1856. A.A.E. Angleterre 706, no. 186.
[2] Morny to Walewski, telegram, 25 Sept. 1856, A.A.E. Russie 212.
[3] Cowley to Clarendon, 28 Sept. 1856, F.O. 27/1135, no. 1169, confidential.
[4] Morny to Walewski, 17 Aug. 1856, A.A.E. Russie 212, no. 4.
[5] Cowley to Clarendon, private, 10 Dec. 1855, Clarendon MSS.
[6] Th. Martin, *The Life of the Prince Consort* (London, 1887), IV, pp. 101 f.

had little interest in Palmerston's Eastern policy. Moreover, in the matter of Bolgrad he considered himself bound by a promise given to Orlov during the congress and later repeated to Brunnow to the effect that Russia should be allowed to retain the capital of the Bulgarian colonies. It was this which the Emperor, in reply to Walewski's enquiry, explained in a personal letter. He recalled that when the Russian plenipotentiaries, during the congress had asked to be allowed to retain the Bulgarian colonies with Bolgrad, their chief town, 'it was determined in courtesy to meet their wishes.' If therefore the Bolgrad now in dispute was in fact the chief town of those colonies, he 'considered himself bound in good faith to admit the Russian claim to it'. If, on the other hand, it was not the chief town, he was under no obligation of this kind. This was in part a question in which his honour was concerned. When, at the beginning of the discussions, a note from Brunnow, claiming new Bolgrad as the capital of the colonies, had been sent to him at Plombières, he had at once replied that he admitted the justice of the claim. On the question of Serpents Island, he shared the British view but considered that, as a new question, it was open to discussion.[1]

The decision of the oracle was at once communicated to St Petersburg and London. 'Nous restons ferme dans notre opinion,' Walewski telegraphed to Morny on 29 September, 'Bolgrad, chef lieu des colonies Bulgares doit rester à la Russie.'[2] To Persigny, he forwarded a copy of the Emperor's letter with instructions to read it to Palmerston and Clarendon at the earliest opportunity.[3] Persigny, on 2 October, acquitted himself of his unwelcome task, omitting 'certain passages . . . which were calculated to produce irritation'.[4] Clarendon replied that he could not but regret the continuation of a discussion, which appeared to him 'non seulement épuisé, mais indigne d'occuper d'avantage les deux gouvernements'.[5] The first round in the duel had thus gone against Palmerston; Gorchakov on the other hand had come a step nearer towards achieving his purpose.

---

[1] Cowley to Clarendon, 2 Oct. 1856, F.O. 27/1135, no. 1191, confidential.
[2] Walewski to Morny, telegram, 29 Sept. 1856, A.A.E. Russie 212, draft.
[3] Walewski to Persigny, 29 Sept. 1856, A.A.E. Angleterre 706, no. 109, confidential, draft.
[4] Clarendon to Cowley, 7 Oct. 1856, F.O. 146/640, no. 1190.
[5] Persigny to Walewski, 2 Oct. 1856, E. A.A.E. Angleterre 706, no. 190, confidential.

VII

In the meantime, Gorchakov had carried his campaign one stage further. In a note dated 19 September and addressed to Walewski, Brunnow formally reiterated the demand 'de réunir à Paris les représentants des Cabinets signataires du traité du 18/30 mars — afin de s'entendre à l'amiable sur les objets en discussion'. Walewski was invited to notify Brunnow of the moment most opportune 'pour réunir en Conférence les représentants autorisés par leurs Cours à prendre part à cette délibération dans le plus bref délai possible.'[1] Relying on the support of France and her faithful satellite Sardinia, and counting on the vote of a friendly Prussia, Russia might hope to achieve in a re-assembled congress a majority against England, Austria and Turkey.

Walewski, in response to the Russian proposal, issued a carefully worded circular to the French diplomatic representatives in London, Vienna, Turin, Berlin and Constantinople. In forwarding to each a copy of Brunnow's note, he instructed them 'de . . . donner lecture et remettre copie de cette dépêche ainsi que de son annexe' to the respective Foreign Ministers and to report their reactions.[2] In addition, Walewski sent telegraphic instructions to Bourqueney, Gramont and Thouvenel, telling them to urge the Austrian, Sardinian and Turkish governments, respectively, to agree to the re-assembly.[3]

The French enquiry was embarrassing to the cabinets to which it was addressed, for it invited them to take sides in a quarrel with which they had little concern. Cavour would have given much to avoid a choice between England and France, his principal allies, but pressed by Gramont he accepted the French demand.[4] Buol, was, if possible, even more embarrassed, for he had himself, in the early stages of the dispute, advocated recourse to the conference.[5] In response to pressure from

---

[1] Brunnow to Walewski, 7/19 Sept. 1856, A.A.E. Russie 212.

[2] Walewski to Persigny, 23 Sept. 1856, A.A.E. Angleterre 705, no. 103. Identical Circulars to Bourqueney, Gramont, Moustier, Thouvenel, drafts.

[3] Walewski to Bourqueney, telegram, 29 Sept. 1856, A.A.E. Autriche 465; Walewski to Gramont, telegram, 1, Oct. 1856, A.A.E. Sardaigne 340; Walewski to Thouvenel, telegram, 29 Sept. 1856, A.A.E. Turquie 327, drafts.

[4] Cavour to E. d'Azeglio and Villamarina, 2 Oct. 1856, *Cavour e l'Inghilterra*, (hereafter quoted as Cavour), Carteggio con V. E. d'Azeglio, a cura della Commissione Reale Editrice (Bologna, 1933), II, 1, p. 58.

[5] Clarendon to Seymour, 8 Jul. 1856, F.O. 7/476, no. 317; and Seymour to Clarendon, 30 Jul. 1856, F.O. 7/488, no. 540.

Bourqueney he now declared that unless there was in London 'opposition absolue' to the French proposal, he would consent to the reassembly.[1] In his official reply, he declared that the Austrian government would join the discussions if a conference was desired unanimously by all the other signatories of the treaty. He did not, he added, consider it likely that such a desire would be expressed.[2] Manteuffel, the Foreign Minister of Prussia, would have preferred the powers to reach agreement without a conference but, 'sur le désir itérativement exprimé du Cabinet de St. Pétersbourg et sur l'invitation formelle et officielle de celui de Paris,' he finally agreed to the reassembly.[3] The Porte, weakest of the signatories, decided after some hesitation to accept the conference 'si *la majorité des ses alliés* lui en faisait la demande'.[4]

The decision, therefore, rested with the British government. Palmerston strongly objected to a meeting of the powers which had signed the treaty of 30 March, as, in his opinion, the question at issue was one which concerned the allies in the late war only. Russia could not have a voice in the decision of the Bolgrad dispute, which involved the question of 'a new & fresh Concession' to her. She had no right to be 'a judge in her own Cause'. Prussia also, whose representatives had been admitted to the deliberations of the congress only after Art. XX had been drawn up, was not 'competent to say what the Congress meant'. England, France and Turkey were the principal parties entitled to express their views, and after them Austria and Sardinia. To a conference composed of these powers only, the British government would be prepared to refer the question.[5] The British ministers, Clarendon accordingly informed Walewski, had asked themselves what was the question to be referred to the congress. The only possible question, it seemed to them, was 'whether the stipulation of Article XX should be changed'. This was a matter which concerned only the allies and should therefore be decided by them alone. 'The question being one whether a new concession should be made to Russia . . . it

---

[1] Bourqueney to Walewski, 9 Oct. 1856, A.A.E. Autriche 465, no. 127.
[2] Clarendon to Cowley, 18 Oct. 1856, F.O. 146/641, no. 1271.
[3] Manteuffel to Werther, 18 Oct. 1856, quoted in Friese, op. cit., p. 129, Footnote 19.
[4] Thouvenel to Walewski, 2 Oct. 1856, A.A.E. Turquie 327, no. 82.
[5] Palmerston to Clarendon, private, 4 Oct. 1856, Clarendon MSS.

ought to be determined by the Representatives of France, England, Austria, Sardinia and Turkey without the presence of either a Russian or a Prussian Member.'[1]

Walewski disagreed. Clarendon, he argued, regarded the question 'à un point de vue que le gouvernement de l'Empereur ne saurait admettre un seul instant'. He professed to consider the French view of Bolgrad 'comme une *concession* que nous aurions faites à la Russie', but, in fact, the question of a concession to Russia had never been involved. What had been discussed among the cabinets was merely 'comment il faut comprendre les intentions du Congrès et nullement d'accorder au cabinet de St. Pétersbourg un avantage particulier en contradiction avec les stipulations du Traité de Paris'. The object of reassembling the congress was to discuss 'une difficulté née de l'exécution même du traité' and to fix 'le sens d'un article du traité'. How could Russia be excluded, seeing that she had taken part in drafting the disputed clause? What result, moreover, would the allies achieve if they reached agreement and if Russia then refused to accept their decision? Would they return to a state of war 'pour un intérêt sans importance'? In such an event, the French government would have been drawn into a war to uphold an opinion which was not even its own.[2]

With the reassembling of the conference blocked by British opposition, the French government undertook a new effort to break the deadlock. Already on 2 October, Walewski had received information that Colonel Besson had put forward in the delimitation commission a plan of his own designed to settle the dispute. Russia in return for abandoning the town of New Bolgrad, was to receive territorial compensation some distance to the north in the territory to be ceded by her under Art. XX of the treaty.[3] Colonel Besson had at once been disavowed by his government even before the details of his proposal had been received in Paris.[4] However, in a despatch to Morny of 15 October, Walewski recommended to the Russian government the 'Besson Plan' for their consideration. 'Sans dévier en rien . . . de notre manière de voir à l'égard de Bolgrad,' he wrote, 'si

[1] Clarendon to Cowley, 7 Oct. 1856, F.O. 146/640, no. 1205.
[2] Walewski to Persigny, 9 Oct. 1856, A.A.E. Angleterre 706, no. 114, draft.
[3] Bourqueney to Walewski, telegram, 2 Oct. 1856, A.A.E. Autriche 465.
[4] Walewski to Bourqueney, telegram, 3 Oct. 1856, A.A.E. Autriche 465, draft; and Walewski to Besson, 4 Oct. 1856, A.A.E. Roumanie, 1856–57, IV, no. 6 draft.

cette combinaison convenait à la Russie et qu'elle crut devoir prendre l'initiative d'une proposition d'échange, nous n'aurions pas pour notre part d'objection à élever, et je vous serais très obligé de me faire connaître son opinion à ce sujet.'[1]

On the same day, in conversation with Cowley, Walewski remarked that he had asked himself whether it would not be possible to submit the question of Bolgrad to the arbitration 'of some disinterested power'. The King of the Belgians might suit all parties, but he himself would not object to any other sovereign the British government might prefer. Cowley promised to transmit the proposal to Clarendon and received, on request, the wording of the question to be submitted to the arbitrator.[2] Cowley himself recommended acceptance of the proposal. If it was declined altogether, he feared that the day would come when John Bull, tired of the discussion, would 'throw your want of conciliation into your teeth'. He might be mistaken but he could not help fearing that if 'this confounded question' was not settled soon, not only would it end in a rupture with France, but public opinion 'with its weathercock tendencies' would some day leave the ministers in the lurch.[3]

Palmerston did not like the French proposal. The question to be decided, he argued, was 'not one of Fact but of Policy'; it was not therefore of a nature to be submitted to arbitration. The issue was whether the allies should accept another town in place of the one intended by the treaty. That was a question of policy which could not be determined by a third party. It concerned the interests of the allies, both present and future, and of those interests they alone could be judges. In their considered opinion, to make the concessions claimed by Russia would be 'seriously prejudicial to their interests'. They were resolved, therefore, not to make that concession, and there was hence no question 'which by its nature could be the subject matter of Reference to an arbitrator'.[4]

Clarendon, for once, disagreed with the reasoning of his chief. He recommended acceptance of the French proposal 'solely with reference to the Alliance for wch I wd not give a ftnight's purchase if matters are not patched up before Parlt

---

[1] Walewski to Morny, 15 Oct. 1856, A.A.E. Russie 213, no. 39, draft.
[2] Cowley to Clarendon, 15 Oct. 1856, F.O. 27/1136, no. 1269, confidential.
[3] Cowley to Clarendon, private, 15 Oct. 1856, Clarendon MSS.
[4] Palmerston Memorandum, 16 Oct. 1856, Clarendon MSS.

meets'. Then people might be disposed to ask whether they ought to have made so great a sacrifice for an object which would be represented to be so very small.[1] Charles Wood, the First Lord of the Admiralty, and after Palmerston, Clarendon and Granville perhaps the most influential member of the cabinet, also favoured arbitration. 'The more I think of your scheme of reference on the Turkish Boundary,' he wrote to Clarendon, 'the better I like it. Warlike as the country was & anxious for the continuance of the war, it wishes now for peace & settlement. You cannot force the Emperor to recede from his word. You had better therefore give up Bulgrad [sic] & take Serpents Island than leave the matter unsettled & if the reference comes even to this conclusion you will be well out of an *unsettled* state.'[2]

The situation was similar to that two months earlier when Palmerston had been dissuaded by the Queen and his colleagues from removing the Russian detachment from Serpents Island, but this time he was resolved to stick to his guns. They ought not, he argued, to fall into the bad ways of John Russell, who was 'stout as a Lion' until the horizon seemed to look clearer, when suddenly he wheeled round and gave up all he had been contending for. Let them 'calmly say to Walewsky' what Palmerston had remarked on the French proposal and see what he said in reply. 'Depend upon it,' Palmerston continued, 'He & the Emperor begin to wish themselves clear of the Difficulty, & if so they will find some way out of it without giving up our Case—at all Events there is still Time enough for us to try on a little longer. We must not conceal from ourselves that Surrender would be a great Loss of Position to us.'[3] As to making King Leopold arbiter between England on the one side and the two Emperors on the other, even if the question at issue were one fit for arbitration 'it would be threadneedle [sic] Street to a china Orange against us—He would give it for the Emperors as sure as Eggs is Eggs.'[4]

Palmerston had his way. Clarendon informed Cowley that Walewski's proposal had received 'the most attentive consideration of Her Majesty's Government', which had regretfully

[1] Clarendon to Cowley, 17 Oct. 1856, Cowley MSS.
[2] Wood to Clarendon, private, 19 Oct. 1856, Clarendon MSS.
[3] Palmerston to Clarendon, private, 17 Oct. 1856, Clarendon MSS.
[4] Palmerston to Clarendon, private, 18 Oct. 1856, Clarendon MSS.

reached the conclusion that the question which remained to be decided was one not of fact but of policy and therefore not 'of a nature to be submitted to arbitration'.[1] Cowley was disappointed. They surely would stand higher, he privately complained, if they could show that they had resorted 'to every possible means for preventing a permanent misunderstanding between the two countries'.[2] He had been told by Napoleon 'with some appearance of soreness' that the British government 'did nothing to help him out of his difficulty—that they had refused every proposal which he made'.[3] It was of no avail. Palmerston explained that the arbiter could hardly know 'what was passing in the Minds of a Lot of Gentlemen at Paris in March last, He not having been present at the Time'. Such a reference would be 'very much like the Question put by old Lord Hertford to Drummonds Banking House Clerks, when he asked them whether the Man whom he had met half an Hour before in Pall Mall was Sir William Stuart or Sir John Stuart'.[4] On 31 October, Cowley handed Walewski the formal reply to his arbitration proposal, which was declared to be 'wholly inadmissible'.[5] So far as the British government was concerned, Napoleon and Walewski had once again drawn a blank.

The reply from St Petersburg, received in Paris two days later, was if more conciliatory in form, scarcely more encouraging in substance. 'Si vous trouvez une compensation *sérieuse* pour Bolgrad,' Morny telegraphed, 'autre que le système Besson, faites la accepter d'avance par l'Angleterre et envoyez la moi; J'espère la faire admettre par la Russie à notre considération. Née ici, elle exciterait les défiances de l'Angleterre qui la refuserait sans doute. Mais ne nous déjugez sur aucun point. Votre autorité à venir en Allemagne et en Russie est à ce prix; croyez moi.'[6] Thus Gorchakov and Alexander II whilst accepting the principle of compensation, had framed their acceptance in such a way as to provoke further disagreements between France and England. As he had done before, Gorchakov, by

---

[1] Clarendon to Cowley, 20 Oct. 1856, F.O. 146/641, no. 1276.
[2] Cowley to Clarendon, private, 20 Oct. 1856, Clarendon MSS.
[3] Cowley to Clarendon, private, 22 Oct. 1856, Clarendon MSS.
[4] Palmerston to Clarendon, private, 23 Oct. 1856, Clarendon MSS.
[5] Cowley to Walewski, 25 Oct. 1856, copy in Cowley to Clarendon, 31 Oct. 1856, F.O. 27/1137, no. 1341.
[6] Morny to Walewski, telegram, 2 Nov. 1856, A.A.E. Russie 213.

accepting a French proposal, had placed on the French government the onus of convincing Palmerston and Clarendon.

As soon as he learnt of the British rejection of arbitration,
Napoleon, in his eagerness to find a solution, put forward another suggestion. He now proposed that 'the Powers who first
assembled in Congress, therefore without Prussia, should meet
in Conference, not for the purpose of voting any resolution,
but of seeing whether their discussions may not lead to a solution of the Questions arising of the non-execution of the treaty'.[1]
It was a desperate expedient, and one unlikely to produce results,
but to Cowley's objection that the discussions might prove inconclusive, he replied that 'if this scheme was not brought to
bear, he knew of no other & shd despair of any termination of
the Question at issue'.[2]

When Clarendon informed the Queen of the new proposal, he
pointed out that the Emperor of the French did not appear to
have 'any definite object in His proposal', but that he now
threw over Walewski in the two points he had most insisted
upon, the admission of Prussia and the decision by the majority
of votes.[3] The Queen, ever critical of Palmerston's proceedings,
expressed her growing impatience. 'The Queen', she wrote,
'hopes that the last proposal of the E. Nap. as explained by Ld.
C. will be accepted by us, as we shall get into a very bad position
if we reject every means offered for a settlement of the Bolg.
question.' The French alliance was 'decidedly on the wane',
France 'never cared at all about the Oriental question' but
used it merely 'as a means to an end'. England cared very much
about it, but had hitherto used the French alliance for its settlement. It was very doubtful whether they possessed the means of
carrying out their policy without that alliance or with France
on the side of Russia, 'certainly not by mere bullying.' Some
mode of action must be found which would enable England
and France to act together.[4]

Palmerston would not budge. They were willing, he wrote, to
make a bridge for Russia 'to retire from her unjust and untenable pretensions', but not prepared 'to make a Bridge for ourselves to leave Russia in possession of her unjust demands'. If

[1] Cowley to Clarendon, telegram, 1 Nov. 1856, F.O. 27/1137.
[2] Cowley to Clarendon, private, 1 Nov. 1856, Clarendon MSS.
[3] Clarendon to the Queen, 2 Nov. 1856, R.A. G 49/54.
[4] The Queen to Clarendon, 2 Nov. 1856, R.A. G 49/56, draft.

the six powers met in conference, and were evenly divided, such a division would merely make matters worse 'by rendering more public the new alliance between France and Russia against Turkey'.[1] Palmerston and Clarendon therefore decided to ask Napoleon for further explanations 'to know a little more clearly what were the E's views in making the suggestion & more particularly in what form the question at issue wd be put to the Conf.'.[2]

In the meantime, Anglo-French relations were steadily deteriorating. In its issue of 5 November, the semi-official *Constitutionnel* carried a note on the policy pursued by the British government. 'De deux choses l'une, en effet,' wrote the paper after discussing British policy over the question of Bolgrad, 'ou l'on veut résoudre la question par voie d'arrangement, au moyen d'un arbitrage; ou bien l'on veut la guerre de nouveau.' The *Constitutionnel* was 'known to receive many of its inspirations from the Foreign Department', and its 'diatribe on English policy' was generally assumed to reflect the views of Walewski.[3] The Anglo-French alliance appeared to be hanging by a thread. 'Fort mécontent de la tournure que prennent les affaires,' Hübner, the Austrian ambassador, noted in his diary. 'Nous voilà en train de sacrifier l'alliance, si précieuse, si difficilement formée avec la France, parceque Bolgrad est une mauvaise frontière stratégique de la Moldavie. En Angleterre, on fait la même faute; mais là on est plus en état de se passer des caprices.'[4] 'We are unpopular in France, whatever we may think,' Granville, who had passed through Paris on his return from the coronation of Alexander II, told Clarendon, '& the Anti-French feeling is pretty strong in this Country. It will require skill on your part to prevent the immense misfortune of a breach of the Alliance.'[5]

VIII

The British government, however, had not yet abandoned hope of winning France over to its views. What Napoleon

---

[1] Palmerston Memorandum, 3 Nov. 1856, Clarendon MSS.
[2] Clarendon to the Queen, 3 Nov. 1856, R.A. G 49/58.
[3] Cowley to Clarendon, 7 Nov. 1856, F.O. 27/1137, no. 1372.
[4] Hübner, op. cit., I, pp. 444 f.
[5] Granville to Clarendon, 7 Nov. 1856, copy in Palmerston to the Queen, 9 Nov. 1856, R.A. G 49/67.

needed, Clarendon felt, was somebody at his elbow who knew what he ought to do and had the courage to tell him. He therefore encouraged Persigny 'to ask for leave to go to Compiègne for three or four days in order to tell the Empr *where France is* & where the *alliance is going to* in this country'.[1] Palmerston agreed that the best move would be 'to send Persigny to Compiègne'.[2] The idea of this mission was linked with another plan. On 27 October, whilst Persigny and d'Azeglio, the Sardinian minister, were staying with the Palmerstons at Broadlands, agreement had been reached on a possible solution to the Bolgrad difficulty. 'I have settled with Persigny & d'Azeglio,' Palmerston told Clarendon, 'that if we were sure of the vote of Sardinia, we should not object to let the Bolgrad Question be referred to the Congress.' If they were quite certain of four votes, they might 'care less as to how many of the Seven were assembled at the Table'.[3]

Persigny reached Compiègne on 3 November, and had several conversations with Napoleon. On the evening of the following day, the Emperor received Cowley, and, with every expression of pleasure and satisfaction in his face said 'that the Bolgrad question was settled—that Pers. had found the means of cutting the Gordian knot & that he had just been putting the finishing strokes to the work in a conversation with V. M.' (Villamarina, the Sardinian minister). He had explained to Villamarina the difficulties in which he was placed by the unguarded expression of his first impressions and his desire to find some means of escaping from his difficulties without forfeiting his word. This, he had remarked, might be done through the agency of Sardinia, who had not yet pronounced an opinion. That opinion, he thought, should be given in support of England. He did not care one farthing about the questions at issue 'but he did wish to maintain unimpaired his good understanding with the Eng. Govt'. Villamarina had replied that this advice would relieve Sardinia of a great anxiety as Cavour was 'like a man in purgatory' being equally anxious to offend neither the French nor the British government. It was agreed that Villamarina should set out instantly for Chambéry,

[1] Clarendon to Cowley, private, 22 Oct. 1856, Cowley MSS.
[2] Palmerston to Clarendon, 26 Oct. 1856, Clarendon MSS.
[3] Palmerston to Clarendon, 27 Oct. 1856, Clarendon MSS.

G

where Cavour was staying, and settle the matter with him, 'the E. requiring above all things for the sake of his honor, that not a trace of the negotiation shd be kept in writing.'[1] He would now, Napoleon told Cowley, renew his proposal for a conference, and Palmerston and Clarendon would accept it after receiving the assurance of the Sardinian cabinet that Sardinia would vote against Russia. Napoleon's decision marked a triumph for Palmerston and for the dogged tenacity with which he had rejected all compromise. Well might Cowley observe that it was 'a source of satisfaction to see to what he (Napoleon) can be brought for the preservation of the English Alliance'.[2]

On 7 November, the official *Moniteur* replied to the attack on British policy which had appeared in the *Constitutionnel* two days before. 'Le Constitutionnel du 5 courant', it wrote, 'contient sur un point en litige des affaires extérieures, un article que nous serions très-fâchés de laisser croire émané du Gouvernement.' England and France, contrary to the impression created by the *Constitutionnel*, were agreed on all major issues, and differed on only one point 'd'un assez faible intérêt'. Would the difficulty be settled by a previous understanding or in conference? That, the *Moniteur* declared, was now the only question. The article, Cowley noted, was written by the Emperor himself and was intended 'to let France understand that the sentiments of His Majesty in regard to the value of the alliance with England have undergone no change'.[3] Five days later when Kiselev, the new Russian ambassador, presented his credentials, Napoleon once again underlined his desire to preserve his alliance with England. He replied to Kiselev's address that 'dès que le traité de paix a été signé, j'ai eu pour constante préoccupation, sans affaiblir mes anciennes alliances, d'adoucir par de bons procédés tout ce que la stricte exécution de certaines conditions pouvait avoir de rigoureux'.[4] This declaration, whilst it did not completely satisfy the British government,[5] gave little pleasure to the Russians. Hübner considered it 'une démonstration en faveur des anciennes alliances'[6] and Cowley reported that the

---

[1] Cowley to Clarendon, private, 5 Nov. 1856, Clarendon MSS.
[2] Ibid.
[3] Cowley to Clarendon, 7 Nov. 1856, F.O. 27/1137, no. 1372.
[4] Cowley to Clarendon, 13 Nov. 1856, F.O. 27/1138, no. 1394.
[5] Clarendon to Cowley, private, 18 Nov. 1856, Cowley MSS.
[6] Hübner, op. cit., I, p. 449.

Russians were furious at it, as they said it was treating them 'en vaincus'.[1]

On 13 November, the British government learnt from Hudson, its representative in Turin, that if the conference were to reassemble, Sardinia would vote with England.[2] It might appear that Palmerston's tenacity had triumphed.

Yet British ministers were not completely reassured by the wording of Walewski's note to Persigny which, in accordance with the Compiègne agreement, was to bring about their acceptance of the conference.[3] Indeed they were 'annoyed at Walewski's despatch' and alarmed at the thought of departing from the line they had hitherto followed 'upon such a slender assurance of the Sardinian vote'.[4] They must, Clarendon told Cowley, have 'some more positive assurances than these' before they took 'the hazardous & *inexplicable* step of assenting to a Conference'.[5]

Whilst the British government was thus seeking further assurances a change had occurred in Paris. This was in part the result of a telegram from St Petersburg. 'Suspendez tout', Morny telegraphed on the 14th, 'jusqu'à l'arrivée de mon courrier parti le 10.'[6] Walewski, who in any case did not like the idea of a conference, took advantage of this development to return to the principle of compensation. He could not, he told Cowley on the 15th, 'look on the meeting as now proposed without apprehension.' How was the matter to be settled if the conference failed to reach a decision? Might not Clarendon, instead, entertain some scheme of compensation by which Russia would recover elsewhere the eight thousand souls she would give up at Bolgrad?[7] Four days later, Walewski reiterated that the conference 'offered so many difficulties that both he and the Emperor had reverted to the idea of compensation . . .'.[8]

The French suggestion formed the basis of some unofficial consultations between Paris and London as a result of which it appeared that agreement might be possible on the compensation

[1] Cowley to Clarendon, private, 17 Nov. 1856, Clarendon MSS.
[2] Hudson to Clarendon, telegram, 13 Nov. 1856, R.A. G 49/77, copy.
[3] Walewski to Persigny, 8 Nov. 1856, A.A.E. Angleterre 706, no. 128, draft.
[4] Clarendon to Cowley, private, 11 Nov. 1856, Cowley MSS.
[5] The same to the same, private, 14 Nov. 1856, ibid.
[6] Morny to Walewski, telegram, 14 Nov. 1856, A.A.E. Russie 213.
[7] Cowley to Clarendon, private, 15 Nov. 1856, Clarendon MSS.
[8] The same to the same, private, 19 Nov. 1856, ibid.

to be offered to Russia.[1] However, as Palmerston still favoured the recall of the conference,[2] the discussions made little progress. To force the pace, Walewski on 22 November officially proposed the adoption of the principle of compensation.[3] The following day, he instructed Persigny to urge this policy on Palmerston and Clarendon.[4] His zeal for compensation had, by this time, been stimulated by causes unknown to the British government.

IX

On 21 or 22 November[5] Morny's courier had reached Paris with the proposal, on Gorchakov's behalf, of a remarkable transaction. The Russian suggestion was transmitted by Morny in the form of three separate documents. The first of these was the draft of a despatch in which Morny would inform Walewski that Russia gave up all claim to New Bolgrad and left the question of compensation entirely in the hands of Napoleon. The second document was the draft of a Franco-Russian convention. By this, the two powers would guarantee

> conjointement et réciproquement les principes 1. de la fermeture des détroits du Bosphore et des Dardanelles 2. de la neutralité de la mer Noire 3. de la garantie collective des principautés de la Moldavie et de la Valachie à l'exclusion de toute protection, ingérence et intervention d'une ou de plusieurs des puissances garantes.

They would consider

> toute infraction à ces stipulations comme impliquant de leur part une entente immédiate sur les mesures à adopter de concert pour en sauvegarder l'exécution et, à cet effet, elles s'assuraient le concours mutuel de leurs forces militaires et navales.

---

[1] Clarendon to Cowley, private, 21 Nov. 1856, Cowley MSS, and Cowley to Clarendon, private, 23 Nov. 1856, Clarendon MSS.

[2] Palmerston to Clarendon, 22 Nov. 1856, ibid.

[3] Cowley to Clarendon, 23 Nov. 1856, F.O. 27/1138, no. 1437, confidential.

[4] Walewski to Persigny, 23 Nov. 1856, A.A.E. Angleterre 706, no. 134, draft.

[5] The exact date of the courier's arrival in Paris cannot be established. He left St Petersburg on the 10th. As correspondence between the two capitals normally took from ten to twelve days and as Walewski's reply to Morny bears the date of 23 Nov., it is not unreasonable to assume that the courier reached Paris on 21 or 22 Nov.

To the draft of the convention was attached a memorandum explaining

> que cette convention était devenu nécessaire en raison de la violation du traité par l'Angleterre et par l'Autriche, qu'elle ne contenait aucun principe nouveau; qu'elle n'était que la simple consécration des stipulations arrêtées dans le traité de Paris; qu'enfin la Russie ne faisait les concessions mentionnés dans le projet de dépêche que sous la condition que le gouvernement français consentirait à signer la convention.[1]

Finally Morny, in recommending acceptance of the Russian proposal, transmitted on behalf of the Russian government a promise of general support for French acquisitions in Europe. 'Sachez bien', Morny wrote,

> que la Russie est la seule puissance qui ratifiera tout aggrandise-ment de la France. J'en ai déjà reçu l'assurance. Demandez donc autant à l'Angleterre! Et qui sait si, avec notre peuple exigeant et capricieux, il ne faudra pas un jour en venir là pour le satis-faire?[2]

Such was the project worked out by Gorchakov, Morny and Alexander II. It derived its significance from the non-execution of the convention of 13 May 1856. Under the terms of this con-vention, signed at Constantinople between England, France and Sardinia on the one side, the Porte on the other, all Otto-man territory was to be evacuated by the allies within six months of the ratification of the Treaty of Paris.[3] The exchange of ratifications had been completed on 28 April and the evacua-tion of Turkish territory should therefore have been completed on 28 October. The British government, arguing that the con-vention could not be carried into effect until the general treaty to which it was annexed had been fully executed, had refused to withdraw British naval units from the Black Sea until Russia

---

[1] V. Boutenko, 'Un Projet d'Alliance Franco-Russe en 1856' in *Revue Historique* (1927), pp. 315 f.

[2] Morny, loc. cit., p. 137. Details of the Russian attitude to French territorial acquisitions had just been outlined in a secret instruction to Kiselev. Should Napoleon direct his attention to the Italian peninsula, Russia 'consentait d'avance à la réunion de Nice et de la Savoie à la France, ainsi qu'à celle de la Lombardie à la Sardaigne'. Should French ambitions be directed towards the 'ancienne frontière du Rhin', Russia 'ne saurait abandonner complètement la Prusse, mais son soutien vis-à-vis de celle-ci n'irait pas au delà de l'emploi chaleureux de ses bons offices'. (Boutenko, loc. cit., p. 298).

[3] For the Convention of 13 May 1856 cf. *B.F.S.P. 1855–56*, XLVI, pp. 27 ff.

should have carried out the terms of the general treaty with regard to Serpents Island and Bolgrad. There had been British naval demonstrations outside Russian Black Sea ports. Austria, on similar grounds, had refused with British encouragement to withdraw her troops from the Danubian Principalities. The Porte, under British pressure, had decided after some hesitation to postpone the closure of the Straits to foreign warships until the full execution of the treaty. The Russian government professed to see in these acts the breach of a formal engagement. The proposed Russo-French convention in its view, would oblige the French government to protest to England, Austria and Turkey against the non-execution of the convention of 13 May. It would formally range France and Russia (and, probably, Sardinia and Prussia as well) against the other three powers and thus destroy, at one blow the victorious Crimean coalition.

In fact, what the Russian government under the guise of a convention for the joint enforcement of the Convention of 13 May was proposing to Napoleon, was nothing less than a quasi-alliance directed against his partners of 15 April. 'Dans ce projet de marché', writes Charles-Roux, 'l'apport de la France consiste dans un service incompatible avec l'alliance anglaise; celui de la Russie dans un concours destiné à prendre la place de cette alliance.'[1] Boutenko remarks that the proposal

cachait sous une forme innocente une arrière-pensée très importante. Eu égard au conflit anglo-russe, cette convention devait être naturellement tournée contre l'Angleterre. Elle signifiait une rupture définitive de la coalition anti-russe et une dissolution possible de l'alliance anglo-française; en ce cas elle devait aboutir inévitablement à la conclusion d'une alliance franco-russe.[2]

Friese similarly writes:

Inhaltlich nur eine Bekräftigung des Pariser Vertrages wäre diese Konvention in der Tat ein wirksamer Gegenschlag gegen den Vertrag vom 15 April gewesen, ja sie bedrohte ernstlich den Bestand der westmächtlichen Allianz.[3]

The import of the Russian proposal, therefore, was clear. Did the Tsar and Gorchakov believe that Napoleon, who was

[1] Charles-Roux, op. cit., pp. 163 f.   [2] Boutenko, loc. cit., pp. 315 f.
[3] Friese, op. cit., pp. 126 f.

certain to see its implications, would accept it? From the French point of view, the arrangement proposed offered a number of attractions. It provided a way out of the difficulties holding up the execution of the Treaty of Paris without recourse to the conference and the doubtful expedient of the Sardinian vote. It held out the prospect of Russian support for action against Austria both in the Principalities and in Italy. Last, but not least, had not Morny, with a view to future economic development and railway construction described Russia as 'une mine à exploiter pour la France'?[1] Against this, however, Napoleon had to weigh the possible dangers to France and his dynasty involved in the destruction of the Franco-British alliance. Whilst both Morny and Walewski clearly attached little importance to its preservation, Napoleon might prove less willing to commit himself to an exclusively Russian orientation.

In fact, Napoleon and Walewski decided to put forward counter-proposals which, whilst weakening the suggested engagement, would yet give the Russians a measure of satisfaction. On 23 November Walewski telegraphed to St Petersburg his approval 'in principle' of Gorchakov's proposal. However, the formal convention was to be replaced by a simple French despatch of which a copy would be left in the Russian archives. 'Comme l'Empereur Napoléon', Walewski wrote ingenuously, 'n'aime pas en politique les combinaisons clandestines, nous vous écririons une dépêche qui contiendrait les trois points dans le sens de la convention et vous seriez autorisé à en laisser une copie.'[2]

The French counter-proposal did not satisfy the Russian government. Russia, Morny telegraphed on the 25th,

> ne désire pas le secret, elle l'offrait pour vos ménagements. La Russie veut garantie de la part de la France contre violation éventuelle du traité de Paris. Elle veut donc outre les 3 points, engagement réciproque d'agir dans ce cas avec force commune. Télégraphiez moi votre dépêche contenant cette clause; je suis sûr de la faire accepter. Aimeriez-vous deux lettres de souverain à souverain?[3]

In response to this message, a courier left Paris on 26 November with a draft despatch prepared by Walewski. It expressed

---

[1] Morny to Walewski, 8 Aug. 1856, A.A.E. Russie 212, no. 1.
[2] Boutenko, loc. cit., p. 320.
[3] Morny to Walewski, telegram, 25 Nov. 1856, A.A.E. Russie 213.

the gratitude of the French government for the spirit of conciliation shown by the Tsar, adding that Napoleon had already opened conversations with London about the compensation to be offered to Russia. It then enumerated the three principles of Gorchakov's original draft, declaring them to be 'des garantis à la fois précieuses et obligatoires pour les parties'. The French government 'serait toujours prêt à se concerter s'il en était besoin, avec celui de l'empereur Alexandre pour en assurer le maintien dans tous les éventualités'.[1] This, although less than the Russians had asked for, yet left open the possibility of future Russo-French co-operation on the basis of Gorchakov's three points.

X

In the meantime however, the diplomatic situation had undergone another change. On the very day on which the courier carrying the French draft left Paris, Cowley read Walewski a despatch from Clarendon, the outcome of a cabinet meeting held on the 24th. In it the British government formally declared its readiness either to accept a reassembly of the conference or to continue the discussions about compensation.[2] To Walewski's enquiry which of the two methods the British government preferred, Cowley replied warily that both courses were equally repugnant to British ministers. It was for France to choose between two plans, both of which had originated with her.[3] At Walewski's request, Cowley left a copy of the British despatch to be shown to Napoleon. That evening at St Cloud, the Emperor decided in favour of the conference.[4]

This decision meant the abandonment both of the principle of compensation and of the consequent French undertaking to Russia. On 27 November, therefore, Walewski telegraphed to Morny that England accepted the conference. 'Ce nouvel incident', he continued,

modifie la situation; l'Empereur n'en est pas moins très touché de la déférence que lui a montré l'Empereur Alexandre. Dites le bien. — Si plutard (sic) on était conduit à revenir au système de

---

[1] Boutenko, loc. cit., p. 321.
[2] Clarendon to Cowley, 25 Nov. 1856, F.O. 146/645, no. 1420.
[3] Cowley to Clarendon, private, 26 Nov. 1856, Clarendon MSS.
[4] The same to the same, private, 27 Nov. 1856, ibid.

compensation, nous serions toujours prêts à donner à la Russie les assurances que contient le projet de dépêche que porte le courrier parti hier et que j'arrête 24 heures à Berlin pour vous envoyer une dépêche supplémentaire concernant la nouvelle situation résultant de l'acceptation de l'Angleterre.[1]

Three days later, Walewski sent Persigny the draft of a circular despatch to French representatives at the signatory courts, inviting the latter to authorize their envoys in Paris to meet to decide the matters in dispute.[2] The following evening the approval of the British government was notified in Paris.[3] That night copies of the circular note were sent out from Paris to the signatory courts.[4]

In the meantime, the Russian government, encouraged by Morny, was impatiently awaiting the messenger from Paris. On 7 December Gorchakov wrote to Kiselev 'avec une satisfaction visible' that Morny expected 'd'une minute à l'autre' the desired assurance from Napoleon. Great, therefore, was his disappointment when 'au lieu de contenir le consentement à la transmission de la dépêche', the Emperor's letter to Morny merely invited Russia 'à entrer dans la triple alliance avec l'Angleterre et la France'. Gorchakov, in a report of 8 December, mournfully informed the Tsar of the collapse of Russian hopes.[5] That day, Alexander expressed his dissatisfaction in conversation with Morny. 'Eh bien', he observed, 'de cette façon nous ne donnons donc suite sous aucune forme à un engagement quelconque entre nous?' Morny replied that, had the negotiations (for compensation) been continued, the most positive assurances 'sous forme de dépêche laissée' would have been given to the Russian government. However, the British acceptance of the conference 'annule l'arrangement et enlève tout motif à la dépêche'. The Tsar, however, insisted. 'Écoutez, monsieur le Comte,' he rejoined with gravity, '... j'ai en vous une excessive confiance, je veux vous parler à cœur ouvert.' He had thought that he was faithfully executing the treaty except for some points 'oubliés ou mal interprétés' on which, moreover, he had been

[1] Walewski to Morny, telegram, 27 Nov. 1856, A.A.E. Russie 213, draft.
[2] Walewski to Persigny, 30 Nov. 1856, A.A.E. Angleterre 706, no. 138, draft.
[3] Persigny to Walewski, telegram, 1 Dec. 1856, ibid.
[4] Cf. Walewski to Thouvenel, 1 Dec. 1856, A.A.E. Turquie 328, no. 86, draft, and to Gramont, 1 Dec. 1856, A.A.E. Sardaigne 340, no. 42, draft.
[5] Boutenko, loc. cit., pp. 321 f.

supported by France. Considering the conduct of England in the Black Sea and of Austria in the Principalities a flagrant violation of the treaty, he had intended to protest against it. Morny had dissuaded him. He had expected a protest from France, but not only had she failed to raise her voice 'mais constamment l'Empereur a ménagé le gouvernement anglais . . .'.

> Franchement je crains [the tsar continued] que ses relations avec l'Angleterre ne dominent tout dans son esprit, même le droit public européen, et je ne vous cache pas mon inquiétude.

This disquiet would be dispelled by an assurance from Paris:

> J'ai fait ce que vous avez voulu, j'ai subordonné ma politique à la vôtre, je suis disposé à agir de même, mais j'aurais besoin d'une assurance qui calmât mes inquiétudes; que sais-je? une dépêche, une lettre particulière écrite à vous qui exprimerait ce que vous m'avez dit, suffirait et me rendrait toute ma confiance.

Morny, in his reply, tried to reassure the Tsar:

> Maintenant Sire [he replied] je connais bien l'Empereur: il aime et estime l'Angleterre, c'est un grand et noble pays; mais j'engage ma tête que s'il survenait une violation évidente, nouvelle, du traité de sa part ou de celle de toute autre puissance, il serait le premier à s'y opposer.

Moreover, he would inform Napoleon of the Tsar's anxiety and felt certain that the Emperor, in his reply, would confirm the assurance just given. In fact, in a private letter, Morny asked Napoleon to do this. By doing so, he added, 'vous lui ôterez un poids de dessus la poitrine et vous lui inspireriez une confiance sans bornes qui pourra vous servir ultérieurement.'[1]

Before Morny's appeal reached Paris, the situation there had undergone yet another change. Walewski, favourable to the principle of compensation and an *entente* with Russia, had begun a campaign to frighten the British government out of the proposed conference. As early as 27 November, he had insinuated in conversation with Cowley that Sardinia might play England false by failing to support her on the Bolgrad issue. The charge, indeed, was without foundation, but Walewski had been fully justified in his further assertion that if the question of compensation were to be raised in conference, Sardinia would be found

[1] Morny, op. cit., pp. 169 ff.

on the side of Russia and France.[1] On 9 December Villamarina, Sardinian representative in Paris and probable spokesman at the conference, read Cowley a private letter from Cavour. In it, the latter confirmed his intention 'so far as the legality of the question goes' to vote against the Russian claim to New Bolgrad. He added, however, and he asked Villamarina to impress the point on Cowley, that 'la saine promesse' to let Russia keep the capital of the Bulgarian colonies also required consideration at the hands of the British government. So long as the discussion was confined to the simple question set out in Walewski's circular, England could count on the Sardinian vote. Nor would Sardinia propose anything herself. However, if Russia or any other power should raise the question of compensation, Sardinia would support it. So certain, in fact, did Villamarina feel that it would come to this that, knowing England to be opposed to compensation and fearing the possibility of an open rupture between her and France, he had represented to Napoleon whether it would not be for the benefit of all parties to avoid a scandalous scene by getting out of the conference altogether.[2] Napoleon, impressed by the difficulties of the situation, had reverted to the idea of compensation.

In England, opinions were divided. Whilst Clarendon, impressed with the dangers of reassembling the conference, was willing to return to compensation,[3] Palmerston held that, being sure of the Sardinian vote, England should 'go boldly into Conference'.[4] It looked at first as if Palmerston's opinion would prevail[5] but an appeal from Napoleon finally turned the scales. On 12 December, Walewski told Cowley that if the British government looked on compensation in the light of a further concession to Russia, then, 'in the name of the Emperor he asked them to make that concession'.[6] The following day, in a private letter, Clarendon accepted the principle of compensation.[7] On the 14th, Palmerston followed suit. An attempt

---

[1] Cowley to Clarendon, private, 27 Nov. 1856, Clarendon MSS.
[2] Cowley to Clarendon, private, 9 Dec. 1856, Clarendon MSS.
[3] Clarendon to Cowley, private, 8 Dec. 1856, Cowley MSS. One reason for Clarendon's attitude was a well-founded doubt about the vote of Turkey.
[4] Palmerston to Clarendon, 8 Dec. 1856, Clarendon MSS.
[5] Clarendon to Cowley, private, 11 Dec. 1856, Cowley MSS.
[6] Cowley to Clarendon, 12 Dec. 1856, F.O. 27/1139, no. 1527 confidential.
[7] Clarendon to Cowley, private, 13 Dec. 1856, Cowley MSS.

should be made, he wrote, to reach agreement on the details of compensation before the conference met. The representatives of the powers would then meet 'only for the Purpose of recording it in some formal shape'.[1] Five days later the British government proposed a new line of frontier in the northern portion of the territory to be ceded by Russia which reduced Russian losses and came close to a line previously suggested by France.[2] A counter-proposition by Walewski further narrowed the difference and on 23 December Clarendon was at last able to inform Cowley that the British government agreed to the latest French proposal.[3]

The following morning, the news was flashed to St Petersburg. Walewski expressed Napoleon's hope that Russia would accept the Franco-British suggestion without delay, as he had had the greatest difficulty in persuading the British government to accept it.[4] Two days later, Morny reported the grudging adhesion of Russia. Gorchakov would have preferred a compromise reached in conference but accepted the present solution in deference to Napoleon.[5] On the 27th, the Tsar, similarly accepted the proposal 'malgré l'insuffisance de la compensation ... par déférence pour l'Empereur Napoléon'.[6] Morny heaved a sigh of relief:

> Voilà donc grâce à Dieu cette affaire terminée et j'espère bien d'ici à la fin de mes jours, ne plus entendre parler de Bolgrad. Je voudrais que vous en fissiez prendre une vue photographiée, et déposer une épreuve dans toutes les chancelleries et dans toutes les ministères des Affaires Etrangères du monde, afin que chacun pût juger, par ses yeux, de l'abominable trou, à propos duquel on a failli mettre de nouveau le feu à l'Europe.[7]

The return to compensation had involved, in the eyes of Napoleon, an automatic return to the idea of a 'reassurance' to the Tsar. Walewski therefore, in a despatch of 23 December, informed Morny:

---

[1] Palmerston to Clarendon, 14 Dec. 1856, Clarendon MSS.
[2] Clarendon to Cowley, private, 19 Dec. 1856, Cowley MSS.
[3] The same to the same, telegram, 23 Dec. 1856, copy in the same to the same, 24 Dec. 1856, F.O. 146/648, no. 1528.
[4] Walewski to Morny, telegram, 24 Dec. 1856, A.A.E. Russie 213, draft.
[5] Morny to Walewski, telegram, 26 Dec. 1856, ibid.
[6] The same to the same, telegram, 27 Dec. 1856, ibid.
[7] The same to the same, 27 Dec. 1856, ibid, no. 24.

Du moment où les puissances se seront entendues sur les points de détail qui nécessitent aujourd'hui la réunion de la Conférence, aucune d'elles n'aura plus le prétexte pour se dispenser de se conformer aux stipulations relatives à l'évacuation des territoires et des eaux de l'Empire ottoman et le Gouvernement de l'Empereur regardera toujours comme un devoir, le Cabinet de St. Pétersbourg peut en être persuadé, de veiller à ce que les engagements solennels que la paix de Paris a consacrés soient strictement observés par toutes les parties.

Morny was to read this despatch to Gorchakov but not to leave a copy.[1]

The rest was a matter of form. On the last day of 1856 the representatives in Paris of the signatory powers met at the Quai d'Orsay under the presidency of Walewski.[2] They held a second meeting on 6 January, at which a protocol was signed embodying the terms of the agreement reached with so much difficulty. Serpents Island was declared to be a part of Turkey, whilst the responsibility for maintaining the lighthouse was placed on the Turkish government under the supervision of the International Riverain Commission. New Bolgrad was incorporated in Moldavia and the boundary in the north of the ceded territory revised in Russia's favour.[3] The dispute occasioned by the execution of the Treaty of Paris was over.

XII

The diplomatic proceedings revolving around Serpents Island and Bolgrad as well as the final solution gave complete satisfaction to neither of the two protagonists. Palmerston's diplomacy since at least 1853 had been based on an understanding with France to check Russian expansion at the expense of Turkey. The disputes about the execution of the Treaty of Paris had revealed the limits of Anglo-French cooperation with regard to the Eastern question. It was clear that, whilst determined to preserve the English alliance, Napoleon at the same time was eager to improve his relations with Russia. Indeed, the Russian propensities of Walewski and Morny had placed a serious strain on the Anglo-French alliance. Palmerston himself took a gloomy view of the future. The 'marriage

[1] Walewski to Morny, 23 Dec. 1856, A.A.E. Russie, no. 56, draft.
[2] Cowley to Clarendon, 1 Jan. 1857, F.O. 27/1187, no. 2.
[3] The same to the same, 7 Jan. 1857, ibid., no. 42 and F.O. 93/110/12.

with France', he predicted, would soon end in 'a separation on account of *incompatibilité de mœurs*'. Considering 'the different private interests of England and France, the different Characters & Habits of the two nations', England should be thankful at having got so much out of the alliance and having maintained it so long, rather than 'be surprized or disappointed at its approaching end'. It might still subsist in name and be useful to England for some purposes and on some occasions, but they must now trust to their own policy and to their own means for carrying them through the difficulties with which from time to time they might have to deal.[1] This was, indeed, a change of attitude from the concept of the grand alliance against Russia of which Palmerston had been the protagonist but nine short months before. Moreover, the idea of 'going it alone' to which he now resigned himself, had failed signally during the recent complications. If the dispute about Bolgrad and Serpents Island had proved anything, it was precisely that England could not deal with Russia single-handed without the assistance of France. Without France, the Crimean settlement would be difficult to maintain. Yet France had just proved that the integrity of the Ottoman Empire was, for her, an object of secondary importance. Contrary to Palmerston's hopes, the recent dispute, far from demonstrating to Russia the firm determination of the allies to enforce the strict observance of the settlement, had helped to underline the differences between them. These differences, even if they had not resulted in the breach hoped for by Gorchakov, had yet been sufficiently marked to raise Russian hopes for the future.

At the same time Gorchakov, like his British rival, had failed to achieve the ultimate object of his diplomacy. If France, on the whole, had shown herself more sympathetic to Russian claims than England, she had yet carefully avoided anything which might endanger the British alliance. As Alexander II had noted in his final conversation with Morny, it appeared that Napoleon continued to regard his understanding with England as the keystone of his policy. No Russian blandishment had been able to wean him from the alliance. The coalition which had forced Russia to her knees in the Crimean war survived and was not to be broken up at Gorchakov's first

---

[1] Palmerston to Clarendon, 10 Dec. 1856, Clarendon MSS.

attempt. At the same time, it was clear that he and his master need not abandon hope. If the knot had not been cut, it had at least been loosened. 'Nous n'avons pas tranché le nœud gordien,' Gorchakov noted, 'c'eût été un effort que trop de sacrifices auraient accompagnés, mais nous le délions progressivement.'[1]

As regards the immediate objects of the dispute, honours had been divided. Palmerston, by his calm determination, had gained the substance of his contention. The Russians had been forced to give up both Serpents Island and New Bolgrad. Against this England had had to accept both compensation to Russia and the recall of the conference. Palmerston's policy of single-handed action had proved a failure. Gorchakov, on the other hand, whilst obliged to abandon two prizes he may never have hoped to retain, had, thanks to Franco-Sardinian support, obtained a tangible consolation prize. He had also established his point that the interpretation of the matters in dispute belonged to the conference as a whole. With pardonable exaggeration, he hailed this as 'un grand résultat pour la politique de l'Empereur'. The credit he modestly gave to his master:

> C'est un fruit de sa fermeté inébranlable, et je puis dire isolée, car même au milieu de nous il y a eu plus d'une défaillance, lorsque le langage arrogant et les démonstrations menaçantes de l'Angleterre[2] pouvaient faire redouter la reprise des hostilités.[3]

The dispute revealed Gorchakov as a shrewd tactician capable of exploiting Anglo-French differences and the benevolent dispositions of Walewski. His tactics of agreeing with the French government and inducing it to plead with that of England on his behalf enabled him to watch with satisfaction the disagreements of his recent opponents. If he over-estimated Napoleon's readiness to break with England and align his policy with that of Russia, he yet perceived and nurtured such Anglo-French differences as were revealed during the dispute. It was due at least in part to his activities that the Franco-British alliance did not emerge strengthened from the crisis.

[1] Gorchakov to Olga Nicolaevna, 30 Nov. (O.S.) 1856, quoted in Friese, op. cit., p. 335.

[2] It may be that British naval demonstrations in the Black Sea had produced serious alarm in Russia. Gorchakov claimed that this was the case in his earlier letter to Olga Nicolaevna (ibid.).

[3] The same to the same, 29 Dec. 1856/10 Jan. 1857, ibid., pp. 336 f.

Palmerston's diplomatic technique as revealed in his handling of the Serpents Island and Bolgrad disputes is characterized above all by his determination not to be stampeded into premature concessions. He was obstinate to the point of inspiring alarm in the Queen, in his colleagues and in an experienced diplomat like Cowley. It was widely felt that he was playing 'fast and loose' with the precious French alliance. Yet Palmerston's 'waiting game' was in fact a masterpiece of cool diplomacy based on a true appreciation of the main elements in the diplomatic situation. His basic assumption that Napoleon would go to almost any length to preserve the British alliance was fully justified by the event. At the same time Palmerston's methods, his 'bullying', naval demonstrations, personal appeals to Walewski, did not achieve their purpose. Although, according to Gorchakov, many highly placed Russians were ready to 'give in' to British threats, Alexander II stood firm and, in the end, successfully called Palmerston's bluff. Again, Palmerston's handling of Walewski was something less than skilful. It was the restraining influence of Clarendon, Granville and the Queen which helped to move British policy from Palmerstonian rigidity in the direction of reasonable compromise. Palmerston, on the other hand, supplied much needed 'stiffening', without which Gorchakov and Walewski might have 'got away' with some very doubtful proceedings.

The dispute over Bolgrad and Serpents Island formed the first test of the Crimean settlement. It was, on the part of Russian diplomacy, a reconnaissance rather than a major engagement, and revealed some disarray in the allied camp and some flaws in the Crimean system. Even though that system successfully withstood this first relatively minor test, it would yet be hard to claim that it was strengthened thereby.

CHAPTER IV

The Russians at Villafranca[1]

If, in the incident of Bolgrad and Serpents Island, the efforts of Russian diplomacy had not been without success, this had been due almost wholly to the approaching complications in Italy. Napoleon III and Cavour, even at the Congress of Paris, had made no secret of their determination to alter the *status quo* in Italy at the expense of Austria. This, by increasing tension between Austria and France, partners in the triple treaty, had weakened the Crimean system. Moreover, with an eye on forthcoming Italian developments, both Napoleon and Cavour were eager to secure the goodwill of Russia, placed in a convenient strategic position to immobilize Austrian forces. As for both the affairs of Italy were now of infinitely greater importance than the Eastern question, they might prove willing to 'pay' in the East for Russian support in the West. The need to retain British sympathies alone put a limit on possible concessions.

This was a situation favourable to the designs of Alexander II and Gorchakov, who now set out to draw from it what advantage they could. The Italian question, in fact, became the occasion of the second Russian offensive against the Crimean system.

In spite of her recent defeat at the hands of the Western allies, Russia's diplomatic position in the Mediterranean region was not, in 1856, an unfavourable one. In the course of the Congress of Paris a friendly understanding had arisen between her representatives and those of the two Mediterranean powers, France and Sardinia, who had but recently been her enemies. What drew the three countries together was clearly a common hostility to Austria. When Stackelberg, the new Russian minister at Turin arrived to present his credentials on the official resumption of diplomatic relations, he was received with

[1] The bulk of this chapter first appeared as an article in the *Slavonic Review* (June, 1952).

H

open arms. On his own part, he showed the friendliest of dispositions. At a dinner given in his honour by Cavour, he drank the principal toast of the evening 'au rétablissement des relations amicales et intimes'. Moreover, on taking his leave of Cavour, he effectively summed up the diplomatic basis of future friendship between Russia and Sardinia. 'Nos deux pays', he declared, 'doivent être bons amis, car ils n'ont pas d'intérêts qui les divisent, et ils ont des rancunes communes, qui les rapprochent.'[1] Stackelberg might with justice have added that not only common hostility to Austria but also a common desire for a close understanding with Napoleon, then at the height of his power, would tend to strengthen the good understanding between the autocratic heir of Nicholas I and the liberal King of Sardinia. France, Russia and Sardinia, united in common antagonism to the Habsburg Monarchy, seemed destined to co-operate in bringing about a reduction of Austrian influence in the Italian peninsula.

I

Within a few months of the resumption of diplomatic relations, the *rapprochement* between Russia and Sardinia received a striking expression. In October 1856, Alexander Fyodorovna, dowager Empress of Russia and widow of the Emperor Nicholas I, arrived in the Bay of Villafranca (outside Nice) on board a Sardinian frigate. Accompanied by one of her ladies-in-waiting and by the Prince de Carignan in full uniform, she drove at once in an open carriage to a villa in the environs of Nice, which had been prepared for her reception.[2]

The imperial lady then settled down to a holiday on the sunny Riviera. The British consul noted that she seemed 'much to enjoy the beautiful weather' and was daily making excursions into the neighbourhood. On one of these she crossed the frontier into France and was received with military honours by the French authorities.[3] Some weeks later, General Rostolan, the divisional commander at Marseilles, called on the dowager Empress to pay his respects on behalf of the Emperor Napoleon.[4]

On 22 January 1857 there arrived at Nice no less a personage

---

[1] Cavour, loc. cit., pp. 21–2.
[2] Lacroix to Hudson, 26 Oct. 1856, F.O. 167/92, unnumbered.
[3] Lacroix to Hudson, 12 Nov. 1856, F.O. 167/92, unnumbered.
[4] Lacroix to Hudson, 16 Dec. 1856, F.O. 167/92, unnumbered.

than King Victor Emmanuel himself. He landed from a Sardinian warship, and having entered Nice on horseback, at once dashed off 'au galop' to pay his respects to the dowager Empress — without even entering his own palace. Alexandra Fyodorovna met the King at the foot of a flight of stairs, embraced him and, if local report is to be believed, assured him that he was 'le roi le plus courteois parmi tous ceux qu'elle avait connus'. The following days were filled with Sardo-Russian dinners, balls, receptions and concerts, and when King Victor left Nice on 28 January the new-found friendship of the two countries had been firmly cemented and demonstrated to the world.[1]

Alexandra Fyodorovna's visit to the Riviera, it soon became apparent, had a political as well as a personal aspect. As early as November 1856 a Russian frigate had dropped anchor in the Bay of Villafranca, and the British consul had learnt that she was to remain there 'until the arrival of a detachment from the Russian fleet at Cronstadt'.[2] Soon two further Russian vessels arrived, and on 22 March they were joined by the *Wiborg*, 'magnifique vaisseau russe de 90 canons.'[3]

Whilst the Russian squadron was gathering in the Bay of Villafranca, Grand-duke Constantine Nikolayevich, brother of the Emperor Alexander II and chief of the Imperial Russian Navy, reached Turin on 26 February 1857. The following day he was invested with the highest Sardinian decoration, the Order of the Annunziata.[4] On 1 March he arrived at Nice 'avec son brillant état major'.[5]

Thereafter Nice, for a time, appeared to have become almost a Russian city. 'On ne voit à Nice en ce moment que des costumes russes', an inhabitant recorded.[6] Russian sailors joined in the festivities on shore and gained the goodwill of the local population. One day the sailors of one of the frigates decided to spend the night on unauthorized shore-leave. 'Le matin, en arrivant à bord, ils ont été fouettés et déjà on avait assommé un de ces malheureux et précipité son corps dans la mer, mais

---

[1] 'Nice d'Antan. Extrait de la Correspondance d'un Niçois en l'An 1857' (*Nice Historique*, no. 5, Nice, Sept.-Oct. 1931).
[2] Lacroix to Hudson, 12 Nov. 1856, F.O. 167/92, unnumbered.
[3] 'Nice d'Antan', loc. cit.
[4] Hudson to Clarendon, 28 Feb. 1857, F.O. 167/98, no. 28, draft.
[5] 'Nice d'Antan', loc. cit.
[6] Ibid.

l'exécution des autres fut arrêtée, car toute la population de Villefranche était sortie en masse sur le quai en criant grâce pour ces pauvres marins.'[1] The Grand-duke, in the meantime, was making good use of his time, and if a later report in an Austrian newspaper is to be believed, 'made frequent expeditions with his officers into the neighbourhood, and surveys were made by them in the presence of Piedmontese Engineers.'[2]

It was rumoured that the Tsar himself would shortly visit Nice, and it was expected that should he do so, the Emperor of the French would come to meet him.[3] However, as the month of March drew on, it became clear that there would be no meeting of the two emperors at Nice. Instead, Victor Emmanuel, the most courteous of kings, came to pay a farewell visit to his imperial guests.[4] On 19 April the Grand-duke left for Toulon on board a frigate, escorted by three other naval vessels.[5] Two days later the dowager Empress embarked for Civitavecchia and Rome 'avec regrets, les larmes aux yeux, enchantée de Nice, de la galanterie du Roi'.[6]

A magnificent reception awaited the Grand-duke in France. At Toulon, a large part of the French fleet was assembled to greet him, and he had the pleasure of launching no less than five vessels which were being built for Russia in the naval yards of the city.[7] When he reached Paris, he found that Napoleon had spared no pains to prepare an impressive welcome. His reception, the British ambassador noted sourly, was 'more that of a Sovereign than of a simple member of an Imperial or Royal Family'.[8]

A similar reception had met the dowager Empress when she passed through Turin on her return journey to Russia. King Victor had met her at the railway station and together they had driven to his palace along a route illuminated and decorated, the British minister noted, with the Russian colours only.[9] On

---

[1] Ibid.

[2] Article in *Ost-Deutsche Post*, 12 Sept. 1858, Translation in Fane to Malmesbury, 16 Sept. 1858, F.O. 7/549, no. 96.

[3] 'Nice d'Antan', loc. cit.

[4] Hudson to Clarendon, 3 Apr. 1857, F.O. 167/98, no. 36, draft.

[5] Hudson to Clarendon, 23 Apr. 1857, F.O. 167/98, no. 42, draft.

[6] 'Nice d'Antan', loc. cit.   [7] Ibid.

[8] Cowley to Clarendon, 17 May 1857, F.O. 27/1196, no. 780. 'Fancy the Emperor going himself to the Gare yesterday', Cowley privately remarked to Clarendon, 'to see if it was properly arranged!' (Cowley to Clarendon, private, 1 May 1857, copy, Cowley MSS.

[9] Hudson to Clarendon, 24 May 1857, F.O. 167/98, no. 53, draft.

the following day, the diplomatic corps had been received at the royal palace to pay its respects to the august visitor. The Empress, on the occasion of her visit, had distributed Russian decorations to many personages of the Sardinian court and government, thus marking in a convincing manner the final reconciliation of the two countries.[1]

Sardinia, Russia and France, in fact, were demonstrating to the world at large that the Crimean War was already forgotten. The reception accorded to the Grand-duke in Turin, Toulon and Paris, and that given to his mother in the dominions of the King of Sardinia, showed that both Napoleon and Victor Emmanuel were courting the Emperor of Russia. Both were aware of the value of Russian support for the realization of their future designs. Russia, therefore, found herself placed in a position where she might turn to advantage the visit of the Grand-duke and his squadron to Mediterranean waters.

II

In the course of the summer which followed the festivities at Nice, Stackelberg, in conversations with Cavour and La Marmora (the Sardinian Minister of War), alluded to the desire of the Grand-duke Constantine for a coaling station in the Mediterranean. Such a station, he explained, would serve the needs of the naval squadrons which it was intended to send regularly into the Mediterranean. La Marmora at once indicated the port of Villafranca as a suitable locality and a part of the old prison of that place as a building 'pouvant servir au but que le Grand Amiral russe avait en vue'.[2] Cavour, however, decided, before taking a final decision, to consult Napoleon III, Sardinia's powerful protector. 'La Russie', he informed Villamarina (the Sardinian Minister in Paris), 'a l'idée d'établir un dépôt et des magasins pour sa marine à Villefranche.' Would Villamarina, 'sans en faire même l'objet d'une communication confidentielle,' sound Walewski, about the attitude of France to this request.[3]

The Sardinian inquiry reached Paris at the very moment

[1] Hudson to Clarendon, 2 Jun. 1857, F.O. 167/98, no. 56, confidential, draft.
[2] Cavour to Sauli, 4 Nov. 1857, M[inistero degli] A[ffari] E[steri], Rome, Archivio Storico, no. 57; Legazione Sarda presso Pietroburgo, no. 28.
[3] Cavour to Villamarina, 20 Aug. 1857, printed in *Nuove lettere inedite del Conte Camillo di Cavour*, ed. Edmondo Mayor (Turin, 1895), p. 278.

that Napoleon was about to meet the Tsar at Stuttgart to discuss with him a common policy for the two empires. He was therefore delighted to be able to render the service asked for. Sardinia, Walewski explained to Villamarina, could not refuse the Russian request. 'Le Gouvernement Français l'accorderait lui même si la Russie en faisait demande.' Both France and Sardinia in the interests of their general policy, had a strong need 'd'être bien avec S. Pétersbourg'.[1]

After receiving this reply the Sardinian government must have indicated privately to that of Russia its willingness to grant the facilities asked for. On 15 October 1857, in consequence, Stackelberg officially requested permission for the use of Villafranca. He had, he declared, already spoken to Cavour 'de l'intention de Mgr le Grand-Duc Constantin d'envoyer régulièrement des escadres d'évolution dans la Méditerranée, et du désir exprimé par son Altesse Impériale d'obtenir dans le port de Villefranche un emplacement qui puisse servir de lieu de dépôt pour le charbon et les vivres de nos navires de guerre.' The friendly reaction of Cavour and La Marmora, 'm'engagent, Monsieur le Comte, à Vous addresser aujourd'hui une demande écrite qui puisse servir de base officielle à la conclusion de cette affaire'. The building indicated by La Marmora 'suffirait parfaitement pour l'établissement de magasins et même d'un petit atelier de réparations'. Stackelberg would be glad to have a plan of the locality for transmission to the Grand-duke, 'en lui faisant part des offres obligeantes du Governement Sarde.' Since it was not intended to send a Russian squadron to the Mediterranean before the following spring, there would be ample time to discuss detailed arrangements before the arrival of the Russian vessels.[2]

Cavour met Stackelberg's request by transmitting to him 'les plans et dessins de la localité dont nous serions disposés à céder la jouissance à la marine russe'. Stackelberg at once expressed 'de vifs remerciemens pour l'empressement que le Gouvernement du Roi a montré de se rendre agréable à la Cour Impériale aussi dans cette circonstance'. Cavour, in reporting these exchanges to the Sardinian representative in St Petersburg, ex-

---

[1] Villamarina to Cavour, 24 Aug. 1857, M.A.E., no. 291.
[2] Stackelberg to Cavour, 3/15 Oct. 1857, A[rchivio di] S[tato in] T[orino], Lettere Ministri Esteri, Russia, mazzo 3⁰.

pressed the hope 'que ce procédé, qui répond au reste aux rapports de bonne amitié qui existent entre les deux Gouvernements, sera non moins apprécié à St. Pétersbourg'.[1]

Thereafter for some months the matter of the Russian coaling station at Villafranca was allowed to rest. Not till August 1858 did the Russian government indicate a desire to avail itself of the facilities placed at its disposal. In a note dated 7 August, Stackelberg announced that a Russian squadron had left Kronstadt for the Mediterranean during the month of July. Some vessels would proceed directly to the ports of the Levant, but the screw line of battleship *Retvitzan* would be stationed in the port of Villafranca 'qui lui servira de point de relâche durant les évolutions qu'il fera dans le cours d'automne et de l'hiver'. Would the Sardinian government therefore give the necessary instructions 'pour que les localités gracieusement concédées à notre marine par le Gouvernement du Roi, soient remises au Commandant du Retvitzan'.[2] On 21 August Cavour informed the Sardinian representative at St. Petersburg that the necessary arrangements had been completed.[3] Gorchakov received the news with pleasure and renewed the expression of his gratitude 'pour cette obligeante concession'.[4]

III

It was at this point that the transaction, which had hitherto been the secret of the three governments more immediately concerned, became known to the world at large. In its issue of 25 August *l'Avenir de Nice* revealed the fact that Russia had obtained privileges at Villafranca. 'Nous savons d'ailleurs par des personnes qui ont suivi cette négociation', the paper remarked, 'que le Piémont et la Russie n'ont eu en vue qu'un établissement commercial destiné à faire concurrence à la marine autrichienne dans les ports du Levant.'[5] Similar information appeared elsewhere and on 7 September the British consul in Nice reported to the chargé d'affaires at Turin that

---

[1] Cavour to Sauli, 4 Nov. 1857, M.A.E., no. 57; Legazione Sarda presso Pietroburgo, no. 28.
[2] Stackelberg to Cavour, 7 Aug./26 Jul., M.A.E., Lettere Ministri Esteri, no. 218.
[3] Cavour to Oldoini, 21 Aug. 1858, M.A.E., Legazione Sarda presso Pietroburgo 28, no. 85.
[4] Oldoini to Cavour, 11 Sept. 1858, A.S.T., Lettere Ministri, Russia, mazzo 24, no. 33.
[5] *L'Avenir de Nice*, 25 Aug. 1858.

several local newspapers had recently discussed the question of a possible cession to Russia of 'the docks of Villafranca'. It was affirmed that the Odessa Steam Navigation Company[1] would be put in possession of the docks and that the object of Russia was to compete in the Mediterranean with the Austrian Lloyd Company. Russia, in addition, was believed to have the intention of establishing at Villafranca 'a supply of spare stores of all kinds for the use of the Russian Navy'.[2]

Before this information reached London, the British government had had its attention drawn to Villafranca by reports in the British press, purporting to describe what had taken place between the Russian and Sardinian governments. The *Globe*, on 10 September, reported the alleged transaction in a message from its French correspondent. 'It is impossible', the paper announced, 'to exaggerate the importance of what has just taken place between Russia and the Government at Turin. All the complimentary interchanges of diplomatic and courtly demonstrations have ended in a solid and substantial fact. Russia has got a lease for 22 years to come, at a fixed rate of 4 million francs annual payment into the Sardinian Exchequer, of all the capital messuage [*sic*] called the town of Villafranca, with water privileges comprising a capacious and well-sheltered harbour, capable of accommodating 30 ships of the line, within 10 miles of France, 2 miles from Nice, and in the most favourite position for becoming a small Sebastopol in the heart of the Mediterranean.' La Marmora had officially announced 'that the seaport of Villafranca is now part and portion of All the Russias' and that the new proprietors were the Russian Steam Navigation Company. The people of Nice were 'delighted at the chance of being a permanent Russian Brighton'. The Sardinians were chuckling 'at the idea of a permanent Russian

---

[1] The Odessa Steam Navigation Company had been founded in Aug. 1856 with the official backing of the Russian Government to promote Russian influence in southern waters, train sailors and provide, in time of war, troop-transports, which might possibly be armed. It was to be supported by large subsidies. (For details of the company see W. E. Mosse, 'Grand-duke Constantine Nicolaevich and the Russian Steam Navigation Company' in *The Journal of Modern History*, xxvi, no. 1, 1954.) In spite of the circumstantial press reports, there is no evidence to show that the company was at this time negotiating with the Sardinian government about the acquisition of special privileges at Villafranca or that such privileges were in fact extended to it. This does not exclude the possibility that there may at this time have been unofficial negotiations between the company and the Sardinian government, which served as the basis for the reports in the French and Sardinian press.

[2] Lacroix to West, 7 Sept. 1858, F.O. 167/104, unnumbered.

fleet being always at hand to protect them against Austria'. Above all, the Kremlin was 'rejoicing in high jubilee at having got as good a footing as even Constantinople for future operations in Syria, Greece, and the Levant', all the while that Europe was 'squabbling over the paltry Principalities and other tomfooleries'.[1]

On the following day, under the heading 'Russian Intrigues', the *Morning Chronicle* repeated the information of the *Globe*. 'For more than a hundred years', the paper remarked, 'the chief object of Russian ambition has been to obtain a naval *point d'appui* in the Mediterranean.' That object, 'so long desired and so strenuously resisted', had been 'at last accomplished . . . by a mere business transaction'.[2]

On 14 September *Le Nord*, of Brussels, recognized as the mouthpiece of the Russian Foreign Office, commented on the news published in the British press. The excitement of the *Morning Chronicle*, *Le Nord* suggested, was part of a campaign by the opposition to upset Lord Derby's Conservative ministry. The facts themselves were harmless and without importance. A steamship company had been established some time ago at Odessa for the purpose of trade with the Levant and the Mediterranean. That company, in need of a depot for its ships and merchandise, had now acquired one on Sardinian soil. 'Quelles puissances', the paper exclaimed, 'pourraient s'y opposer si ce n'est celle où cet entrepôt existe, ou celle que cet entrepôt avoisine? Or, ces deux puissances, qui sont la Sardaigne et la France, ne se plaignent pas, et c'est l'Angleterre qu'on voudrait faire intervenir dans une pareille transaction, d'un caractère tout commercial.' In a moment of political aberration, France and Europe 'ont pu se laisser entraîner à faire les affaires de l'Angleterre, au point de défendre à la Russie d'avoir des vaisseaux de guerre dans la mer Noire. Voudrait-on peut-être maintenant les amener à interdire à la Russie le droit d'avoir des navires de commerce? . . . Nous conseillons au Morning Chronicle d'exhorter ses patrons à lui fournir de meilleures thèses.'[3]

On the evening of 15 September Palmerston, then in opposition, met Corti, the Sardinian chargé d'affaires, at a dinner he

---

[1] *Globe*, 10 Sept. 1858.
[2] *Morning Chronicle*, 11 Sept. 1858.   [3] *Le Nord*, 14 Sept. 1858.

was giving for a Turkish diplomat. Palmerston attacked the conduct of Sardinia 'avec une vivacité extrême', and when Corti asked him to await the official explanation of the Sardinian government, he rejoined that the statements in *Le Nord* left no doubt in his mind about the substance of the news. The Odessa Steam Company was simply 'un subterfuge employé par le Gouvernement Russe pour éluder le traité de Paris, qui imposait de certaines limites aux forces qu'il pouvait entretenir dans la mer Noire'. Its vessels 'pouvaient à un moment voulu, être transformés en bâtimens de guerre', and that was why the Russians were 'si désireux d'avoir un entrepôt dans la Méditeranée'.[1] Palmerston was very angry indeed, and there can be little doubt that, had he been in power, nothing could have saved Sardinia from an impressive demonstration by the Royal Navy and an official demand for explanations.

The British government, however, took a calmer view of the matter. The *Morning Herald*, which was held to represent its views, adopted a moderate tone. On 18 September Malmesbury, the Foreign Secretary, received reassuring information. The Sardinian government, he learnt from the British representative at Turin, had granted permission to the Russian government 'to establish a depot of coal and provisions in the Bay of Villafranca'. All offers on the part of Russia to purchase the station had been refused, and no charter or document existed which could 'in any way be construed into an act of cession of the port to Russia'. West also transmitted a declaration which the Sardinian government had inserted in the official gazette. 'The pretended cession to Russia of the port of Villafranca spoken of by some newspapers', the Sardinian government declared, 'is nothing more than the gratuitous grant which His Majesty's Government has made, of the use of the locale of the ancient bagno of Villafranca which has long been unoccupied, to serve as a depot for coal and provisions, in the same manner as some years ago a similar permission was given to the government of the United States of America in the Gulf of Spezia.'[2]

The French government, as might have been expected, refused to intervene. When on 20 September Cowley privately

[1] Corti to Cavour, 16 Sept. 1858, Cavour, loc. cit., pp. 230 ff.
[2] West to Malmesbury, 15 Sept. 1858, F.O. 67/236, no. 15, confidential and enclosure.

inquired about its attitude, he was told 'that the matter had been referred to the Minister of Marine, who saw no cause to call in question the proceedings of the Sardinian government'.[1]

Malmesbury therefore felt reassured and on 24 September told the Queen that in his view the excitement about the alleged cession had been exaggerated. 'The strange, but harmless cession of a wharfage at Villafranca to the Russian Lloyds', he wrote, 'is a piece of mean spite of Cavour against the Austrian Lloyds, but the people who will most suffer are the Co. of the *French* Messageries at Marseilles.'[2]

IV

Cavour in the meantime had decided to ignore the clamours of sections of the British press. On 18 September he assured Oldoini in St Petersburg that the attacks in the British papers had caused no change in Sardinian policy. Oldoini, in conversation with his colleagues, should deny the inaccuracies and exaggerations which had been published. 'Vous aurez soin toutefois', Cavour added, 'de faire entendre de la manière la plus positive que les injustes colères de la presse Anglaise et voir même la mauvaise humeur de certains diplomates sont loin de nous faire regretter ce que nous avons fait pour le Gouvernement de l'Empereur, et qu'au contraire ce que vient de se passer, loin de refroidir nos sentiments envers Sa Majesté Impériale et son Gouvernement, auraient plutôt pour effet, si cela était possible, de les rendre plus forts et plus durables.'[3]

The Russian government did not hesitate to reciprocate Cavour's assurances of goodwill. On 1 October, Alexander II gave the Sardinian General d'Angrogna, who had been sent to Warsaw to compliment him, a personal message for King Victor Emmanuel. Tell the King, the Tsar remarked, 'combien je suis heureux des bonnes relations qui existent entre les deux pays

---

[1] Cowley to Malmesbury, 20 Sept. 1858, F.O. 27/1259, no. 1235, confidential. In a private letter to Malmesbury, Cowley had expressed his annoyance. 'What do you say', he had written, 'to Cavour's giving the Russians a coal depot on Sardinian Soil? pretty well I think for a man who signed the Treaty of Paris to put down Russian Maritime Supremacy in the Black Sea, and who knows that the Russian Lloyds is nothing else but a vast scheme to have a large armed fleet available at the shortest notice. I see that, with their usual Russian tendencies, they are not disposed to find fault with Cavour here' (Cowley to Malmesbury, private, 17 Sept. 1858, Cowley MSS, drafts, xx, pp. 145 f.).
[2] Malmesbury to the Queen, 24 Sept. 1858, R.A. J 30/92.
[3] Cavour to Oldoini, 18 Sept. 1858, M.A.E., no. 586.

que j'espère se resserront de plus en plus. — J'espère que la flotte et le Grand-Duc Constantin seront bien accueillis à Villefranche. Ce dernier a déjà été en mesure de connaître les bontés du Roi à son égard.'[1]

On 16 November the long-awaited Russian battleship steamed into the Bay of Villafranca,[2] and two days later the former 'bagno', complete with fixtures valued at 5271.90 francs, was formally handed over to Captain Taube, commander of the *Retvitzan*.[3] The 'cession', which had caused so much excitement, had become an accomplished fact.

On 3 December Grand-duke Constantine arrived at Turin, accompanied by his wife and eldest son. On the following day he was the guest of honour at a formal dinner given by King Victor Emmanuel.[4] Two days later the Grand-duke, who had embarked at Genoa, reached Villafranca on board the *Retvitzan*. His landing was delayed by two hours and a half owing to the late arrival of one of the two escorting vessels. The Grand-duke, 'greatly displeased at this', immediately 'placed the whole Ship, Officers and men under arrest'.[5] He then drove into Nice, where rooms had for some time been reserved for him at the Hotel Victoria. He was accompanied by the Grand-duchess and his son, and Stackelberg also arrived from Turin to join the grand-ducal party.[6]

One of the first concerns of the Grand-duke was the setting up of the depot in the ancient 'bagno'. In this he received the full co-operation of the Sardinian military engineers, with whose officers he had several long conversations.[7] Another task to which he devoted himself was that of supervising the preparation of a model 'of Villafranca, its Bay, Military Buildings, and adjacent Country'.[8] Villafranca had become—though on a modest scale—a Russian naval base.

[1] d'Angrogna to Cavour, 1 Oct. 1858, M.A.E. Régistre des pièces déchiffrées N.21, no. 481, copy.
[2] Commando Generale della Divisione Militare di Nizza to Ministero della Guerra, 16 Nov. 1858, A.S.T., Sezione IVa, no. 1055, Ministero della Guerra.
[3] Hudson to Malmesbury, 9 Dec. 1858, F.O. 67/236, no. 186.
[4] Hudson to Malmesbury, 5 Dec. 1858, F.O. 67/236, no. 181.
[5] Lacroix to Hudson, 7 Dec. 1858, F.O. 167/104, unnumbered.   [6] Ibid.
[7] Genio Militare Direzione di Nizza to Ministero della Guerra, 16 Dec. 1858, A.S.T., Sezione IVa, no. 1055, Ministero della Guerra.
[8] Hammond to Secretary of the Admiralty, 26 Apr. 1859, P.R.O., Ad[miralty] Papers Ad 1/5719. By April 1859 the Foreign Office had secured a facsimile of the model prepared for the Grand-duke Constantine, which early in 1860 was deposited in the Admiralty Library.

V

The British government had observed with suspicion and disapproval the Russian activities at Villafranca. Disapproval had turned to alarm when early in January 1859 information reached London that the Russian government intended to establish coaling stations similar to Villafranca in other parts of the Mediterranean. Malmesbury now decided that steps must be taken to forestall the Russian designs.

On 11 January telegrams were accordingly sent to the British representatives at Madrid and Constantinople telling them that Russia would ask or had already asked of Naples, Spain and Turkey 'a Port like Villa Franca to be lent or let to them'. The British government was entirely opposed to this, and the envoys must 'oppose any such cession as most distasteful to Her Majesty's Government'.[1] In addition the Foreign Secretary tried to enlist the support of the French government. The Russians, he privately wrote to Cowley, were 'trying to get ports in Spain, Sicily and Egypt like Villafranca—that is, military ports'. Cowley should quietly ask Walewski how that would suit France. It was indeed well known that relations between France and Russia were close, but did France really wish to have Russia 'a maritime Power in the Mediterranean?' Russia was openly boasting that the allies had overreached themselves, 'because she was blocked up at both ends before for nine months, and at one end all the year,' while now she could keep a fleet all the year round in the Mediterranean.[2]

On the following day the British envoy at St Petersburg was informed of the alleged Russian schemes and told that they would be extremely distasteful to England. Such an extension of Russian occupancy in the Mediterranean might 'lead in the event of war with Russia to very embarrassing questions with the countries in which Ports so occupied by her might be situated'. In any case it would render necessary 'the continued maintenance in the Mediterranean of a larger British Naval Force than it might always be convenient for us to keep in that

---

[1] Malmesbury to Buchanan, 11 Jan. 1859, F.O. 185/345, no. 6, and Malmesbury to Bulwer, 11 Jan. 1859. F.O. 195/614, no. 37.

[2] Malmesbury to Cowley, 11 Jan. 1859, printed in Malmesbury, *Memoirs of an Ex-Minister*, 2 vols. (3rd edition, London, 1884), II, pp. 147–8.

Quarter, since it is evident from the present accumulation of Russian Naval Force under the shelter of Villafranca, that the possession of other similar Ports would probably lead in a great measure to a transfer of the Russian Fleet from the Baltic to the Mediterranean'. The British government, therefore, would do its utmost 'to dissuade other Mediterranean Powers from making any such concession to Russia', and Crampton was instructed quietly to direct his attention to this matter, so that the government might obtain through him 'the earliest information of any steps which Russia may be taking to carry out the project imputed to her'.[1] That same day, a despatch in similar terms was sent to Madrid[2] and on the following day another to Constantinople.[3] Finally the British representative in Vienna was instructed by telegraph to ask the Austrian government to make representations to that of Naples 'to prevent Russia from obtaining any such further footing in the Mediterranean'.[4]

The replies received by Malmesbury were of a reassuring nature. The Austrian government promised to make strong representations at the court of Naples and declared that its interests in the matter were identical with those of England.[5] Calderón-Callantes, with typical Spanish bravura, replied that he 'could not believe that Russia would ever make such a proposal to Spain, and if she did the answer would be a short one— as the Spanish Nation were no more disposed to let their harbours in Europe than to sell their Island in America'.[6] Fuad Pasha, in accordance with the customs of his country, gave a somewhat ambiguous reply. He did indeed assure Bulwer 'that no approaches had as yet been made by Russia for the loan or hire of any harbour in Turkey' and that, whenever such an application was received, the Porte would decline it. If, however, Russia should merely demand for her Steam Navigation Company equality of treatment with those of France and Austria, that is 'the privilege . . . of hiring stores and building wharves in some of the Ottoman Ports', such a request could not well be

---

[1] Malmesbury to Crampton, 12 Jan. 1859, F.O. 181/353, no. 23, confidential.
[2] Malmesbury to Buchanan, 12 Jan. 1859, F.O. 185/345, no. 11, confidential.
[3] Malmesbury to Bulwer, 13 Jan. 1859, F.O. 195/614, no. 43, confidential.
[4] Malmesbury to Loftus, 18 Jan. 1859, F.O. 120/362, no. 36.
[5] Loftus to Malmesbury, 20 Jan. 1859, no. 47, copy in Malmesbury to Crampton 5 Feb. 1859, F.O. 181/355, no. 53.
[6] Buchanan to Malmesbury, 24 Jan. 1859, F.O. 72/954, no. 26.

refused. Bulwer, thereupon, warned Fuad that a demand of this nature 'ought not to be granted without singular caution', and that it would be well 'that in each case the opinion of Her Majesty's Government were previously taken'.[1] With these assurances the British government was satisfied, and nothing more was heard of Russian plans for the acquisition of further footholds on the shores of the Mediterranean.

VI

In the meantime the war which France and Sardinia were planning to wage on Austria was rapidly approaching. In July 1858 Napoleon and Cavour met at Plombières and agreed on joint military operations at an early date. In December Napoleon entered into a formal engagement, obliging him to join Sardinia if the latter should become involved in a war with Austria.[2] By the end of December, Napoleon informed the Tsar that, according to his information from Sardinia, hostilities were likely to open the following May.[3]

Parallel with his negotiations with Cavour, Napoleon in the autumn of 1858 had opened talks with the Russian government with a view to Franco-Russian co-operation in the coming war. This was the moment for which Gorchakov and Alexander II had been waiting, for it might now become possible to strike a further blow at the hated Crimean system. When in September 1858, Prince Napoleon[4] visited Warsaw to sound the Russian government, Gorchakov at the first interview had dwelt on the humiliation inflicted on Russia by the neutralization of the Black Sea. Whilst rejecting all thought of active Russian participation in the impending conflict, he was ready to consider an armed demonstration or diversion on the Russian frontier with Austria. Prince Napoleon refused to make any promises about the Black Sea clauses. Indeed, he carefully avoided anything which might alarm or offend England. The draft of a possible

---

[1] Bulwer to Malmesbury, 31 Jan. 1859, F.O. 78/1428, no. 75.

[2] Charles-Roux, op. cit., p. 245.

[3] Quoted in Ernst Schüle, 'Die Verhandlungen zwischen Russland und Frankreich vor dem italienischen Kriege 1858–9' in *Zeitschrift für ost-europäische Geschichte* VIII, Neue Folge, Band IV (Königsberg-Berlin, 1934) p. 203. For a detailed description of the Franco-Russian negotiations cf. B. H. Summer, 'The Secret Franco-Russian Treaty of 3 March 1859' in the *English Historical Review*, XLVIII (London, 1933).

[4] Napoleon's cousin, J. C. P. Bonaparte. For the following cf. B. H. Sumner, loc. cit.

agreement which emerged from these mutual reticences failed to satisfy the wishes of the Emperor of the French.

Napoleon, therefore, sent to St Petersburg a confidential agent to submit his counter-suggestions. It was now proposed that, in the event of war in Italy, Russia should observe a neutrality benevolent to France. She should, moreover, concentrate on her Galician frontier with Austria sufficient forces to immobilize one hundred and fifty thousand Austrians. In exchange for these services France, at an eventual peace conference, would support the abrogation of the Black Sea clauses. Should Russia join in the war, Napoleon would assist her in acquiring Austrian Galicia. In return, the Russian government would consent to the absorption of Nice and Savoy by France with compensation for Sardinia in northern Italy.

These proposals were not of a nature to attract the Russian government. As Gorchakov explained to the French agent, Russia had no desire whatever to add to her Polish populations by the acquisition of Galicia. It would be a different matter if she were offered the retrocession of southern Bessarabia, as its loss had been an affront to her honour. Moreover, Gorchakov wished to raise Russia's price for the armed demonstration on the Austrian border. France, in return should promise not merely every assistance in securing the abolition of the Black Sea clauses in a future conference, but she should also declare immediately that, as for herself, she already regarded them as null and void. In exchange for the territorial adjustments desired by France, she should acquiesce in the retrocession of southern Bessarabia. It is difficult to believe that Gorchakov seriously expected Napoleon to accept terms such as these.

In fact, the French government submitted a counter-draft. The Tsar, Napoleon wrote, required a partial revision of the Treaty of Paris, he, himself, changes in the Treaty of Vienna. Both treaties would remain in force until the war produced a congress. He therefore suggested that at the congress each party should strongly support (*faire triompher*) the interests of the other. In a private letter to Gorchakov, Prince Napoleon added that the Russian request for the immediate and unilateral denunciation by France of the Black Sea clauses was unreasonable. All that could be expected of Napoleon was that he should take the first favourable opportunity pour tâcher de faire revenir de plein gré les grandes puissances sur les articles de ce traité que vous considérez comme portant atteinte à la souveraineté de l'empereur de la Russie dans la Mer Noire.[1]

In accordance with these views, the counter-draft proposed that, in exchange for Russia's consent to her acquisition of Nice and Savoy, France at the peace conference would champion Russia's claim for a revision of the Black Sea clauses. There was no mention of southern Bessarabia. Moreover, even before the messenger bearing the new proposals reached St Petersburg, a telegram from Paris had further reduced their scope. The final French proposal was so vague as to be almost meaningless: it simply provided for future consultations about a joint policy at an eventual peace conference.[2] There was little in this to tempt Gorchakov and the Tsar.

In further exchanges, Gorchakov vainly attempted to make the immobilization of Austrian troops in Galicia conditional on a French promise of full support for the annulment of both the Black Sea clauses and the Bessarabian cession. In the end, all mention of Russian troop concentration was omitted from the draft. Under the terms of the treaty finally signed on 3 March 1859, Russia merely undertook to maintain a benevolent neutrality in the event of a Franco-Austrian war. The vague and non-committal French formula about mutual good offices at a future congress was incorporated. Shortly before the treaty was signed, the Tsar, rather ingenuously, remarked:

Of course I don't want war, but if it breaks out I shall not draw back and I believe that Napoleon in his turn will perform what he has promised: the abrogation of the Treaty of Paris which is, for me, a lasting nightmare.

More realistically, Gorchakov in April 1859, told the French ambassador

ce que nous voulons, ce n'est ni vous qui pouvez nous le donner

---

[1] It might well be doubted to what extent, under this vague engagement, France would in fact support Russian claims in the face of certain opposition from England, Austria and Turkey.

[2] 'Leurs Majestés s'entendront sur les modifications aux traités existants à faire prévaloir en commun dans l'intérêt des deux Empires lors du règlement de la paix.'

I

ni l'Autriche. La guerre actuelle ne peut pas nous le donner et c'est pourquoi nous ne nous en mêlerons pas.[1]

Russia, therefore, would maintain a neutral attitude.

VII

The decision affected the position of the Russian squadron wintering at Villafranca. In her first draft of the proposed treaty of alliance, France had stipulated that, in the event of war, the Russian vessels then in the Mediterranean would remain in specified French and Sardinian ports. Their presence at these ports was considered a moral support.[2] Gorchakov, in his counter-draft, had tried to limit the Russian obligation. 'Les vaisseaux russes se trouvant actuellement dans la Méditerranée,' article 3 of the Russian counter-propositions stated, 'y resteront jusqu'à ce qu'il ait été jugé à propos de leur donner, d'un commun accord, une autre destination, et pourront toujours au besoin entrer dans les ports français.'[3] When it finally became clear that France would not accept Russia's demands about the Black Sea clauses and that Russia therefore would remain neutral, Gorchakov became increasingly concerned about the presence of Russian vessels in the Mediterranean. These he considered, would constitute a pledge in the hands of France (*zalog v rukakh Frantsii*) and might even become involved in the fighting. He therefore decided to prevent the dispatch of further warships to the Mediterranean, and refused to accept any engagement committing Russia with regard to the future location of her squadron.[4]

Such caution on the part of the Russian government seemed indicated also for another reason. France, as Gorchakov knew, had reached agreement with the Sardinian government that at the conclusion of a successful war in Italy she would acquire Nice and Savoy. Russia, at an early stage in the negotiations, had consented to this transfer of territory. So far, therefore, as the depot at Villafranca was concerned, Russia in the event of

---

[1] Montebello to Walewski, 20 Apr. 1859, quoted in Schüle, loc. cit., pp. 210–11.
[2] Ibid., p. 195.
[3] Schüle, loc. cit., p. 213.
[4] 'Zapiski Ministra inostrannykh del kn. Gorchakova o sekretnykh peregovorakh za 1859 g.', printed in F. Rotstein, 'K istorii franko-russkogo soglasheniya 1859 g.' in *Krasny Arkhiv* 88 (Moscow, 1938), pp. 191–2.

Franco-Sardinian victory would have to deal with a first-rate European power in place of the weak and compliant government of Sardinia.

It was this situation which offered Gorchakov the opportunity of curbing the activities of the Grand-duke Constantine, whose repeated excursions into the field of foreign policy had been, for some years, a source of irritation to the Russian Foreign Office.[1] Russia's decision to remain neutral had in a large measure destroyed the basis of the Grand-duke's policy in the Mediterranean, and Gorchakov was delighted at the opportunity to restrain his unwelcome rival.

When war finally broke out in May 1859 Russia, as she had promised, assumed an attitude of neutrality benevolent to France and Sardinia. Down to the outbreak of hostilities the Russians had made use of the facilities put at their disposal by the Sardinian government. News was received at the Foreign Office in London that they were 'landing Stores and Guns at Villafranca by Night'.[2] Shortly after the declaration of war, however, a surprising development occurred. On 22 June 1859, the British consul at Nice reported that an event was taking place at Villafranca which had astonished him 'as it must all who are acquainted with the fact'. The Russian government 'after having caused to be conveyed to that Port all sorts of Ships' Stores for the supply and repair of their Ships of War', had suddenly 'sent Frigates to remove every single article from the place'. One vessel, the *Ryurik*, had already left Villafranca. Another, the *Polkan*, was still in the port, taking the remaining things on board. Even a large quantity of coal, brought to Villafranca during the preceding winter by a Hanoverian vessel and which might easily have been disposed of on the spot without loss, had that morning been put on board and was about to be removed with the rest of the objects referred to. The few sailors and men who had been left in charge of the locality were also to be embarked and taken away. It was understood that the two frigates had come from Smyrna and that they were proceeding directly to Kronstadt.[3]

---

[1] For the rivalry between Gorchakov and the Grand-duke Constantine cf. Friese, op. cit., pp. 153 f., and Wodehouse to Malmesbury, 27 Mar. 1858, F.O. 65/517, no. 29, secret and confidential.
[2] Admiralty to Vice-Admiral Fanshawe, 11 May 1859, Ad. 13/7, no. 270, secret.
[3] Lacroix to Hudson, 22 Jun. 1859, F.O. 167/110, unnumbered.

The British government, surprised at this report, decided to make inquiries in Paris. Walewski replied that he had heard nothing about the matter. He considered that if the report was true, which he seemed to doubt, Russia's conduct was to be attributed to her 'displeasure at the proceedings of Sardinia in Italy'.[1]

The war in Italy ended a few weeks later, with an armistice signed at another Villafranca, and there was thus no further need for Gorchakov's policy of caution.

VIII

In October 1859 the dowager Empress of Russia returned to her beloved Nice 'au bruit des canons de la frégate *La Svetlana*, à hélice, de quarante canons, sur laquelle la souveraine s'était embarquée'. The frigate anchored in the Bay of Villafranca in the presence of a large crowd, and the Empress began a stay which was to last for seven months.[2] Stackelberg once more took advantage of her presence at Nice 'pour faire de cette ville sa résidence ordinaire'.[3] In January 1860 the Orthodox Church in the rue Longchamp, the construction of which had been begun in 1857, was inaugurated under the patronage of the Empress.[4]

In March 1860 came the moment when, under the Treaty of Turin, Nice, and with it the port of Villafranca, was to be transferred from Sardinia to France. The Russian colony at Nice was passionately opposed to the transfer, and the dowager Empress herself made no secret of her sentiments. 'A Nice', Cavour recorded in February 1860, 'la colonie russe est passionément antiséparatiste. Le mot d'ordre vient du Palais de l'Impératrice.' Count Viechorski, 'grand-maître de la maison de l'Impératrice,' was even reported to have joined the demonstrators in the streets of Nice 'les soirs de manifestation'.[5]

In spite of the feelings of the local Russian colony, however, Nice and Villafranca, now Villefranche, passed into the possession of France. Although the dowager Empress had openly

[1] Cowley to Russell, 27 Jun. 1859, F.O. 27/1298, no. 48.
[2] Léon Sarty (Comtesse de Sauteron de Saint Clément), 'Nice d'Antan. Notes et Souvenirs,' in *Nice Historique* (Nice, 1921).
[3] 'Autour de l'Annexion. Souvenirs du Capitaine Segretain sur Nice (Avril-Mai, 1860)' in *Nice Historique*, no. 2 (Avril-Juin, 1949).
[4] Léon Sarty, loc. cit.
[5] Segretain, loc. cit.

shown her hostility to the transfer, the position with regard to the former prison was not affected, and the Russian navy, as hitherto, was allowed to make use of the building.

The great days of Russian naval activity in the Mediterranean, however, were now drawing to a close. After 1860 the Grand-duke Constantine, the moving spirit behind the establishment at Villafranca, steadily lost his influence over the Emperor Alexander and his credit with the Russian public. Moreover, costly internal reforms called imperiously for retrenchment and for the adoption of a passive policy abroad. There was no longer room for the wilder schemes of the adventurous Grand-duke. When in 1870 Russia freed herself from the restrictions imposed on her sovereignty by the Treaty of Paris, the Mediterranean lost much of its importance for Russian naval strategy. The Russians, nonetheless, continued until 1917 to maintain their foothold in the former prison of Villefranche.

IX

The Italian crisis thus failed to realize the more ambitious hopes of Alexander II and Gorchakov. Once again, as in November 1856, it had proved impossible to wean Napoleon from the British alliance. The sole price he was willing to pay for an armed Russian demonstration on the Austrian frontier was a promise, couched in general terms, to support Russian desires for revision at a future conference. The undertaking, however, might still have proved valuable if, at the widely expected congress, Russia had been able to make her acquiescence in the French acquisition of Nice and Savoy conditional on the revision of the Black Sea clauses. Moreover, the Russian government might have hoped to gain a measure of support from Prussia and even England in return for its readiness to associate itself with them in an intervention of the neutrals. These hopes, however, were doomed to disappointment. The sudden Austro-French armistice greatly reduced the prospects of success. Palmerston's return to office, moreover, removed whatever slight chance there might have been of British concessions. In the end it became clear that, for different reasons, none of the powers desired a congress at all and that the new arrangements would, therefore, be made on a bilateral basis.

Indeed, at least British opposition to a possible congress was due largely to the fear that, in one form or another, the issue of the Black Sea clauses would be raised. Nor did it, finally, prove possible to obtain 'compensation' for the French annexation of Nice and Savoy and the aggrandizement of Sardinia. Even the foothold at Villafranca, the one tangible Russian gain, lost much of its value in Russian eyes in consequence of the French annexation.

Yet there had been intangible benefits. Even though no practical consequences had followed, it might prove useful in the future that Napoleon had formally indicated that, in his eyes, the neutralization of the Black Sea was 'negotiable'. Moreover, some time after the armistice Rechberg, Buol's successor, had in his turn offered as the price of a restoration of friendly relations between Russia and Austria, Austrian support for a future revision of the Treaty of Paris. Although Austria, for the present, was too weak for this to be anything but a Platonic gesture,[1] it was yet an indication that for her also, neutralization was 'expendable'. Two of the three partners of 15 April had thus formally indicated how little intrinsic value they attached to the Black Sea clauses.

Nor did the end of the Italian crisis leave the triple alliance in a healthy state. Two of its three partners had just fought a brief but bloody war. Moreover, the circumstances of the French annexation of Nice and Savoy had imposed a severe strain on Anglo-French relations. Whilst Russell used strong language in Parliament, Palmerston in private conversation had actually threatened the French ambassador with war.[2] It was hard to believe that these strains would not weaken the action of the triple alliance in the East.

This, however, so far as Alexander II and Gorchakov were concerned, was a matter of future hope rather than present fact. So far as the Italian crisis was concerned, Russian gains had been small. Only the next European crisis would show whether Russian diplomacy had come appreciably closer to the achievement of its objectives.

---

[1] Gorchakov aptly, if inelegantly, remarked in private conversation that he did not seek his allies 'dans la pourriture' (Engel-Jánosy, *Graf Rechberg*, Berlin, 1927, p. 73).

[2] H. Temperley and L. Penson, *Foundations of British Foreign Policy* (London, 1938), pp. 211 f.

Part 3

THE DECLINE AND FALL
OF THE CRIMEAN SYSTEM

During the Italian crisis, the Russian government had appeared, rather incongruously, as the ally of Napoleon and revolutionary nationalism. Russian hopes, however, of securing with the help of this alliance a revision of the Treaty of Paris had been disappointed. Moreover, the vigour of the Italian national movement as well as its democratic and revolutionary features had taken Alexander II and Gorchakov by surprise and aroused their misgivings. These were confirmed when in 1861, under the impact of the Italian movement, the European ferment of nationalities spread to the streets of Warsaw. When, early in 1863, the Poles rose against Russian rule, they received diplomatic support not only from Napoleon backed by French public opinion but also from the British government.[1] Even the Austrian government, reluctantly, took part in their joint remonstrances. Moreover, as the crisis deepened, Napoleon left no stone unturned to turn diplomatic into military intervention. Only the reluctance of the British government held him back. In fact, throughout the later months of 1863, a French landing on the Baltic coast was a distinct possibility. With the joint diplomatic intervention of the three powers, a new Crimean War, a renewal of the Crimean coalition, appeared to loom on the horizon. As in 1854, conservative Prussia, on account of a natural solidarity of interests, stood out as Russia's only friend. Even the relative ill-success of the famous Alvensleben Convention could not disguise the fact.

In the event, the Crimean War was not renewed. The Russian government firmly rejected every attempt at Western intervention. Napoleon, tied down by his Mexican adventure and 'left in the lurch' by his British and Austrian partners lacked the determination to intervene single-handed. Bitter Anglo-French recriminations followed the unsuccessful intervention. Russia, during 1864, was able to crush the Poles.

The Polish crisis with the Western diplomatic campaign against Prussia and Russia profoundly affected the alignment of the powers. It changed the basis of Russian foreign policy.

[1] For a detailed description of Western intervention during the Polish insurrection see W. E. Mosse, 'England and the Polish Insurrection of 1863' in the *English Historical Review*, January 1956.

The Russo-French *rapprochement* inspired by the Italian crisis came abruptly to a close. Instead, Russia now began to look to Bismarck's Prussia, seemingly conservative, authoritarian and anti-revolutionary. Even when the revolutionary implications of Bismarckian statesmanship in Germany began gradually to emerge, Alexander II and Gorchakov found consolation in the fact that this was, at least, the 'conservative' alternative to German unity under national-liberal-revolutionary auspices. From an ideological point of view — and ideological considerations were becoming increasingly prominent in Russian foreign policy — Bismarck remained the least unsatisfactory of all possible partners.

In fact, the Russian government had now completely forsworn its earlier revolutionary 'aberrations'. Alarmed at the violence of national and democratic passions in Italy, Hungary, Roumania, Denmark, Germany and last but not least Poland, the Tsar and Gorchakov were turning to a policy of monarchical solidarity directed against France, the patron of revolutionary nationalism. This solidarity included even the hated Habsburg monarchy. From having been the 'accomplice' of Cavour, the Tsar was now turning into a staunch defender of the European order established by treaties and began to speak nostalgically of the times of the Holy Alliance.

Russia's new-found respect for the European treaties had, of course a paradoxical corollary. If the Russian government was consistent in its new policy, respect for treaties must embrace not only the Treaty of Vienna but that of Paris as well. In fact, at least after 1863, Alexander and Gorchakov became, for a time, defenders of *all* treaties, not excluding even the one primarily directed against Russia herself. This stand, dictated by consistency, at the same time offered the only hope of drawing England into a defensive conservative grouping directed against France and European nationalism. This, temporarily, became the major object of Russian diplomacy. Only the isolation of France could prevent her intervention in Poland. To this object, the remaining aspects of Russian foreign policy must, at least for the time being, be subordinated. Late in 1863, during the discussions on Napoleon's proposal for a European congress, Gorchakov — probably sincerely — assured the incredulous Napier that, in the event of the congress assembling he did not 'as at present minded', see any cause for 'bringing the state of the East under review'.[1] Concern for Poland and distrust of France were beginning to dominate Russian policy to the virtual exclusion of other considerations.

In consequence, throughout the Danish crisis Gorchakov worked indefatigably — if without marked success —to preserve and strengthen his (largely imaginary) quadruple grouping of Russia, England, Austria and Prussia. Russia, indeed, was the last of the powers to abandon formally the Treaty of London of 1852. As long as she maintained this demonstratively 'European' attitude, whilst she might, in favourable circumstances, attempt to secure a revision of the Treaty of Paris with the consent of her fellow-signatories, she was unlikely to help to discredit any international instrument, however unpalatable. It was in this conservative frame of mind that Alexander II and Gorchakov entered the great European crisis of 1866.

---

[1] Napier to Russell, 9 Nov. 1863, no. 692, confidential, copy in R.A. J 80/23.

CHAPTER V

England, Russia and the Roumanian Revolution of 1866[1]

La Sainte Alliance . . . qu'on a tant attaquée a cependant donné à l'Europe 50 ans de paix. Ne nous attachons pas au nom, mais le système offrait des garanties, et je regrette qu'on ne puisse y revenir.

ALEXANDER II, 10 April 1866

La Russie ne marchandera pas son bon vouloir à la Puissance qui s'engagera à appuyer dans un futur Congrès le rappel des stipulations du traité de Paris relatives à la Mer Noire. C'est là le but principal de la vie diplomatique du Prince Gortchakoff, et je suis convaincu qu'il ne travaillera sincèrement à réunir le concert européen que le jour où il croira pouvoir atteindre ce grand objectif de la politique étrangère russe.

BARON DE TALLEYRAND, 14 August 1866

. . . la victoire de Königgrätz fut, après la guerre d'Italie, le second coup porté à la validité du traité de coalition du 15 avril 1856.

P. SABUROV

The crisis of 1866 which marked a further and decisive stage in the revolt of the nationalities against the European treaties was set off by the revolution which, early in that year in defiance of the Treaty of Paris, placed on the throne of the United Principalities of Moldavia and Wallachia, Prince Charles of Hohenzollern-Sigmaringen. The Roumanian revolution, involving as it did a major modification of the Crimean settlement, was a challenge to the powers who had signed the Treaty of Paris and, more particularly, to the signatories of the Triple Treaty of 15 April 1856. The question set before these powers by the Roumanian revolution was whether they would condone a further unilateral infringement of the order they had painfully established ten years before. Indeed, although the fact was perhaps not generally realized, the future of the Crimean system was at stake.

[1] The bulk of this chapter first appeared as an article in the *Slavonic Review* (December 1960).

I

On the night of 22–23 February 1866 Prince Alexander John,[1] who since 1859 had ruled with indifferent success over the United Principalities, fell victim to a palace revolution[2] and was forced to abdicate.[3] On the following day the two houses of the Roumanian parliament, in joint session, proclaimed the Count of Flanders, nephew of the King of the Belgians, Prince Philip I of Roumania. The Prince, indeed, almost immediately declined the proffered honour, but in issuing the invitation, the Roumanians had thrown down the gauntlet to the protecting powers. By electing the Count, they had demonstratively ignored the convention of 1858 by means of which the treaty powers had sought to prevent the election of a foreign prince.[4] Events in Bucarest, therefore, now made it incumbent upon the powers to redefine their positions.

Turkey, the suzerain power, felt alarm at the turn of events. At Constantinople it was feared that if the Principalities obtained a foreign prince, a similar claim would be put forward by Serbia. Indeed it was considered likely that all the outlying provinces would demand independence or quasi-independence and that the 'dissolution' of the empire would follow.[5] To meet the threatened danger, the Porte resolved to take its stand on the strict application of the convention of 1858. It accordingly proposed to its co-signatories that a Turkish commissioner accompanied by delegates of the powers should at once repair to Bucarest to deal with the situation on the spot. The proposal was vetoed in Paris.[6] Drouyn, the French Foreign Minister, proposed instead the calling of a conference (in Paris) to con-

---

[1] In 1859, as Col. Alexander Cuza, he had been elected *hospodar* (prince) of both Moldavia and Wallachia in the celebrated double election by means of which the Roumanian patriots had outwitted the protecting powers.

[2] The revolution had not come as a bolt out of the blue. Green, the British consul in Bucarest, had repeatedly warned the Foreign Office of impending developments (Lyons to Clarendon, private, 6 and 20 Dec. 1865 and 3 Jan. 1866, Clarendon MSS, dep. c. 101).

[3] For details of events in Bucarest cf. T. W. Riker, *The Making of Roumania* (London, 1931), pp. 491 ff.

[4] For details of the convention cf. W. G. East, *The Union of Moldavia and Wallachia, 1859* (Cambridge, 1929), pp. 140 ff.

[5] Lyons to Clarendon, private, 28 Feb. 1866, Clarendon MSS.

[6] Riker, op. cit., pp. 508 f.

sider the future of the Principalities.[1] This counter-proposal was received at Constantinople without enthusiasm. In telegrams to London and Paris, the Porte insisted that, if there was to be a conference, it must be based on the observance of the treaties. The question of a foreign prince must be excluded unequivocally from the deliberations.[2] The British government rejected this reservation.[3] Clarendon, the Foreign Secretary, wished to reserve his freedom of action. He was reluctant to separate himself from France and felt, moreover, that it would be disloyal to the other signatories to prejudge the issue.[4] However, if the Porte had no success in London, it found support for its attitude in an unexpected quarter. The Russian government — an unlikely defender of the Treaty of Paris — expressed itself in a sense favourable to Turkish wishes. Gorchakov's reply to the French invitation was that Russia would not join in a conference unless the Porte expressly desired one.[5] Informed of Turkey's conditional acceptance he, in turn, declared his willingness to attend a conference 'with the reservation, however, that the Convention of 1858 shall form the basis of its deliberations'.[6]

In adopting this unexpected, attitude, the Russian government was actuated by a number of motives. In the first place, it feared that the disappearance of Cuza might open the door, directly or indirectly, to annexation of the Principalities by Austria. What caused particular concern was a plan, much canvassed in the European chanceries, to compensate Austria

---

[1] An ambassadorial conference on the navigation of the Danube was already meeting in Paris under Drouyn's presidency. All that was needed, therefore, was for the governments to issue full powers and supplementary instructions to their representatives.

[2] 'Nous pensons', declared Aali Pasha, 'et c'est la question principale pour nous, qu'il faut décider avant tout le principe de faire respecter les Traités et les arrangements existants.' Turkey would then be ready to meet her co-signatories, 'pour délibérer sur les moyens d'exécution'. The Porte must insist on this condition, 'parce qu'il nous serait excessivement difficile de nous trouver dans une réunion sans être sûrs d'avance de ne pas y rencontrer la question du Prince étranger sous quelque titre que ce soit' (Aali to Musurus, telegram, 27 Feb. 1866, confidential, copy in Clarendon to Cowley, private, 28 Feb. 1866, F.O. 519/180).

[3] Clarendon expressed the view that 'the Turk must join the conference and then ask what he pleased' (Ibid.).

[4] Clarendon wrote: 'I thought I should not be acting with good faith towards the other Governments if I said any thing upon a point of so much importance without their [illegible]' (the same to the same, private, 1 Mar. 1866, ibid.).

[5] Buchanan to Clarendon, 3 Mar. 1866, F.O. 65/698, no. 92.

[6] The same to the same, 6 Mar. 1866, ibid., no. 100.

on the Danube for the eventual cession of Venetia to Italy.[1] This Alexander II was determined to prevent, if necessary by force of arms.[2] Complications of this nature would be forestalled by strict adherence to the protocol of 1858.

A further reason for Russia's insistence on the convention was that the union of the Principalities under Cuza had proved unsatisfactory. Indeed, the Tsar had not hesitated to stigmatize it as 'une œuvre bâtarde'.[3] In the time of the late Prince, it was claimed, Bucarest had become a hot-bed of Polish conspiracy and revolutionary agitation.[4] If, however, the two Principalities were again to be separated (as provided for in the convention), Russia might hope to exercise a preponderant influence at least in Moldavia.[5]

Again, alarmed by recent events in Poland and the Elbe duchies, the Russian government had come to see in the observance of international engagements an element of much-needed stability. There can be little doubt of the Tsar's sincerity in lamenting to Buchanan[6] that 'a tendency to disregard international engagements was one of the great dangers of the day'.[7] Nor was Gorchakov necessarily hypocritical when he told Ignat'yev at Constantinople[8] that 'it would be inexpedient under present circumstances that any step should be taken which might invalidate existing treaties or

---

[1] The possibility had been mooted as early as 1864, when Lord John Russell had sounded the French government about it. The suggestion had been accepted in principle in Paris but had foundered on the rock of Turkish opposition. Napoleon III subsequently revived the proposal but met with firm opposition in Vienna (Riker, op. cit., p. 511). Cuza's abdication had reopened the issue. The proposal was still regarded with favour in Paris (Cowley to Clarendon, private, 25 Feb. 1866, F.O. 519/232). One of the schemes under consideration was to make the (Habsburg) Duke of Tuscany ruler of the Principalities (the same to the same, private, 9 Mar. and 22 Mar. 1866, ibid.). The Italian government was 'pushing' the proposal in London and Paris (Riker, op. cit., pp. 511 f.). British and Austrian reactions, however, were cool.

[2] Buchanan to Clarendon, 14 Mar. 1866, F.O. 65/698, no. 115, most confidential. In the margin of a document mentioning the possibility, the Tsar was reported to have written 'inadmissible jusqu'à la guerre' (the same to the same, 27 Feb. 1866, ibid., no. 69, most confidential).

[3] The same to the same, 13 Mar. 1866, ibid., no. 109, confidential.

[4] The same to the same, 25 Apr. 1866, F.O. 65/699, no. 190, confidential.

[5] It was the opinion of Tillos, the French consul in Bucarest, that Russia had sufficient influence to have a *hospodar* of her own choice elected in Moldavia (Cowley to Clarendon, private, 23 Mar. 1866, F.O. 519/232, summarizing a report from Tillos to Drouyn). Cf. also Buchanan to Clarendon, 13 Mar. 1866, F.O. 65/698, no. 109, confidential.

[6] The British ambassador in Petersburg.

[7] Ibid.

[8] In a private letter which he read to Buchanan.

disturb existing territorial and international arrangements in the East'.[1]

There was, moreover, an afterthought concealed behind Russia's ostensible concern for the faithful execution of the treaty. Stremaoukhov, the head of the Asiatic department of the Ministry of Foreign Affairs, 'let the cat out of the bag' when he told Buchanan in private conversation that if the arrangements of 1856 were to be maintained, it must be in every respect

> for if they were to be violated in points, to the maintenance of which Russia attached importance, it was not to be expected that she would consider herself bound by others which humiliated her, or that she would in such circumstances continue to endure Treaty stipulations which precluded her from keeping ships of war in the Black Sea, while her coasts were left entirely open to to aggression on the part of the Turkish fleet lying at Constantinople.[2]

'I sometimes suspect,' Buchanan reflected, that

> the *respect* shewn to the Treaty of Paris here arises from a hope that its violation by others may give Russia a right to claim that the most galling of the stipulations against her power in the Black Sea should be modified.[3]

Whatever the turn of events, therefore, it was clear that, from the Russian point of view, insistence on the convention of 1858 would pay dividends. Either Russia would obtain a settlement consonant with her interests or, were this to fail, she would strengthen her case for a further revision of the treaty. Russia, therefore, urged the Porte to insist on the application of the convention. It was for Turkey, Gorchakov informed the Turkish minister, 'to show Europe whether it still had *couilles* or not.'[4]

Russian policy at the impending conference, therefore, seemed settled when an unforeseen *contretemps* suddenly raised a doubt. Budberg, the Russian ambassador in Paris and plenipotentiary designate for the conference, was at this moment on leave in St Petersburg. When presented with his instructions and an order to repair at once to the French capital, he chose

---

[1] The same to the same, 25 Apr. 1866, F.O. 65/699, no. 190, confidential.
[2] The same to the same, 14 Mar. 1866, F.O. 65/698, no. 114, confidential.
[3] The same to the same, private, 28 Mar. 1866, Clarendon MSS.
[4] Riker, op. cit., p. 509.

the moment to bring to a head his long-standing feud with the
Foreign Minister. The rivalry of the two, while partly personal,
also involved an element of policy. Support for Turkey and the
Convention of 1858, while likely to align Russia with Turkey
and England, would certainly place her in opposition to the
Emperor of the French. This, though acceptable to Gorchakov
and the Tsar, was anathema to Budberg. The ambassador,
therefore, while arguing that the duty of representing Russia at
the coming conference could be performed equally well by a
chargé d'affaires, also

> criticized the instructions which were prepared for him and
> maintained that the policy of Prince Gortchakov in seeking a
> more intimate understanding with England was an error and that
> everything possible should rather be done to promote cordial
> relations with France.

The quarrel was referred to the Tsar who, very properly, took
the part of his Foreign Minister. Budberg was ordered to call on
Gorchakov and assure him that he would obey his instructions
in future.[1]

The incident had a twofold importance. It meant in the first
place — as Gorchakov would later discover with annoyance —
that the Russian plenipotentiary at the conference would be
lukewarm in carrying out his instructions. More important, the
inevitable delay in Budberg's departure for Paris gave the
Roumanian nationalists valuable time in which to consolidate
their position. Soon an exasperated Clarendon would be blaming the Russian government for delaying the work of the conference.[2] There is an element of truth in the charge made by the
Foreign Secretary that Budberg's tactics played into the hands
of the Roumanians.

The British government, in the meantime, had attempted to
define its policy. On 5 March, in the House of Commons,

---

[1] Buchanan to Clarendon, 14 Mar. 1866, F.O. 65/698, no. 120, secret.
[2] 'The delay and its consequences', he told Brunnow, 'have been mainly caused
by your Government 1st by the Russian Plenipotentiary not proceeding to his post
and 2nd by his not having sufficient instructions' (Clarendon to Brunnow, 1 Apr.
1866, copy in Clarendon to Cowley, private, 3 Apr. 1866, F.O. 519/180). Budberg's
demand for further instructions referred to by Clarendon was simply a dodge to
cause more delay. An indignant Gorchakov informed Buchanan that as for Budberg requiring further instructions, 'he was saturated with them!' (Buchanan to
Clarendon, 11 Apr. 1866, F.O. 65/698, no. 169).

Gladstone[1] announced that England would enter the conference

> holding it our main duty to keep in view not only the precise
> words of the stipulations but also the general scope and purpose
> of the Treaty of 1856. Subject to the provisions and policy of that
> treaty, it must be the desire of every British Government to see the
> local institutions of that country developed in accordance with the
> well-ascertained opinions of the inhabitants.

With regard to the question of a foreign prince,[2] he must
decline to commit himself.[3]

Vague and ambiguous though it was, this statement was
received enthusiastically in Bucarest, where the municipality
drew up an address to Gladstone 'thanking him for the bene-
volence with which he spoke of the Principalities'.[4] In fact, the
declaration, in its studied ambiguity, concealed the basic
dilemma facing British diplomacy. The problem, seemingly incapable of solution, was that a choice might have to be made
between two objects almost equally dear to the hearts of
British statesmen: 'the precise words of the stipulations' and
'the well-ascertained wishes of the inhabitants'. Gladstone, in
his declaration, had carefully evaded this issue.

The Chancellor's statement, with its refusal to face the basic
problem, in fact reflected the views of a divided cabinet.
Russell, the Prime Minister, considered that as long as the
Principalities neither proclaimed their complete independence
of Turkey[5] nor elected a 'Russian Viceroy'[6] they should be
allowed to 'go in "pursuit of happiness" as the Americans say
to any shop they like'.[7] Force should be used only to meet a

---

[1] Gladstone was Leader of the House of Commons. Both the Prime Minister
(Russell) and the Foreign Secretary (Clarendon) had seats in the House of Lords.
Gladstone, moreover, had previously shown some interest in the affairs of the
Principalities (Clarendon to Cowley, private, 13 Mar. 1866, F.O. 519/180).

[2] 'A question which has been connected with great difficulties in the discussions
of former times.'

[3] Gladstone in the House of Commons on 5 Mar. 1866, *Parl. Debates*, CLXXXI, cc.
1519 f.

[4] Green to Clarendon, 15 Mar. 1866, F.O. 78/1920 no. 38. Another
similar address was displayed in one of the churches for signature by the general
public.

[5] 'We must resist independence of Roumania and employ Turkish and Austrian
troops if needs be in the name of the European Powers to put it down.'

[6] 'We must likewise in conjunction with France resist the Duke of Leuchtenberg
or any other Russian Viceroy.'

[7] Russell to Clarendon, private, 28 Feb. 1866 (1), copy in Clarendon to Cowley,
private, 28 Feb. 1866, F.O. 519/180.

declaration of independence, 'short of which we should content ourselves with friendly advice'.[1]

Clarendon held somewhat different views. Though eager for a strict application of the convention, he yet wished at all cost to avoid a disagreement with France.[2] His first programme, outlined to the trusty Cowley, was 'to keep the Powers in concert and save the Principalities from a foreign Prince — to allow their separation again to be a debatable question and not to invite Couza back'.[3] This plan, omitting as it did all reference either to the convention or to the wishes of the inhabitants was purely 'diplomatic'. The selection of a foreign prince Clarendon considered impracticable.

> The sooner the phantom of a foreign Prince is laid aside the better — we never shall find a Xan Gentleman-Prince willing to put himself at the head of 2 millions of pauper brigands in order to become a vassal of the Sultan, and if we did, the Powers would be sure to disagree 1st about his appointment and next, if he was appointed, about the independence he would endeavour to secure for himself.[4]

It was 'much better to go in for the practical rather than keep harping upon the impossible'. The 'practical' meant 'as close an adherence as we can to the Convention which is known and recognized in the Principalities as the work of the Great Powers and from which any divergence might be considered an innovation that the people might resist'. The convention laid down the procedure to be followed in the event of a vacancy in the *hospodarship*. The assemblies of the two provinces should meet separately *ad hoc* for the purpose of holding elections. If they chose different men, this would prove their desire for separa-

---

[1] Russell to Clarendon, private, 28 Feb. 1866 (2), copy, ibid. Russell spoilt what was in itself a reasonable approach by a most unrealistic suggestion which aroused the scorn of Clarendon and Cowley. 'But I don't see', he wrote, 'why Maximilian of Mexico, or one of his brothers should not accept the Principality under the Sultan' (Russell to Clarendon, private, 28 Feb. 1866 (1), copy, ibid.). This was too much for Clarendon who told Cowley 'I could not resist sending [illegible] R's notes upon the settlement of the Principalities as curiosities which I was sure would amuse you' (Clarendon to Cowley, private, 3 Mar. 1866, F.O. 519/180).

[2] A little later he would tell Cowley: 'Of course it is an immense object thus to pull well with France upon this as upon all questions, but the bad faith and habitual lying of Drouyn almost render an entente impossible' (the same to the same, private, 26 Mar. 1866, ibid.). Cf. also the same to the same, private, 10 Mar. and 13 Mar. 1866, ibid.

[3] The same to the same, private, 3 Mar. 1866, ibid.

[4] The same to the same, private, 1 Mar. 1866, ibid.

tion, if the same man, their wish to preserve the union. If this course were now followed, it would save the powers a great deal of trouble. 'We have no objection to the Union', wrote Clarendon, 'and should be inclined to it rather than have a wrangle with the French, but it will entail a departure from the Convention and some new form of election will have to be devised.'[1]

Armed with these instructions, Cowley had a long conversation with Drouyn. Napoleon's Foreign Minister declared that his master had previously supported the wish of the Principalities to be united under the rule of a foreign prince. 'What the Emperor had thought good then, he continued to think good now.' However, he had been prevailed upon to desist from expressing an opinion now in favour of a foreign prince. As for the question of union, however, France would feel obliged to support it in conference even single-handed. Cowley rejoined that, if France had a preconceived opinion, so had the British government:

> Would not the best course to take be to consult the wishes of the populations themselves which might be easily done by putting into force the 11th and 12th articles of the Convention of 1858, made expressly to meet the case of the vacancy of the Hospodariat?[2]

Let the two provinces decide for themselves. If there were to be a double election as before, he had no doubt but that the British government would respect it. If, on the contrary, each province chose its own separate *hospodar*, why should not France, who was always putting forth the doctrine of respect for popular opinion, abide by the decision? Drouyn rejoined that the Convention of 1858 'was made for a state of things which no longer existed'. To put the articles into force now, it would be necessary to begin by creating separate governments and separate chambers. Could this be done without courting, in the first place perhaps a refusal of the central government to dissolve itself and, in the second, a disturbance of the popular tranquillity by going to fresh elections? Moreover, the electoral law had since been changed. Was the old or the new one to be applied? Cowley and later Clarendon could not but concur in

---

[1] Clarendon to Cowley, private, 10 Mar. 1866, F.O. 519/180.
[2] Cowley to Clarendon, private, 12 Mar. 1866, F.O. 519/232.

the justice of these objections.[1] With this admission on their part, the Convention of 1858 was dead.

Nothing daunted, Clarendon now declared that the British government had 'no objection whatever to the Union' but wished first to know whether it was desired by the peoples. It could not be admitted that separation was to be a barred question but if there were 'reasonable grounds for believing that the Union would not be obnoxious beyond endurance to the Moldavians, we ought I think to close with it'.[2]

A similar exchange of views was meanwhile taking place between the cabinets of London and St Petersburg. Buchanan informed the Tsar that, in the view of the British government, it would be expedient to carry out the stipulations of the Convention of 1858 'as far as they might be consistent with existing circumstances'. Much of the recent trouble must be ascribed to the setting aside of the convention by the double election of Cuza. Alexander II agreed, observing that 'a tendency to disregard international engagements was one of the great dangers of the day'. At once, however, Buchanan revealed the ambiguity of the British attitude by adding that 'accomplished facts were . . . difficult to deal with' and by alluding to Gladstone's statement in the House of Commons that 'while Her Majesty's Government would regulate their views as far as possible by the stipulations of the Convention of 1858, they would also be disposed to take into fair consideration the wishes of the people of the Principalities'. The Tsar, confident that the majority of Moldavians at least opposed the union, replied that he did not object to a popular vote and felt confident about the result.[3] In fact, there seemed to be a measure of agreement between the British and Russian points of view, but while the Russian government was taking its stand squarely on the convention, Clarendon was floundering unhappily between the French and Russian positions. It was clear that agreement among the powers in conference would not prove easy to reach.

---

[1] Ibid., and Clarendon to Cowley, private, 14 Mar. 1866, F.O. 519/180.

[2] The same to the same, private, 17 Mar. 1866, ibid.

[3] Buchanan to Clarendon, 13 Mar. 1866, F.O. 65/698, no. 109, confidential. It would presently be shown that while the objections of the Moldavians to union under a native *hospodar* were indeed insuperable, this did not apply to union under a foreign prince. For the views of the Moldavians and a discussion of the separatist demonstrations of 15 April 1866, cf. Riker, op. cit., pp. 501 ff.

II

It was while negotiations were in this state that the conference opened in Paris. The first session, held before Budberg's arrival from Petersburg, was a purely formal one.[1] Safvet, the Turkish plenipotentiary, announced that his government joined in the conference on the understanding that all discussion of a foreign prince would be excluded. Not until nine days later did the conference meet again to hold its first working session. Budberg then proposed that the Convention of 1858 should be accepted as the basis of deliberations. Drouyn objected that it had already been modified more than once by subsequent international acts; Goltz, the Prussian, supported the objection. Budberg, however, drew the attention of the conference to article 13 which provided for separate native *hospodars*. Cowley then expressed regret that the conference had delayed notifying the provisional government in Bucarest of its objection to the election of a foreign prince. Budberg reiterated that Russia would not tolerate such a prince. In reply to a question from Goltz as to what she would do if the Principalities elected one in defiance of the conference, he said that she would occupy them.[2] Discouraged and unhappy, the representatives of Turkey and Austria sat silent.[3] Nothing was decided and Cowley, after the meeting, observed that the commencement of the conferences did not augur well for the end of them.[4] He himself favoured fresh elections[5] and an enquiry to ascertain 'the real position of the Moldavian deputies at Bucharest'.[6]

---

[1] It took place on 10 March. For the protocols of the Paris conference on the Principalities, cf. *Nouveau Recueil des traités, conventions et autres transactions remarquables, servant à la connaissance des relations étrangères des puissances et des états dans leurs rapports mutuels*, edited by Samner and Hopf (Göttingen, 1876–1908), vol. 18, pp. 166 ff., and *Archives diplomatiques: recueil de diplomatie et d'histoire*, Paris, 1860 et seq., 1867, vol. 2, pp. 6611 ff.

[2] There was a precedent for such an occupation in the events of 1848–9.

[3] Cowley wrote: 'Unfortunately, as is usual when we have to defend the interests of the Porte, the Turkish representative is a fool. He never opens his lips and we can derive no assistance from him. The other representatives with the exception of Budberg are all afraid of and want to conciliate France, and although I think that Metternich [the Austrian ambassador in Paris] would support the Turk, if the Turk would speak, the Turk's silence involves his silence also' (Cowley to Clarendon, private, 20 Mar. 1866, F.O. 519/232).

[4] Ibid.

[5] He considered that this was 'the safest ground on which to proceed for us and that we should hold it as long as we can' (ibid.).

[6] Ibid.

The latter suggestion had in fact already been anticipated by Clarendon.[1] The Foreign Secretary had learnt from the British consul in Bucarest that if the powers vetoed the appointment of a foreign prince, the provisional government was expected to proclaim the independence of the Principalities, both to prevent their separation and to curb the personal ambition of native boyars. Russian influence was at work to create confusion and promote separation. Its task would be facilitated were it to become known that the conference vetoed the selection of a foreign prince. At present, national sentiment was so strong that no native dared put forward his candidature openly; but if there were to be an election there would, in all probability, be numerous candidates. There would almost certainly be serious disturbances 'compelling armed intervention'. The consul concluded, 'The maintenance of the Union of the Principalities under a native Prince I fear is impossible, nor do I think that the nomination of a native Hospodar . . . by the great Powers could be carried out.'[2]

The news from the Roumanian capital impressed both Clarendon[3] and Drouyn.[4] It put an end to hopes of an Anglo-French compromise solution based on union under a native prince. So alarmed was Clarendon at the prospect of a Roumanian declaration of independence, followed by disturbances and outside intervention, that he began to consider seriously — at least in theory — the possibility of accepting a foreign prince. 'In the abstract', he grudgingly admitted,

> I see no objection to a foreign Prince, though his being a foreigner implies ignorance of the Principalities and his being a

[1] Clarendon told Green (the British consul) that the conference would not sanction a foreign prince and asked how the Principalities would react to this refusal (Riker, op. cit., p. 514).

[2] Green to Clarendon, 19 Mar. 1866, F.O. 78/1920, reporting telegram.

[3] Tillos, the French consul in Bucarest, had reported that there existed but one feeling in the Principalities, the desire to place themselves under a foreign prince. Nothing short of force — which would be resisted — would induce them to elect another native ruler. The members of the provisional government were honest men, resolved to resist to the utmost. If a foreign prince was positively refused them, the two provinces would probably separate. Russia had sufficient influence to have a *hospodar* of her own choice elected in Moldavia. In Wallachia, where universal suffrage prevailed, some low person would probably be named or the army, tired of the state of things, would name and put in the government someone from the ranks. In the meantime a national guard was being formed. Over 4,000 men had already enrolled in Bucarest (Tillos's dispatch to Drouyn, summarized in Cowley to Clarendon, private, 23 Mar. 1866, ibid. A copy, at Cowley's request, was officially transmitted to Clarendon).

[4] Clarendon to Cowley, private, 24 Mar. 1866, F.O. 519/180.

Prince implies deficient education — and if a decent man could be found willing to bind himself to *all* the necessary conditions, we should not persist in our opposition.

Cowley, 'need not put a veto quite as absolute as hitherto upon the foreign Prince'.[1] However, he should still make Drouyn feel 'all the inconvenience of not insisting that the Principalities should abide by the Treaties made in the interests of Europe as well as the Principalities'. It must also be for Drouyn to overcome 'the strong and not unnatural aversion both of Russia and the Porte to the arrangement he proposes'. Finally, would the French minister have the goodness to explain who the prince was whom France intended to send to the Principalities 'for nothing shall make me believe that Drouyn has not one in his eye'.[2]

Among the reasons for Clarendon's *volte face* was the fear that the Principalities would checkmate the conference by declaring their independence. If they then failed to find a foreign prince,[3] 'they might perhaps announce a republic.'[4] Indeed, the news from Bucarest was hardly reassuring. The provisional government, without awaiting the verdict of the Paris conference, dissolved the chambers and announced its intention of holding new elections. At a hastily convened meeting of the conference, Drouyn thereupon insisted that further delay had become impossible and urged the selection of a foreign prince. Budberg, however, announced that he was awaiting fresh instructions; thus no decision could be reached. According to Cowley all the plenipotentiaries felt the ridicule of their position, 'Drouyn & Co. less than the others, because what had been done coincided with their views.' 'It seems to me', Cowley observed, 'that it would be most undignified to go on discussing at Paris while events in the Principalities are outstripping our discussions, and we should either have authority given us to enforce our decisions,

---

[1] Cowley himself, fresh from the impression of Green's report, urged that 'the safest course for us to pursue is to give way to the undoubted wishes of the Principalities and allow them to elect a Foreign Prince if they can find one'. Such a course had as many inconveniences as any other, but 'this at least has the advantage of being asked for by the people, while any other would be more or less imposed upon them' (the same to the same, private, 22 Mar. 1866, ibid.).

[2] Clarendon to Cowley, private, 24 Mar. 1866, F.O. 519/180.

[3] 'Who must be a bold man to put himself at the head of that nation of Brigands in defiance of the Suzerain and the guaranteeing Powers.'

[4] Clarendon to Cowley, private, 28 Mar. 1866, F.O. 519/180.

which could only be done by the application of force or adjourn
and await the development of events.' The application of force
would be so difficult and might be attended with such evil
consequences that it ought not seriously to be taken into consideration at present. On the other hand, a declaration by the
conference, that 'while abstaining from immediate interference,
it is not the intention of the Great Powers to permit their
solemn engagements to be set aside by any decisions which the
new Chamber may take', might have some effect in checking
the aspirations for independence which were probably the
order of the day. They must make a stand somewhere and it
was better to do it on a principle than on anything else. He felt
more convinced every day that they would, in the end, be
forced to accept a foreign prince.

> If the result of these new Elections, spite of all we may do, is a
> declaration in favour of it, what will John Bull say? You know
> this better than I can pretend to do, but of one thing I am certain
> that the Principalities can make out a good case for themselves
> and that France knows how to profit by it.

He was, therefore, for 'burning our fingers as little as possible,
unless we are determined that what we decide shall be law'.[1]

It was in accordance with this programme, and 'upon the
supposition that the conference ought to suspend its sittings'
that Cowley drafted two papers to be presented to the plenipotentiaries at the next meeting. The first, a declaration to be
made by the conference, was kept 'purposely general and vague,
in order that there may be no loophole for the Provisional
Government to give it a complete slap in the face'. The second,
an identical dispatch to the consuls in Bucarest, was 'much
more precise', and, at all events, gave the Principalities to
understand what would not be permitted. Since the consuls
could be told to use this dispatch only as a guide, any action of
the Principalities in opposition to what was therein laid down
'would not have the same importance as if it had been addressed
to the Provisional Government'. It was, Cowley admitted,
hardly a dignified course for the conference to follow. 'This
retreat is certainly not very honourable', he wrote, 'but it is
better than a permanent struggle with the demagogues of the

---

[1] Cowley to Clarendon, private, 31 Mar. 1866, F.O. 519/232, copy.

Principalities, who, if left to themselves, may perhaps become more reasonable.'[1]

Cowley's drafts were approved in London with only minor alterations but not without a significant tussle between Russell and Clarendon. While the former strongly urged 'the elimination of the Veto upon the Foreign Prince as ... if such a one was found who would comply with all necessary conditions and constitute himself bonâfide a Vassal of the Porte, he might be accepted', Clarendon, expressed dissent 'not only because such a man is unfindable, but because Russia and Turkey will never accept him and that we should be creating endless troubles for ourselves out of the Principalities as well as in them'. In the end, however, he withdrew his objections[2] and Russell's alteration was allowed to stand.[3]

There followed 'the longest and most futile session of the Conference',[4] at which Cowley's proposals were adopted. Six identical telegrams were duly sent to Bucarest. The conference then adjourned pending further news from the Roumanian capital. It was agreed to reconvene at the demand of any of the plenipotentiaries. The initiative was thus left to the Roumanians.

III

The provisional government in Bucarest, in the meantime, had not let the grass grow under its feet. Having failed to secure the Count of Flanders, it had cast around for another princeling willing to assume the burden of ruling the Principalities. With the assistance of Napoleon III, its patron and protector, it had unearthed a new candidate.[5] On 10 April in reply to a question

[1] The same to the same, private, 2 Apr. 1866, ibid., copy. The following day Cowley 'dotted the "i"'s' when he told Clarendon 'Perhaps it is as well on the whole as the Conference is quite powerless to enforce its decisions, that its language should be as mild as possible' (the same to the same, private, 3 Apr. 1866, ibid., copy).

[2] Since he had no opportunity of arguing the point with Russell, who was at Windsor, Clarendon wearily told Cowley, he let the elimination stand.

[3] Clarendon to Cowley, private, 3 Apr. 1866, F.O. 519/180.

[4] Riker, op. cit., p. 525.

[5] For the genesis of the Hohenzollern candidature cf. Riker, op. cit., pp. 527 ff. While some obscurity still surrounds the origins of the candidature, it seems practically certain that it originated in Paris. Sigmaringen was acceptable to Napoleon on account of his Bonapartist connections. His maternal grandmother had been Stéphanie de Beauharnais, adopted daughter of the great Napoleon, his other grandmother a Murat. The Roumanian patriots and their backers had hit upon an ideal candidate combining suitably remote Hohenzollern and Bonaparte connections.

from Cowley, Napoleon, with more modesty than accuracy, confessed that while he had no candidate himself, 'the Principalities themselves had tried it on with the hereditary Prince of Sigmaringen, and that both his father and the King of Prussia had given a qualified acquiescence.'[1] Already on the following day, a proclamation of the provisional government called on the Roumanian nation to vote in a plebiscite on an invitation to Charles-Louis of Hohenzollern-Sigmaringen to assume the government of the Principalities as Charles (Karol) I. On 15 April, by 685,969 votes to 224, the Roumanians declared for the Prince. However, in spite of encouragement from Bismarck,[2] Prince Charles still hesitated, for William I, the cautious head of the Hohenzollern family, was reluctant to give his consent.

This delay gave the powers a further opportunity to meet the challenge of the Principalities. The British attitude remained ambiguous. While Layard announced in the House of Commons that 'the treaties on this subject bound the great Powers of Europe, in conjunction with Turkey, to provide for the election of a native prince',[3] Cowley told Clarendon: 'Of course there is danger of the treaty of 1856 becoming a dead letter, but unless we are prepared to go to war again to prevent it, I do not see how it is eventually to be upheld.'[4] The Russian government, in spite of the plebiscite, maintained its former position. Gorchakov still objected to anything tending to the establishment of Moldo-Wallachian independence, which he regarded as the signal for the dismemberment of the Turkish empire.[5] He declared that

> though Russia had not been the champion of the integrity of Turkey and although the Crimean War had been waged against her and the Treaty subsequently concluded had been directed against her . . . it would be inexpedient under present circum-

---

[1] Cowley to Clarendon, private, 10 Apr. 1866, F.O. 519/232.

[2] In the early stages of the candidature, Bismarck's attitude had been one of caution. Now he counselled boldness. He told the Prince: 'You have been unanimously elected by a whole nation. Obey the summons. Proceed at once to the land, to whose government you have been called. When once Your Serene Highness is in Roumania, the question will soon be solved; for, if Europe sees herself confronted by a *fait accompli*, the interested powers will, of course, protest, but a protest stands on paper, and the fact cannot be undone' (quoted in Riker, op. cit., p. 536).

[3] Layard in the House of Commons on 20 Apr. 1866, *Parl. Debates*, vol. CLXXXII, cc. 1774 f.

[4] Cowley to Clarendon, private, 20 Apr. 1866, F.O. 519/232.

[5] For which Russia was not, at this time, prepared.

stances, that any step should be taken which might invalidate existing treaties or disturb existing territorial and international arrangements in the East.[1]

Russia's stand, moreover, was beginning to impress the Turks. Lyons reported from Constantinople that there was 'a good deal of discussion . . . as to a change of policy with regard to Russia'. The Turks seemed to look upon France as their enemy and upon England as 'a lukewarm and weak friend', and to think that, since under these circumstances they were powerless to resist Russia, they had better make the best terms they could with her. With this view, they were talking of selling the Principalities to Russia, thinking, or pretending to think, that this would appease her craving for Ottoman territory. Russia would then be satisfied if she could exercise in the rest of Turkey a predominant influence which would enable her to protect her own church. She would have no desire to come to Constantinople herself and would defend it against other powers. He could hardly suppose, Lyons added, that any influential men had really become converted to 'a policy so suicidal' but the fact that the idea had been suggested and was seriously discussed was itself a symptom worth noting.[2]

It was in these circumstances that the conference met once again in Paris on 24 April. Budberg, at whose request the meeting had been called, reiterated his demand for the strict observance of the convention and the setting up of two separate assemblies. In the name of Gorchakov, he called for a formal pronouncement that in no circumstances would the conference countenance the election of a foreign prince. When Cowley inquired what was to happen if the provisional government refused to annul the recent elections, Budberg replied that in such an event the protocol[3] must be applied. Since this would almost certainly involve the use of force, Drouyn protested and so did Cowley. The British government, it was shown, had finally abandoned the defence of the treaty and aligned itself with Napoleon and Roumanian nationalism. Russia and Turkey —

---

[1] Gorchakov to Ignat'yev, private, quoted in Buchanan to Clarendon, 25 Apr. 1866, F.O. 65/699, no. 190, confidential.

[2] Lyons to Clarendon, private, 18 Apr. 1866, Clarendon MSS, dep. c. 101.

[3] The protocol of 6 Sept. 1859 by which the powers 'condoned' the double election of Alexander Cuza as an exceptional proceeding and laid down the procedure for future elections (cf. Riker, op. cit., pp. 247 f.).

ironically — stood alone in incongruous alliance. In the circumstances, all the plenipotentiaries could do was to refer to the
cabinets the draft of a declaration to be presented separately by
the consuls to the provisional government.

At a subsequent meeting, the conference formally declared
that, in bringing about through the recent plebiscite the
nomination of a foreign prince, the provisional government had
contravened the Convention of 9 August 1858, article XII of
which vested the election of a *hospodar* in the assembly. The
conference, therefore, decreed 'that the task of solving the
question of the maintenance of union should be left to the
assembly which is going to convene'. If the majority of either
Moldavian or Wallachian deputies requested it, they should
have the right of voting separately. If the majority in either
assembly should then pronounce against union, this would
have as a consequence the separation of the Principalities.
Once this question was disposed of, the assembly should proceed
to the choice of *hospodars* 'which according to article XIII ought
to fall only on a native'. The consuls were to watch in common
accord over the free conduct of the voting.[1]

The Roumanian reply to these 'instructions' was resounding.
On 10 May the new assembly without a dissentient voice declared Roumania to be one and indivisible and proclaimed
Charles of Hohenzollern-Sigmaringen hereditary Prince of the
United Principalities. When the result was announced, many
deputies broke into cheering: 'Long live Roumania! Long live
Charles I!' On the following day the Prince, secretly and
incognito left Düsseldorf; on the 22nd he was acclaimed in his
new capital.

IV

Faced with these events and despairing of the Paris Conference, the Turkish government, in the meantime, had under-
standably lost patience. On 21 May Aali warned Lyons that
'the submissiveness with which the Porte had subscribed in
opposition to its own views of good policy and in derogation of
its Treaty rights to all their [the powers'] counsels and resolu-
tions since the deposition of Prince Couza' must not lead them
to expect it 'to go as far as to abandon the principle of the

[1] Printed in Riker, op. cit., pp. 540 f.

integrity of the Empire'. If the Principalities persisted in their election of a foreign prince, 'it would be the right and duty of the Porte to use force to prevent the accomplishment of so flagrant a violation of the Treaties.'[1]

The following day, Musurus[2] notified Clarendon that the Porte had decided to send troops into the Principalities 'in order to compel the Moldo-Wallachians to fulfil their obligations towards the Suzerain Power and to eject Prince Charles of Hohenzollern who had placed himself at the head of an insurrection against the Sultan'. Clarendon was embarrassed. He could not but admit that 'in accordance with the Convention of 1858 the People of the Principalities were bound to elect a native for their Hospodar'. Yet, he asked, would the Porte feel an insuperable objection to setting aside that provision of the convention and recognizing Prince Hohenzollern in the event of his acknowledging himself a vassal of the Sultan? Musurus rejoined that the object of the Roumanians in electing the Prince had been only too frankly avowed. It was to shake off Turkish suzerainty and create an independent kingdom. Were this to be tolerated, it would lead other provinces to follow their example and end in the dismemberment of the Ottoman Empire. Clarendon could not deny this, but insisted that armed intervention by Turkey without the consent of the guaranteeing powers would be 'a manifest violation of the Treaty of 1856'. He therefore strongly urged the Porte to reconsider its determination or, at all events, not to act upon it without having formally brought it under the consideration of the conference. Musurus made the inevitable reply that to do so would be simply to invite a veto 'and as the Conference had already shown its small regard either for the Treaty of 1856 or the Convention of 1858, the Porte had a right to follow the example and to take its own measures for the protection of its vital interests'. There was little more to say. Clarendon could only reply that whatever the conference had or had not done, that was no reason why the Porte should violate treaty engagements by which it was bound. He could not, on the part of Her Majesty's government, give his assent to armed intervention in the Principalities. No measures of this kind should be taken until the necessity for

---

[1] Lyons to Clarendon, 22 May 1866, F.O. 78/1909, no. 182, confidential.
[2] The Turkish ambassador in London.

them had been acknowledged by the powers represented in the conference.[1]

The discussion was resumed three days later,[2] when Musurus laid before Clarendon a telegram from Aali, re-stating the Turkish determination to occupy the Principalities. The Foreign Secretary replied that if a military occupation had in fact taken place without communication or concert with the guaranteeing powers, it was to be deeply regretted. Such an act of precipitation on the part of the Porte was certain to be disapproved by the conference. Musurus replied that those powers represented at the conference who, he assumed, were friendly to the Porte, could have little idea of the injury inflicted on the Sultan by the present state of affairs in the Principalities. The different measures proposed by the Porte for restoring order after the expulsion of Cuza — all of them in strict conformity with the convention — had been rejected by the conference. The delegates, having been ridiculed and practically defied by the provisional government in Bucarest, had taken no measures to assert their authority. A foreign prince elected by a plebiscite had surreptitiously crossed the frontier. Having assumed the reins of government and taken command of the Moldo-Wallachian troops, he had placed himself at the head of an armed insurrection against the Sultan, whose suzerainty over the Principalities was guaranteed by the great powers of Europe. This was not only an encouragement to the other European provinces of Turkey to revolt, but also an insult to the Sultan, who had become an object of derision to his Moslem as well as his Christian subjects. An insurrection at Constantinople was a dangerous possibility. Was not the Sultan, in these circumstances, justified in taking measures to protect the interests secured to him by treaty? Clarendon could only repeat that 'the Porte was bound by Treaty not to interfere by force in the Principalities without the consent of the guaran-

---

[1] Clarendon to Lyons, 22 May 1866, F.O. 78/1904, no. 188, draft.
[2] The Turkish government, in the meantime, had officially learnt on the morning of 22 May the news of Prince Charles's arrival in Bucarest (Lyons to Clarendon, 22 May 1866, F.O. 78/1909, no. 182, confidential). On the 23rd, the Turkish council of ministers met for several hours without reaching a decision. The following evening it finally resolved to send troops across the Danube (the same to the same, 24 May 1866, ibid., no. 189). Apprised of this fact by Aali, Lyons had telegraphed the news to London (the same to the same, 24 May 1866, ibid., no. 188, reporting telegram).

teeing Powers'. The present state of the case should be brought before the conference and the Porte should abide by the result of its deliberations.[1]

Clarendon's two conversations form a landmark in the evolution of British policy. Concern for the integrity of the Ottoman Empire, the ostensible cause of the Crimean war, had now been thrown to the winds. Not only was England trying to dissuade the Porte from occupying the Principalities, but Clarendon had actually made himself the *advocatus diaboli*, pleading for the recognition of Prince Charles. Moreover, as soon as he came to realize that the Turkish government had not yet taken an irrevocable decision,[2] Clarendon had begun to apply pressure at Constantinople. It was probable, he told Lyons, that Russia would break up the conference unless some decided step was taken to sustain the Porte in its objection to Prince Charles. This, in the present state of Europe, might drive the prince into the arms of Russia. It might be worth the consideration of the Porte whether the extreme probability of such a result was not more dangerous for the independence of Turkey than would be the admission of Prince Charles as successor to Cuza. 'You might,' concluded Clarendon,

> suggest to the Porte whether, looking at the two dangers, the latter may not be held to be the least; and you might find out confidentially whether if Prince Charles were to do homage in the usual way to the Sultan and engage for fidelity and for the observance of Treaties with other Powers, the Porte would not be disposed to reconsider the adverse decision which it has formed to the acceptance of the Prince's election.

Lyons, however, should take care not to commit the British government in anything he might say in the matter.[3]

The Porte, confident in the assurance of Russian support,[4] refused to listen to British advice. On 11 June Musurus handed Clarendon a further note 'formally declaring its [the Porte's] determination to have recourse to military measures in the

[1] Clarendon to Lyons, 25 May 1866, F.O. 78/1904, no. 193, draft.
[2] Lyons to Clarendon, 30 May 1866, F.O. 78/1909, no. 198.
[3] Clarendon to Lyons, 6 Jun. 1866, F.O. 78/1904, no. 204, reporting telegram.
[4] Gorchakov declared that while Russia would not engage in punitive action single-handed, such was the manifest duty of the conference. If the latter accepted the *fait accompli*, Russia would withdraw her representative (Riker, op. cit., p. 551). Buchanan expressed his belief that Russia was working for a Turkish occupation (Buchanan to Clarendon, 14 Jun. 1866, F.O. 65/700, no. 288).

Principalities'. Clarendon, who took a serious view of this new threat, could only reiterate 'that in accordance with the Treaties, military measures could not be adopted without the consent of all the guaranteeing Powers, which consent had not been given'. For the rest, he regretted 'the final determination which the Porte appeared to have taken'. Musurus in his reply not only used arguments with which by this time Clarendon was painfully familiar but also drew attention to the dangers of a religious conflict in the Ottoman Empire. He further expressed the belief that the Moldo-Wallachians would not resist a Turkish occupation.[1]

But Clarendon had not yet reached the end of his resources. On the 12 June he informed Lyons by telegraph that his French colleague would communicate with him regarding joint advice to the Porte on 'the expediency of accepting Prince Charles if he will come to Constantinople to do homage to the Sultan as his Suzerain, will engage to be faithful in his allegiance to the Sultan, and to observe the Treaty engagements between the Porte and other Powers'.[2] In consequence of these instructions, Moustier and Lyons called on Aali and Fuad and used every argument they could muster to persuade the Porte to accept Prince Charles.[3] On 14 June, Lyons reported that matters were taking a hopeful turn. The Sultan, it appeared, was disposed to confer upon Prince Charles the government of the Principalities if the Prince in his turn would subscribe to certain conditions to which it was intended to subject his recognition.[4] Clarendon was delighted. There could, he wrote, be little doubt that Russia was seeking to come to some separate understanding with the Principalities, the basis of which would be their independence of the Porte under Prince Charles.[5] The probability of such a

---

[1] On 7 June the Roumanian provisional government addressed to the foreign consuls in Bucarest a circular 'indicating unequivocally' the intention of the Turks to invade Roumania. The following day, some 10,000 Roumanian troops left Bucarest for the Danube. But, reported Green, if they put up any serious resistance to an invader, they would 'astonish themselves as much as their enemies' (Green to Clarendon, 8 Jun. 1866, F.O. 78/1921, no. 98). But there was doubt, also, about the fighting capacity of the Turkish forces opposed to them (cf. Riker, op. cit., p. 553).

[2] Clarendon to Lyons, 12 Jun. 1866, F.O. 78/1904, no. 210, reporting telegram.

[3] Riker, op. cit., p. 554. Cf. also Lyons to Clarendon, private, 20 Jun. 1866, Clarendon MSS, dep. c. 101.

[4] Clarendon to Lyons, 18 Jun. 1866, F.O. 78/1904, no. 218, draft.

[5] Prince Charles had, in fact, established unofficial contacts with the Russian government to overcome its hostility.

result should be a further inducement to the Sultan to determine for himself the pending questions and not to afford an
opening for a third party to settle them in a manner prejudicial
to the interests of the Porte.[1]

Clarendon's joy was premature. Although Aali himself now
appeared to be disposed to favour recognition of Prince Charles,
he had still to contend with those who held the occupation of
the Principalities 'to be absolutely necessary for the Sultan's
dignity'.[2] On 22 June Clarendon sent a further telegram urging
that unless the Porte made up its mind soon to recognize Prince
Charles, it must be prepared for his recognition by Russia without reference to itself.[3] By this time, the Foreign Secretary was
about to make room for a conservative successor.[4] If only, he
sighed, he could 'leave the Office with that vile question of the
Principalities settled'. He anxiously awaited the telegram from
Constantinople which would tell him whether the Prince would
be recognized, 'believing that of the several bad alternatives
that would be the least mischievous to Turkey.' When no
answer arrived, he sadly reflected that the Porte had either not
been able to make up its mind or the Prussian had not proved so
much of a vassal as he pretended.[5] Actually, by this time, the
powers had more important matters to attend to than the future
of Moldo-Wallachia. Both the Porte and the Principalities,
Cowley wrote to Lyons, were 'lost sight of in the tremendous
conflict which is going on in central Europe'.[6]

In view of the Austro-Prussian conflict and in the face of
feelers from Bucarest, Russia, the determined upholder of the
treaties, was withdrawing from her advanced position. On 12
June Budberg had received instructions to demand the dissolution of the conference.[7] Four days later Ignat'yev grudgingly
informed the Porte 'qu'il avait ordre de s'abstenir désormais de
tout conseil et de garder une attitude d'observation'.[8] On 22
June Drouyn noted with satisfaction 'l'attitude beaucoup plus

[1] Ibid.
[2] Lyons to Clarendon, private, 20 Jun. 1866, Clarendon MSS, dep. c. 101.
[3] Clarendon to Lyons, 22 Jun. 1866, F.O. 78/1904, no. 224, draft reporting telegram.
[4] On the fall of Russell's administration.
[5] The same to the same, private, 28 Jun. 1866, Clarendon MSS, dep. c. 143.
[6] Cowley to Lyons, 29 Jun. 1866, F.O. 519/233.
[7] Riker, op. cit., p. 553.
[8] Moustier to Drouyn, telegram, 16 Jun. 1866, Origines, vol. 10, p. 191.

L

réservée du Baron de Budberg'.[1] The following day Gorchakov himself invited the British government to join him in keeping peace in the Balkans.[2] Finally, on 25 June, Budberg formally proposed to Drouyn the closing of the conference.[3] An exchange of letters between the two ended the ignoble farce.

The withdrawal of the powers left the Roumanians and the Porte face to face. While the danger of international complications was greatly reduced, no agreement was yet in sight. Prince and Sultan now entered upon a truly oriental round of bargaining about the terms of recognition. The urgency, however, had gone out of the situation. What had begun as an international crisis of considerable gravity had shrunk to a minor incident with a strongly Ruritanian flavour. And on 23 October 1866 an imperial *firman* at last recognized Prince Charles as hereditary ruler of the United Principalities under the suzerainty of the Sultan. Yet another blow had been struck at the treaty of 1856; Roumania had taken a decisive step on the road to independence.

V

The success of the Roumanian revolution revealed the weakness of the defenders of the *status quo*. Apart from Turkey, supported somewhat unexpectedly by Russia, the Crimean settlement had found no consistent champion. British policy in particular had vacillated in a surprising manner. Riker is unjust in accusing Clarendon of discounting unduly 'the force of public sentiment in Bucharest' and of consistently placing 'the legal rights of Turkey above the welfare of the Principalities'.[4] No such consistency is to be found either in the Foreign Secretary's private correspondence or in his official policy. The keynote of that policy was embarrassment and vacillation resulting from the attempt to achieve conflicting objects. On the one hand, there was a natural desire to prevent alterations in a settlement which had been bought with British blood and which was held to embody important British interests. It was

---

[1] Drouyn to Moustier, 22 Jun. 1866, ibid., p. 248.
[2] He complained to Buchanan that French and Italian agents were trying to push Serbia into a declaration of independence. England should urge the Porte to be careful in its dealings with Serbia (Buchanan to Clarendon, 23 Jun. 1866, F.O. 65/700, nos. 301 and 302).
[3] Budberg to Drouyn, 13/25 Jun. 1866, *Origines*, p. 266.
[4] Riker, op. cit., pp. 514 f.

clear that, invalidated in some of its provisions, the Treaty of Paris would lose much of its binding force. On the other hand, once the wishes of the Roumanians had been clearly pronounced, there was a strong desire, expressed more particularly by Russell, to promote their welfare and national aspirations. The Foreign Secretary was pulled in the same direction by his desire to maintain co-operation with France. The policy which emerged from the clash of personalities and views was one of opportunism and drift. The fundamental issue, the conflict between treaty engagements and 'national self-determination', was never squarely faced. British preoccupations were of a more practical kind. The Roumanian revolution opposed to each other — unhappily from the British point of view — two of England's Crimean allies, the Porte and France. With which of the two was British policy to align itself? There could be little doubt about the ultimate answer, for even Clarendon, the theoretical champion of legality, was penetrated with the overriding need for maintaining an understanding with France. The state of Europe, indeed, appeared to render this imperative.

In these circumstances not only the strict observance of treaties but also the interests of the Porte went by the board. England openly abandoned — except in a purely formal sense — her Turkish ally, the time-honoured principle of the integrity of the Ottoman Empire, the 'Palmerstonian system'. Not only did Clarendon fail to support the Turkish reservation on the eve of the Paris conference; he severely discouraged the Porte from asserting its unquestioned treaty rights by force of arms and finally joined with France in urging upon the Sultan the need to accept Prince Charles. The Turks could complain with some justice that they had been 'left in the lurch'.

It is to be presumed that Clarendon did not lightly abandon a system of which he had been himself one of the principal architects. What determined his policy, apart from a desire to work with the French government, was the fear that any disturbance in the Principalities would enable Russia to fish in troubled waters. Russian influence was strong in Moldavia. The Russian government, moreover, was known to desire, at an opportune moment, the retrocession of southern Bessarabia, lost in 1856. With Austria, Prussia and Italy and, to a lesser extent, France preoccupied with the affairs of central Europe, a disturbance in the Principalities might afford Russia a convenient opportunity to resume her advance in the Balkans. Russia, therefore, must be deprived of all pretext for intervention. There must be no disorders and no declaration of independence. At the same time, neither Porte nor Principalities must be driven to despair which might lead them to throw themselves into the arms of Russia. It was a situation which, as Clarendon knew only too well, bristled with dangerous possibilities.

Considering the dangers of the situation, British diplomacy aided by some luck operated with considerable success. All immediate dangers were averted. British opposition probably prevented a Turkish occupation of the Principalities and helped to smooth the path for the eventual recognition of Prince Charles. At the same time, British advice at Bucarest and Paris helped to prevent a 'premature' declaration of independence on the part of the Principalities. It may have had some influence on Prince Charles in his negotiations with the Porte. British empiricism, therefore, did much to turn aside the dangerous possibilities inherent in the situation. There was no 'Eastern crisis' to complicate the one about to break out in central Europe.

But if, on a short-term view, British policy achieved complete success, there was yet a price to be paid. In the first place Clarendon's policy at the time of the Roumanian revolution weakened British influence at Constantinople. The Porte, chastened by bitter experience, would henceforth pursue a more independent course than in the days of Palmerston and Stratford. More seriously, the establishment of Prince Charles at Bucarest struck a fatal blow at the moral validity of the Treaty of Paris. If that treaty could be violated with impunity as regards the Principalities, why not with regard to the neutralization of the Black Sea? It is from this time that Gorchakov — who had so recently defended the treaty — begins to speak of it as an instrument which, owing to repeated violations, had lost much of its binding force.[1] Had not the British Prime Minister himself admitted that if the treaty was altered contrary to Russian wishes with regard to the Principalities, Russia would

---

[1] Cf. Gorchakov to Budberg, 20 Aug. 1866, quoted in K. Rheindorf, *Die Schwarze Meer (Pontus) Frage, 1856–1871*, Berlin, 1925, p. 51.

be entitled to compensation?[1] In fact, even before the Sultan's final recognition of Prince Charles, the Russian government had prepared a circular denouncing the Black Sea clauses of the Treaty of Paris. It had rested its case principally on the repeated violations of the treaty with regard to the Principalities.[2] In the end, the project had been abandoned as inopportune, but Gorchakov at least regarded this simply as a postponement.[3] Four years later, at the time of the long-anticipated Franco-Prussian war, the circular taken from its pigeon-hole and launched upon embattled Europe. It was Russia's belated 'bill' for accepting the election of Prince Charles. The attitude of the powers towards the Roumanian revolution had further impaired — as Gorchakov had hoped from the start — the validity of the treaty. After 1866 it was unlikely that the remaining portions of the Crimean settlement either could or would be effectively defended. One more blow had been successfully struck at the fast-vanishing 'respect' for treaties and treaty obligations.

[1] Brunnow reported his conversation with Lord Russell:

Finalement, la partie la plus remarquable de mon entretien avec le Premier Ministre est celle qui se réfère à l'éventualité d'un changement apporté à la situation des Principautés Danubiennes, contrairement aux stipulations du Traité de Paris. J'ai soutenu qu'un pareil changement ne saurait s'effectuer au préjudice des intérêts directs le la Russie. Elle serait en droit d'insister sur les compensations et sur les gages de sûreté que nécessiterait tout arrangement nouveau destiné à modifier le status quo. De droit et de fait, la révision du Traité de Paris deviendrait la conséquence directe d'un pareil changement.

Lord Russell a non seulement abondé dans ce sens, mais il m'a dit que la Russie serait alors en droit 'de reprendre sa frontière naturelle'. Il est allé plus loin. Il a admis, que le cas échéant, la Russie aurait à demander 'une extension territoriale en Moldavie' (Brunnow to Gorchakov, 30 Apr./12 May 1866, no. 91, très secrète, Archives of the Russian Ministry of Foreign Affairs in Moscow).

[2] For Gorchakov's project to denounce the Black Sea clauses at this time cf. C. W. Clark, 'Prince Gorchakov and the Black Sea Question 1866' (*American Historical Review*, XLVIII, no. 1, New York, 1954).

[3] Gorchakov to Oubril, 5/17 Nov. 1866, ibid., p. 57.

CHAPTER VI

The End of the Crimean System: England, Russia and the Neutrality of the Black Sea, 1870-1871[1]

But if they looked into the history of such treaties, they would find that like pie-crust, they were made to be broken, and always had been broken when opportunities presented themselves to the aggrieved parties to denounce the obligations they imposed. . . . As in the Treaty of 1856, when a great Power found itself placed under peculiar disadvantages it was impossible to expect that such Power would not avail herself of the earliest opportunity to put an end to the Treaty.

MR MUNTZ in the House of Commons, 30 March 1871

. . . if Europe sees herself confronted by a *fait accompli*, the interested powers will, of course, protest, but a protest stands on paper, and the fact cannot be undone.

BISMARCK to Charles of Hohenzollern-Sigmaringen, April 1866

The crisis of 1866 had once again disappointed Russian hopes. Although even Lord Russell in conversation with Brunnow had admitted that Russia would be entitled to compensation if the arrangements governing the Principalities were set aside against her wishes, his promise had proved purely 'Platonic'. In fact, Russia had failed to extract any tangible advantage whatever from the Roumanian revolution. The weakening of the moral validity of the Treaty of Paris, although a long-term gain, could hardly be considered an immediate benefit.

Similarly, Russia had emerged empty-handed from the events which brought about the reorganization of Germany. Again, the Tsar and Gorchakov had hoped to secure the abrogation of the Treaty of Paris, this time in exchange for their consent to the destruction of the Germanic Confederation established by the Treaty of Vienna. Since, however, matters had been settled once more without recourse to a congress, it had proved im-

[1] The bulk of this chapter first appeared as an article in the *Historical Journal*, IV, no. 2 (1961).

possible even to raise the question.[1] Russia's only gain was that, as a result of General Manteuffel's mission to St Petersburg, she obtained a 'private' promise, in exchange for her consent to Bismarck's reorganization of Germany, of Prussian support for the future. In view of Prussia's new strength and importance, her declaration that she had no interest in the continued neutralization of the Black Sea was indeed a valuable asset but one which would be of use only at some future date. A similar gesture from Beust, the Austrian Foreign Minister, eager to draw Russia into the anti-Prussian camp, was of little immediate advantage. Indeed, more significant than the conditional Austrian promise was the fact, communicated by Beust to the Russian government, that Napoleon, anxious not to offend England, had declined to associate himself with the offer.[2]

The Crimean system had thus survived the crisis of 1866. Though weakened by the events of Bucarest and the Prussian promise to Russia, it was still solidly based on British determination to defend it and on French reluctance to antagonize the British government. However, it now seemed probable that the question of the Black Sea would be reopened in the course of the Franco-Prussian crisis expected in the none too distant future.

I

When the long-awaited war in the West finally broke out in the summer of 1870 the Russian government, in the beginning, was preoccupied almost exclusively with securing the neutrality of Austria and Denmark. When this seemed assured, Gorchakov, following the first French defeats, approached the British and Austrian governments with proposals for joint measures to protect the integrity of France and preserve the balance of Europe.[3] In these circumstances, the Eastern question and the possibility of treaty revision were discreetly kept in the background.

Gorchakov's attempts to rally the neutrals for the protection

[1] When it became clear that there would be no opportunity of raising the question of treaty revision in an international congress, Gorchakov with the encouragement of the Tsar had drawn up a circular unilaterally denouncing the Black Sea clauses. The project had encountered opposition from the Ministers of War and Finance, afraid of possible complications, and in the face of their resistance had been finally abandoned (cf. C. W. Clark, loc. cit.).

[2] Cf. W. E. Mosse, *The European Powers and the German Question, 1848–1871* (Cambridge, 1958), pp. 259 f.

[3] Ibid.

of France alarmed the Grand-duchess Helen,[1] head of the small pro-German faction at the Russian court. At the beginning of August she suggested to Reuss, the North German minister, the possibility of diverting the Tsar from his anti-German activities by directing his attention to the revision of the Treaty of Paris. Bismarck, to whom this advice was transmitted, instructed Reuss to explore privately the possibility of a bargain. Prussia, in return for the abandonment of Russian efforts to preserve the integrity of France would, at a future conference, champion Russia's wishes with respect to the Black Sea.[2] The Tsar and Gorchakov were reluctant to abandon their 'European' approach but the German triumph at Sedan forced them to renounce all hope of a 'European' solution. In the new circumstances created by the German victory, a 'deal' with the victor was clearly the best method for bringing closer the day when Russian warships would again sail the Black Sea.

In fact, six days after Sedan, Gorchakov in conversation with Reuss alluded for the first time to the subject of treaty revision.[3] Russia, he declared, had stood quietly by whilst the Treaty of Paris had been violated and ignored by all the other powers.[4] Now he, in his turn, would abandon his silence and denounce at an early moment arrangements offensive to the dignity of Russia. The articles restricting Russia's sovereign rights in the Black Sea must be annulled. To this Reuss replied that, when the time came for action, Russia could count on Prussian sup-

---

[1] Widow of one of the Tsar's uncles, this former Württemberg Princess had for ten years been a leading champion of German interests at the Russian court.

[2] This, of course, would be merely a confirmation of the promise already made to Russia four years before during the Manteuffel mission in return for her acquiescence in the reorganization of northern and central Germany under Prussian auspices.

[3] Stremaoukhov, head of the Asiatic department in the Ministry of Foreign Affairs, had already explained to Reuss Russia's desire to see the Black Sea opened to the flags of war of all nations. No congress, he said, was needed. The Russian government would simply issue a declaration stating that, in its view, the much flouted Treaty of Paris had ceased to operate with regard to the Black Sea. With open support from Prussia, no opposition need be feared. British protests would probably remain Platonic. Russia was unlikely either to refortify Sevastopol or to maintain a strong squadron in the Black Sea. She would content herself with the resumption of her sovereign rights and the removal of the stain of 1856 (Reuss to Bismarck, 9 Sept. 1870, printed in Rheindorf, op. cit., p. 149 f.).

[4] This cryptic observation, it would soon appear, referred principally to the manner in which arrangements relating to the Danubian Principalities had been repeatedly set aside with the connivance or at least acquiescence of the powers. In the second place, Gorchakov was alluding also to a number of alleged violations of the neutrality of the Black Sea in connexion with the entry into the Straits — with the consent of the Porte — of small naval vessels of different nationalities.

port.[1] Bismarck, apprised of Gorchakov's intentions, consulted the King in the presence of the Crown Prince. Both repeated their already well-known readiness to support the Russian wishes. They would prefer however, to see the matter settled without recourse to a congress.[2]

Although thus assured of Prussian support, the Tsar and Gorchakov still hesitated. However, with the weakening of French resistance to the invading Germans, the conviction gained ground in St Petersburg that the moment for action had come. On 27 October, Alexander II informed his ministers in the strictest confidence of his resolve to denounce the Black Sea clauses. The moment, he declared, was favourable. France was laid low. Prussia had repeatedly pledged her support. Austria[3] had more than once indicated that she attached little importance to neutralization. Italy was preoccupied with domestic matters.[4] Serious opposition need be expected only from England. Even this, however, would be a war of pen and ink. England was dangerous by reason of her navy and her wealth. The former, at this time of year, could not operate effectively in the Baltic; in the Black Sea, it would find nothing to destroy. England might try to subsidize an Austro-Turkish force, but it was doubtful whether Austria would allow herself to be dragged into hostilities. Turkey, by herself, was no danger. If, deprived of her French ally, England confined herself to protests, the Porte also would finally acquiesce.[5] The ministers unanimously approved the Tsar's decision. The matter was too popular and of too national a character for them to voice the misgivings some may privately have felt.[6]

In consequence of the Tsar's decision, Gorchakov drew from its pigeon-hole his draft circular of 1866 which, with some minor

---

[1] Ibid.

[2] 'Werden sie [Russian wishes] in dem Umfang gehalten, wie sie ohne Kongress faktisch durchführbar sind, ist es um so leichter . . .' (Bismarck to Reuss, telegram, 16 Sept. 1870, ibid., pp. 149 ff.). In the light of Stremaoukhov's and Gorchakov's explanations, the subsequent surprise expressed by the Prussian government at the mode of procedure adopted by Russia appears disingenuous.

[3] For the sake of convenience, this term is used to describe the Austro-Hungarian Monarchy after 1867.

[4] The incorporation of Rome.

[5] Reuss to Bismarck, 2 Dec. 1870, confidential, ibid., pp. 151 ff. Reuss received his account of the meeting directly from one of the participants.

[6] As the council was breaking up, some of the ministers were in fact asking themselves whether a decision which might have serious consequences had not been too lightly taken (ibid.).

alterations, was despatched to Russia's principal missions abroad. The treaty of 1856, Gorchakov argued, had lost much of its validity. It had been set aside more than once in respect of the Principalities whilst Turkey, under a variety of pretexts, had repeatedly permitted foreign men-of-war to enter the Straits. The Russian government could not admit that a treaty, violated in several essential clauses, should remain binding in others directly affecting its interests. His Majesty the Emperor of Russia, therefore,

> ne saurait se considérer plus longtemps comme liée aux obligations du Traité du 18/30 Mars, 1856, en tant qu'elles restreignent ses droits de souveraineté dans la Mer Noire.

At the same time, he was ready to concert with the other signatories of the treaty

> soit pour en confirmer les stipulations générales, soit pour les renouveler, soit pour y substituer tout autre arrangement équitable qui serait jugé propre à assurer le repos de l'Orient et l'équilibre Européen.[1]

Accompanied by a covering dispatch addressed more specifically to the British government,[2] this note was delivered at the Foreign Office on 9 November. Granville, the Foreign Secretary, informed Brunnow[3] that he would have to consult his colleagues on this important matter, 'the more so in consequence of the suddenness of such a communication'.[4]

II

In actual fact, the Russian note found the British government neither unforewarned nor unprepared. Even before the outbreak

---

[1] Gorchakov to Brunnow, 19/31 Oct. 1870, printed in *Correspondence respecting the Treaty of March 30, 1856*, Parl. papers, C. 245 (1871), hereafter quoted as *Corr.*, no. 1.

[2] In this dispatch Gorchakov said that Granville would not contest the fact that the treaty of 1856 had undergone serious modifications. With the precedent of the Principalities before her, what value could Russia attach to the efficacy of the treaty and the pledge of security she believed herself to have obtained by the neutralization of the Black Sea? The balance of power established in the East by the treaty of 1856 had been disturbed to the detriment of Russia: her present resolution had no other object than to restore it. The British government would not consent to leave the safety of its shores to the mercy of an arrangement which it no longer respected. It was too equitable not to concede to Russia the same duties and the same rights (the same to the same, 20 Oct./1 Nov. 1870, ibid., no. 2).

[3] The Russian ambassador in London.

[4] Granville to Buchanan, 9 Nov. 1870, ibid., no. 3.

of the Franco-Prussian war Buchanan[1] had expressed the view
that the Russian government would seek an early opportunity
for repudiating the Black Sea clauses.[2] On several occasions
since he had repeated the warning.[3] It had, moreover, been
reinforced by the reported language of the Russian ambassador
in Constantinople.[4] By the beginning of October, Gladstone
had reached the conclusion that British Eastern policy must be
reviewed

> for the number and variety of symptoms that come up convey to
> me the impression that there is little time to lose. Everybody at a
> time like this looks out for booty: it will be hard to convince
> Continental Europe that Turkey is not fair prize.[5]

The Turkish government also was beginning to feel concern.
Musurus, its ambassador in London, told Granville that peace
between France and Prussia seemed likely to be concluded
under the auspices of a congress, in which Russia intended to
raise the question of the treaty of 1856. The Turkish government
proposed that, before a congress assembled, England, Austria
and Italy should formally pledge themselves to prevent all discussion of the subject. The Foreign Secretary sensibly replied
that it would be premature to lay down conditions of a congress
'before the proposal for holding one was seriously entertained'.[6]

In his despatch reporting this conversation to Sir Henry Elliot[7]
Granville added an inquiry about the ability of Turkey to defend
herself single-handed against Russia 'or possibly Austria'. In
what way could England most effectively assist her? How could
she best warn the Turks of the need for caution on their part?[8]

[1] The British ambassador at St Petersburg.

[2] 'I have no doubt, however, that on the first favourable opportunity, Russia will
claim the abrogation of the stipulations of the Treaty of Paris, which close the
Black Sea to her ships of war' (Buchanan to Clarendon, 16 Jun. 1870, F.O.
65/802, no. 226, confidential).

[3] Buchanan to Granville, 15 Aug. 1870, F.O. 65/803, confidential; 21 Sept. 1870,
F.O. 65/804, no. 354, confidential; and 18 Oct. 1870, ibid., no. 406, secret and
confidential.

[4] Elliot to Granville, 23 Aug. 1870, F.O. 78/2124, no. 164. For the language held
by Ignatiev, cf. S. Goriainov, *Le Bosphore et les Dardanelles* (Paris, 1910), pp. 194 ff.

[5] Gladstone to Granville, 4 Oct. 1870, *The Political Correspondence of Mr Gladstone
and Lord Granville, 1868–76*, ed. A. Ramm (1952), I (Camden third series, LXXXI),
pp. 136.

[6] Granville to Elliot, 6 Oct. 1870, F.O. 195/959, no. 207.

[7] The British ambassador at Constantinople.

[8] The same to the same, ibid., no. 208, confidential. The inquiry was the result of
consultations between Granville and Gladstone (cf. Granville to Gladstone, 8 Oct.
1870, Ramm, loc. cit., p. 141).

Before this inquiry reached Constantinople,[1] Aali, the Grand-Vizier, had already spoken 'very seriously' to Elliot about Turkey's position in the event of a Russian attack. He did not anticipate immediate aggression but had been given to understand that Russia claimed to have grounds of complaint against Turkey. Whilst Turkey would give no ground for attack, pretexts could always be found or created. Looking forward to the possibility of such an event, it was necessary to ascertain the means available for resisting it especially as, in the present position of Europe, Turkey might have to rely on her own resources. He was particularly anxious with regard to finance and the supply of arms and wished to know 'whether in case of attack he could look to Her Majesty's Government for assistance in reference to them'.

Elliot replied that not only was the available supply of breech-loading rifles limited but that should England, in a Russo-Turkish war, declare her neutrality, arms could not be supplied without departing from it. Aali rejoined with some warmth that England being 'a party to a solemn guarantee of Turkey, the case was very different from what it would otherwise be'. He could understand circumstances arising which might prevent a country fulfillings its engagements to the letter

> but it would continue to be bound to render any assistance in its power, and he hoped that the sympathies of Great Britain, which had never been wanting to Turkey, might again be calculated upon if the occasion called for it.[2]

Before Aali's enquiry reached London, Gladstone, in a memorandum, had discussed the difficulties of Turkey's position. Of her defenders, France might be considered out of the case. In England,

> the whole policy of the Crimean War is now almost universally, and very unduly depreciated, and the idea of another armed intervention on behalf of Turkey, whether sole or with allies, is ridiculed.

Austria might be presumed to have goodwill for Turkey, but whilst she had her own troubles to deal with, 'she might have that good will converted by her territorial interests, and almost

---

[1] On 25 Oct.
[2] Elliot to Granville, 17 Oct. 1870, F.O. 78/2125, no. 242, confidential.

necessities, into one very different'. Northern Germany might or might not be friendly. In the past, Turkey had been 'habituated to look to external aid'. Of this, there was now 'no prospect on which any sane man can rely'.[1]

Elliot, in the meantime, had prepared his reply to Granville's first inquiry. In it he pleaded that Turkey should not be left to her fate. It was this belief which had caused the Crimean War and it might again be followed by a similar result. What the Porte, in the absence of more material aid, would hope to obtain from England was arms and money. In addition, some active young officers in the British service might be seconded to the Turkish navy.[2] Before the dispatch reached London,[3] the expected emergency had arisen.

III

On 9 November, Gorchakov's circular was delivered at the Foreign Office. The following day, the cabinet met and decided to reject the Russian mode of proceeding, to keep the door open as to the substance of the question and to urge on the Russian government the propriety of bringing its wishes under the collective consideration of the powers.[4] A memorandum in this sense, drawn up by Gladstone,[5] was converted by Granville into a dispatch to Buchanan protesting in strong terms against the Russian announcement but 'with a docquet open at the end to friendly discussion'.[6] The issue, in the view of the British government, was

> not whether any desire expressed by Russia ought to be carefully examined in a friendly spirit by the co-signatory powers, but whether they are to accept from her the announcement that, by her own act, without any consent from them, she has released herself from a solemn convenant.

In the circumstances it was impossible for the British government to sanction the course announced by Russia.[7]

---

[1] Gladstone to Hammond, 28 Oct. 1870, P.R.O., G.D., 59/58.
[2] Elliot to Granville, 17 Oct. 1870, F.O. 78/2125, no. 242, confidential.
[3] On 14 Nov.
[4] Gladstone's notes on decisions of the cabinet, 10 Nov. 1870, Add. MSS 44638 (in the British Museum, London).
[5] Printed in Ramm, op. cit., pp. 134 ff.
[6] Granville to the Queen, telegram, 11 Nov. 1870, R.A. H 4/162.
[7] Granville to Buchanan, 10 Nov. 1870, *Corr.*, no. 4.

On the morning of 16 November, Buchanan read the British note to Gorchakov, who reiterated the assurance that the circular had 'no motives but to remove a stain on the honour of Russia', and, at the same time, 'to establish more securely the amicable relations of Turkey and Russia'. He also recapitulated and developed the arguments on which he founded Russia's right to denounce certain articles in the treaty of 1856. Buchanan rejoined that these observations were 'entirely irrelevant' as Granville objected

> *in limine*, to any Power arrogating to itself the right to terminate a Treaty without the assent of the other Parties to it. It was not therefore, ... to the question of the revision of the Treaty, but to the form in which it had been presented to them, that Her Majesty's Government objected. ...

Gorchakov replied that the Tsar's decision was irrevocable. Turkey would consult her best interests by assenting to it, as she would then secure the future goodwill of Russia. If, however, she followed a different course, 'either spontaneously or by the advice of other Powers', she would expose herself to the most serious dangers. The Christian populations of the Ottoman Empire 'whose past tranquillity was greatly to be attributed to the influence of Russia', would rise in arms against the Sultan 'on the first misunderstanding between the two Governments'. Buchanan refused to discuss this matter, as Granville's dispatch fully explained the British view. He expressed a hope that Gorchakov would find in the British arguments 'reasons for endeavouring to remove the difficulty which now stands in the way of the consideration of the question'.[1] The Russian government, however, could no longer retreat from the position

---

[1] Buchanan to Granville, 16 Nov. 1870, *Corr.*, no. 25. Buchanan, another of the 'Palmerstonian' ambassadors, had received much of his diplomatic training in tussles with Bismarck in Berlin. His language, on this occasion, did not err on the side of moderation. He noted with satisfaction that during the reading of Granville's note, Gorchakov's feet and legs shook with a nervous tremor (the same to the same, private and most confidential, 16 Nov. 1870, R.A. H 4/175 abstract). Gorchakov, with some justice, remarked during the interview that the British government would never have made concessions in response to diplomatic requests but was too prudent and desirous of peace not to accept a *fait accompli* (ibid.). He also argued, again with some justice, that he was surprised at the sentiments at present expressed by the British government with regard to the abrogation of treaties, 'as they had accepted without remonstrance the changes which had taken place in Germany in 1866 by the extinction of the German Confederation and the Kingdom of Hanover' (the same to the same, 16 Nov. 1870, *Corr.*, no. 25).

it had taken up. On 15 November, the text of Gorchakov's circular had been published in the 'Official Messenger'.[1] It had been received with enthusiasm by the Russian public. The press of St Petersburg, Buchanan reported, was 'unanimous in favour of the declaration which the Country, if necessary, will support by arms'.[2]

In England also, public opinion was aroused.[3] The press all but unanimously was denouncing the Russian proceedings. Papers were demanding an ultimatum to Russia to withdraw her circular. The 'bluster of the newspapers' aroused the fears of John Bright;[4] Gladstone expressed himself 'much disgusted with a good deal of the language . . . in the newspapers' about immediate war with Russia.[5] There was a widespread demand for military preparations and it required the greatest tactical skill on Gladstone's part to hold at bay an angry public opinion. Assisted by Granville, he still hoped for a peaceful solution. The situation, however was critical. Much would depend on the attitude of the other interested powers.

IV

The power affected most directly by Gorchakov's circular was Turkey, on whose reaction would depend, in no small measure, the outcome of the crisis. In Constantinople it had at first been believed that Russia had demanded the retrocession of southern Bessarabia and relief was felt when it became clear that this was not the case. The denunciation of the Black Sea clauses was received in the Turkish capital 'with much less

---

[1] The same to the same, 15 Nov. 1870, ibid., no. 24.

[2] The same to the same, 16 Nov. 1870, F.O. 65/805, no. 464, reporting telegram. Commercial men felt that the Emperor could not retreat from the position he had taken up (ibid.). This did not prevent a widespread feeling that Gorchakov had opened the question 'clumsily and indiscreetly' (the same to the same, 15 Nov. 1870, ibid., no. 462, reporting telegram). Persons attached to the Foreign Office described the circular as 'an impotent attempt' which would not be supported by action and would end in failure, if it met with decided opposition from England (the same to the same, 14 Nov. 1870, ibid., no. 458, reporting telegram). This last statement is probably exaggerated. Buchanan was trying to influence the British government in favour of an uncompromising stand.

[3] For a detailed description of British reactions to Gorchakov's circular, cf. W. E. Mosse, 'Public Opinion and Foreign Policy' in *Historical Journal* (Spring 1963).

[4] Bright to Gladstone, 18 Nov. 1870, Gladstone Papers in the British Museum London, Add. MS 44112, fol. 163.

[5] Gladstone to Granville, 19 Nov. 1870, Ramm, loc. cit., p. 161.

indignation'.[1] Aali considered that 'a war against Russia under the circumstances of the case must be of offensive, and therefore disadvantageous character'. The Porte was 'quite ready to join its allies in one', but would not 'look upon itself as deserted in its emergency' if they decided that a policy of simple protest would be 'the best and safest in the interests of Turkey'.[2] Musurus suggested to Granville that England should say she could do nothing without Turkey and Turkey she could do nothing without the powers. If the Russians refused to withdraw their circular, Turkey should say:

> These are words. We answer by words, you denounce the special convention, we denounce all our treaties by which you have consuls, capitulations, liberty for your commerce through the Canal of the Bosphorus. If you act upon your words, then we do the same.[3]

Gladstone expressed satisfaction at Turkish moderation,[4] the Russians were openly delighted.[5]

Next to Turkey, France and Austria as co-signatories of the treaty of 15 April were the powers most immediately concerned. The French Provisional government, whilst scarcely in a position to pay much attention to the 'Eastern question', hoped that the resentment of the great powers would lead them 'to assert themselves in a manner which will check Russia and Prussia and, at least, bring on a Congress'. It therefore declared its readiness to support any British action.[6]

In Vienna, opinion was divided. Whilst Beust was reluctant to put himself forward in the matter, Andràssy urged a joint protest of the signatories. The Emperor took the view that the dual monarchy must not venture further than its

---

[1] Elliot to Granville, telegram, 17 Nov. 1870, R.A. H 4/179. The Turkish reaction completely falsified Elliot's earlier forecast which, however, may have been influenced by wishful thinking.

[2] The same to the same, telegram (2), 17 Nov. 1870, ibid., H 4/178. Aali's language convinced Elliot 'that he desires avoiding a rupture if the Powers consider it can be done without too much loss of credit' (the same to the same, telegram, 20 Nov. 1870, ibid., H 4/199).

[3] Granville to Gladstone, 18 Nov. 1870, Ramm, loc. cit., p. 159.

[4] 'The Turks seem to be temperate' (Gladstone to Granville, 19 Nov. 1870, ibid., pp. 160 f.).

[5] Buchanan reported that the news from Constantinople had 'greatly increased the arrogance of the official class of Russians' (Buchanan to Granville, 23 Nov. 1870, F.O. 65/805, no. 489, reporting telegram). The acquiescence of Turkey considerably weakened the force of the British remonstrance.

[6] Lyons to Granville, telegram, 14 Nov. 1870, R.A. I 67/32.

co-signatories[1] and, in fact, Austria's reply to Russia closely followed the line of Granville's note.[2] A tentative sounding in London about the possibility of a joint protest produced a negative reply.[3] The discussions among the powers drew attention to the importance of Prussia. Would Bismarck, as he had repeatedly promised, support Russia, or would motives of expediency lead him to align himself with the defenders of the Treaty of Paris? Prussia's first reaction to Gorchakov's circular had been one of surprise not unmixed with disapproval.[4] However, after an unavailing attempt to delay its publication,[5] Bismarck decided to make good his repeated promises of support.[6]

In the meantime, the news Bismarck received from London was disturbing. Bernstorff reported that the situation was becoming grave. Granville's language was stern: Disraeli considered the position very serious (*sehr ernst*) and thought the country might pronounce for war. The final decision rested

---

[1] For the discussions in the council of ministers of 14 Nov. 1870, cf. H.H.S.A.V., Ministerrath für gemeinsame Angelegenheiten, Präsid. Sektion Dep.I, R. M. Protokoll 1869–71, xxx, p. 275.

[2] Beust to Chotek, 16 Nov. 1870, *Corr.*, no. 27.

[3] Granville to Bloomfield, 30 Nov. 1870, F.O. 120/481, no. 115.

[4] King William declared: 'Ich habe aber immer diese Frage als vor einen Kongress gehörig nach unserem Frieden mit Frankreich betrachtet. Jedenfalls habe ich nie daran gedacht, dass eine *Kündigung* ohne vorhergegangene *Verständigung* mit den Unterzeichnern möglich sei' (marginal note on Reuss to Bismarck, 9 Nov. 1870, Rheindorf, op. cit., pp. 152 f.).

[5] Bismarck pleaded for delay on the ground that, a few weeks later (i.e. after the final defeat of France) Prussia would be in a better position to support Russia (Bismarck to Reuss, telegram, 8 Nov. 1870, Bismarck, *G[esammelte] W[erke]*, 6 vols. in 8, Berlin, 1924 et seq., vi*b*, p. 590). Gorchakov replied that delay was impossible. All necessary steps had been taken, 'et le moment est venu de mettre à l'œuvre les bonnes dispositions que vous nous avez manifestées à diverses reprises sur cette question de dignité et d'honneur national — et dont je puis dire vous avez même pris l'initiative (against which Bismarck observed in the margin: 'In dieser Form sicher nicht!') (Reuss to Bismarck, 9 Nov. 1870, Rheindorf, op. cit., pp. 153 f.).

[6] Although critical of Gorchakov's methods, Bismarck was resolved to honour his promises. From Prussian headquarters in Versailles he informed the Foreign Ministry in Berlin: 'Ich habe die russische Form ist nicht geschickt, aber wir können gegen die Sache nicht auftreten. Europa hat Frankreichs Angriff auf uns nicht gehindert, und England seiner Neutralität einen für uns ungünstigen Charakter verliehen. Dass Oesterreich nicht dasselbe tat, hinderte nur Kaiser Alexander. Der König ist letzterem dankbar, wir haben an dem Vertrag von 56 wenig Interesse und nur einen äusserlichen, von England damals bekämpften, Anteil' (Bismarck to Foreign Ministry, telegram, 18 Nov. 1870, ibid., p. 154). Bismarck accordingly arranged for Prussian papers to publish Beust's dispatches of 1867 and other correspondence tending to show that Austria-Hungary supported Russia (Bismarck to Thile, telegram, 14 Nov. 1870, ibid.). The Russian minister in Berlin received an assurance that Prussia would not join in any action directed against Russia (Bismarck to Foreign Ministry, 18 Nov. 1870, ibid.).

M

with Parliament, whose attitude alone would show whether the country as a whole was as warlike as the capital appeared to be.[1] It was widely believed that Russia would recede from her position if Prussia showed her disapproval.[2] However, the conviction was gaining ground that Russian intransigence would provoke a conflict in which England might find herself placed at the side of Prussia's enemies.[3] The decision at Versailles, therefore, was awaited with impatience.

Bismarck, by this time, was thoroughly alarmed at the possibility of further complications. He resolved, therefore, in Prussia's own interest, to settle the 'Eastern' conflict. With this end in view, he proposed to the Russian government[4] the convocation at Constantinople or elsewhere of a conference of ambassadors to seek a peaceful solution.[5] Gorchakov, alarmed at the tone of the British and Austrian communications, expressed his agreement in principle. He would, however, prefer the conference to be held at St Petersburg.[6]

Having obtained Russian agreement, Bismarck next set out to secure the adhesion of England. Odo Russell, then Under-Secretary at the Foreign Office, was about to visit Versailles to discuss pending questions.[7] These, of course, would include Gorchakov's circular. The two men had their first meeting on

---

[1] 'Es wird sich dann zeigen, ob die Meinung des Landes wirklich so kriegerisch ist, wie die der Hauptstadt in diesem Augenblick.'

[2] Bernstorff to Bismarck, confidential, 18 Nov. 1870, [Die] G[rosse] P[olitik der europäischen Kabinette] (Berlin, 1922), II, p. 12.

[3] 'Man sieht mit äusserster Spannung der Entscheidung in Versailles entgegen, wovon, wie man überzeugt ist, die ganze Wendung der Dinge abhängt. Wenn wir mit den andern Vertragsmächten die einseitige Aufkündigung Russlands für unzulässig erklären und jedes Einverständnis mit ihm verleugnen. so glaubt man, dass Russland sich besinnen wird. Wo nicht, hält man den Krieg für unvermeidlich, welcher sich fast über ganz Europa erstrecken dürfte, und worin England jedenfalls tatsächlich der Bundesgenosse unserer Feinde sein würde' (the same to the same, telegram, 19 Nov. 1870, ibid., p. 13).

[4] On 20 Nov.

[5] Bismarck, G.W., op. cit., p. 604.

[6] Ibid.

[7] Russell's mission to Versailles, 'to ascertain a little of what was going on', had been decided on before the Russian action (Granville to Gladstone, 15 Oct. 1870, Ramm, loc. cit., pp. 147 f.). Gorchakov's circular greatly enhanced its importance. On 12 Nov., Granville informed the Queen it was proposed 'merely to send Bismarck the British answer to Gorchakov's circular and to tell him that Russell would give him all further explanations he might require' (Granville to the Queen, 12 Nov. 1870, R.A. H 4/167; QVL, op. cit., pp. 82 f.). Bismarck attached great importance to Russell's visit. He told the Foreign Ministry in Berlin: 'Sagen Sie den Diplomaten, die fragen sollten, dass wir uns erst nach Russells Herkunft äussern würden' (Bismarck to Foreign Ministry, telegram, 18 Nov. 1870, Rheindorf, op. cit., p. 154).

21 November. Bismarck explained that the Russian note had taken him by surprise: he regretted it, but could not interfere. He recommended 'Conferences at Constantinople before hostilities' and was most anxious to prevent war.[1]

Russell demurred:

> On returning to him in the evening when we had two hours' and a half's more talk, I felt that I knew him better and could express more easily all that I had determined to say to convince him that unless he would get Russia to withdraw the circular, we should be compelled, with or without allies, to go to war. He was long obstinate and would not believe we could ever be roused to action — but as he gradually admitted the truth of the consequences to which a pacific acceptance of the Russian kick must inevitably lead, he came round to our standpoint and felt that in your place he could not recede.
>
> The evil consequences to Germany of a European War before Paris was taken, the moral support the Tours Government might get from a renewal of the old Anglo-French Alliance, the opportunities war might give to Beust to play a more important part in European questions and the increasing difficulty of bringing the Franco-Prussian conflict to a speedy and satisfactory close, together with the stern fact that England *must* fight and that he, *Bismarck*, alone could prevent it which I endeavoured to bring as forcibly as I could before his mind, gradually worked the change in his mind which has led him to support the cause of Peace and England against Gortschakoff and his circular.[2]

---

[1] Odo Russell to Granville, telegram, Versailles, 21 Nov. 1870, dispatched at 9.42 p.m., received at 3 a.m. the following day, in F.O. 65/807.

[2] Bismarck was, in fact, delaying his offer of mediation in the hope of striking a bargain with England about the Franco-Prussian war: 'He repeatedly said that in his opinion in politics "one hand should wash the other" (*dass eine Hand die andere waschen muss*) and seemed to wait anxiously and attentively for my reply. Of course I took no notice and turned a deaf ear to his insinuations and dealt with the question on its own merits only, without offering him any other advantage for Germany but the choice between Peace and War with Russia on our part' (the same to the same, private, 30 Nov. 1870, R.A. I 67/54, copy).

When Gladstone heard of Russell's language, he expressed disapproval. He was much concerned to see the envoy had won Bismarck 'by a representation about our going to war which really had not the slightest foundation' (Gladstone to Granville, 6 Dec. 1870, Ramm, loc. cit., p. 176).

Granville, however, defended Russell's conduct: 'I am afraid our whole success has been owing to the belief that we would go to war, and to tell the truth I think war in some shape or other sooner or later, was a possible risk after our note. In any case, I would reassure nobody now. Promising peace is as unwise as to threaten war. A sort of sentiment that the bumps of combativeness and destructiveness are to be found somewhere in your head has helped us much during the last five months' (Granville to Gladstone, 8 Dec. 1870, ibid., pp. 179 f.).

On the following day, Bismarck officially notified Bernstorff of Russia's willingness to discuss the matter in conference.[1]

Early on 23rd, a telegram from Buchanan brought the news that Gorchakov 'if he could ascertain confidentially that the claim of Russia would be granted . . . would not refuse to do everything possible to remove objections of Her Majesty's Government as to the manner in which it had been brought forward'.[2] A message from Versailles announced Bismarck's willingness 'to take the initiative in proposing a conference at St Petersburg'.[3] The following morning, Bernstorff formally repeated the offer.[4]

Granville perfectly understood that England was being invited to give up her demand for the withdrawal of Gorchakov's circular:

> He [Bismarck] offers, if we ask him, to ask the Russians, after the slap in the face which they have administered to us, to receive the whole of Europe in their capital in order [sic] with the assistance of Prussia they may get all they want. On the other hand Prussia has always thought this an unfair proviso, they owe Russia a debt of gratitude for keeping the Austrians quiet, but they wish to help a peaceful conclusion of the matter, and make a proposal which, with certain modifications, might be accepted.[5]

He therefore told Bernstorff:

> That I could not anticipate the judgment of my colleagues as to the possibility of a Conference in the present state of affairs; that supposing my colleagues were in favour of one, St Petersburg appeared to be out of the question; that it would be necessary to consult the other Parties to the Treaty; and that the Conference could not be agreed to subject to any foregone conclusion as to its results.[6]

The cabinet, on the 25th, also adopted this view. The outcome of its deliberations was an instruction to Odo Russell in Versailles:

> Speaking for themselves, Her Majesty's Government have no objection to enter into a Conference for the purpose of considering

---

[1] Bismarck to Bernstorff, telegram, 22 Nov. 1870, *G.P.*, op. cit., pp. 16 f.
[2] Buchanan to Granville, 22 Nov. 1870, F.O. 65/805, no. 842, reporting telegram.
[3] Odo Russell to Granville, telegram, 22 Nov. 1870, F.O. 65/799.
[4] Granville to Loftus, 24 Nov. 1870, *Corr.*, no. 35.
[5] Granville to Gladstone, 23 Nov. 1870, Ramm, loc. cit., p. 167.
[6] Granville to Loftus, 24 Nov. 1870, *Corr.*, no. 35.

any adequate statement of the grounds on which Russia may wish to bring before the co-signatory Powers a proposal for the revision of the Special Convention between herself and Turkey, annexed to and embodied in the Treaty of 1856.

However, they could join such a conference only on the express understanding 'that it should be in no way prejudiced by any previous assumption as to the result of its deliberations'. They would, at the same time, feel bound, in concert with the other powers, to weigh with fairness and without bias any claims which Russia might advance and any proposals she might make. With regard to the place of meeting, St Petersburg and Constantinople were unacceptable, whilst the continuation of the war in France also ruled out Berlin. The British government would agree to the choice of Vienna, Florence or London or, if a non-signatory capital was preferred, to The Hague, Brussels or Berne.[1]

Prussian diplomacy, meanwhile, had been busy at St Petersburg. On the night of the 25th, Reuss assured Buchanan on Gorchakov's behalf that a conference would not, as Granville appeared to fear, meet simply to register a Russian declaration. Its object, on the contrary, would be to place on a more secure footing than at present the peace of the East and the independence of the Porte. Russia would willingly contribute to this result. If the choice of St Petersburg for the conference was repugnant to Granville, Gorchakov would not object to London to satisfy British national sentiment. 'The Prussian Minister says this concession, made at his instance, costs His Excellency much.'[2] This message was received in London early on the 26th. Another, from Versailles, confirmed Bismarck's acceptance of 'the basis laid down by Her Majesty's Government for the proposed Conference and ... London as the place of meeting'.[3] With this, the acute phase of the crisis was

---

[1] Granville to Odo Russell, 25 Nov. 1870, *Corr.*, no. 37. On 25 Nov. also, Gorchakov's reply to Granville's note had been delivered at the Foreign Office. In it Gorchakov, whilst maintaining his circular 'in principle', repeated Russia's readiness 'to join in any deliberation having for its object the general guarantees destined to consolidate the peace of the East', and expressed the conviction that 'fresh guarantees would be obtained if, a permanent cause of irritation between the two Powers [Russian and Turkey] being removed, their mutual relations were to be re-established on the basis of a good and solid understanding' (Gorchakov to Brunnow, 8/20 Nov. 1870, ibid., no. 36).

[2] Buchanan to Granville, 25 Nov. 1870, F.O. 65/805, no. 496.

[3] Granville to Odo Russell, 27 Nov. 1870, *Corr.*, no. 39.

over;[1] diplomacy, in the face of considerable odds, had saved the peace of Europe.

The merit for the solution was shared by the principal actors. Gladstone and Granville had persuaded their colleagues to waive the demand for a formal withdrawal of the Russian circular.[2] Bismarck, for the first time in his career as a European statesman, had acted as the 'honest broker' in the Eastern question. Gorchakov, faced with varying degrees of disapproval, had shown a conciliatory disposition. Their joint efforts had resulted in a compromise not totally unacceptable to any one.

V

The decision to hold a conference was followed by weeks of intensive diplomatic preparation. Two separate issues dominated the negotiations. In the first place, a way must be found to reassert the principles of international law and morality violated by Gorchakov's circular. That was the reparation required by England. In addition, arrangements satisfactory to the signatory powers must be found to replace the neutralization of the Black Sea. That was the compensation owed to Turkey. Neither quest, in fact, proved an easy one. The weeks which followed the decision to meet in conference remained full of anxiety. One cause for the continued tension was the British determination not to accept Russia's wishes without adequate compensation. Granville, in fact, declined repeated Russian requests to state in advance the British attitude on the point of substance. He told Brunnow:

That the authority I held from you [Gladstone] and from the Cabinet was only to enter the Conference on conditions with

[1] That Gladstone seriously believed in the possibility of war is shown by a letter to Earl Spencer in which he wrote: 'I trust the war cloud is floating away' (Gladstone to Spencer, 28 Nov. 1870, Add. MSS 44539, copy). Cf. also Gladstone's letters to Rt. Hon. C. E. Fortescue of 26 and 28 Nov. 1870, ibid., copies.

[2] This was the ostensible reason for the resignation of Otway, the disgruntled Under-Secretary at the Foreign Office. 'We have now [he wrote] at the instance of Prussia accepted a Conference with the other Powers co-signatories of the Treaty of 56. We have done this after our reply to Prince Gortchacow's note, and after the Russian rejoinder, containing no retraction of a claim which has given just offence, created great alarm, and caused that intimation from our Government to Russia which was hailed with almost universal satisfaction in this country. I cannot but think that we neither go in well nor shall we come out well of this conference. I fear that it will entail on us humiliation or war...' (Otway to Gladstone, private, 27 Nov. 1870, Add. MSS 44428).

which he was acquainted and to listen with fairness to what Russia had to say.

That I could give him no further answer as to the ultimate decision whether he put the question as an Ambassador or as an individual to me. . . . Although I could give him no assurance as to the result, yet I thought he ought not to conclude that it was impossible by sense and moderation on both sides to come to a satisfactory conclusion.[1]

In face of Granville's skilful pressure, the Russian government declared its willingness to meet British wishes about the re-affirmation of international engagements.[2] Brunnow and Granville joined in drafting a declaration on the subject, to be presented by the former at the opening of the conference.[3]

With this obstacle removed, the powers could turn their attention to the question of substance. If Russia were to be relieved by the conference of her disabilities in the Black Sea, what arrangements should be made to take their place? The logical consequence of ending neutralization would be for both Tsar and Sultan to resume their sovereign rights. This, however, was not generally accepted. Aali at first favoured closing the Straits in time of peace by international treaty.[4] Elliot objected 'that a very material support would be given to the Porte by allowing her to call in the Fleets of her Allies when she was menaced instead of being obliged to shut them out till she was actually at war'.[5] Gladstone agreed.[6] Granville, however, argued that if the Tsar recovered the whole of his sovereign right, it would 'be disagreeable to give the Turk only a portion

---

[1] Granville to Gladstone, 5 Dec. 1870, Ramm, loc. cit., pp. 174 f. Three days later Granville repeated: 'I shall decline telling him our views till after the first conference' (the same to the same, 8 Dec. 1870, ibid., p. 179).

[2] 'He [Brunnow] was perfectly aware that public opinion in England must be satisfied as well as that in Russia' (the same to the same, 5 Dec. 1870, ibid., p. 174).

[3] On 5 Dec., Brunnow communicated to Granville the draft of his proposed statement, and readily accepted the Foreign Secretary's alterations (ibid., p. 176, n. 1).

[4] Elliot to Granville, private, 18 Nov. 1870, P.R.O., G.D. 29/102.

[5] The same to the same, private, 21 Nov. 1870, ibid. Elliot set to work to convince Aali and thought he had been successful. 'Aali is I think beginning to incline a good deal to my opinion that it may be well to modify the rules for closing of the straits against ships of war so as to leave the sultan the power of inviting them in case of danger' (the same to the same, private, 2 Dec. 1870, ibid.).

[6] 'I think Elliot hits the point in the suggestion that the Sultan should not resume an unbounded discretion but one to be exercised in case of menace, or to use our word in the Naval Reserve Act, in case of "emergency" ' (Gladstone to Granville, 3 Dec. 1870, Ramm, loc. cit., p. 170).

of his'.[1] Both stuck to their guns[2] until, in the end, a majority of the cabinet decided in favour of Granville.[3] The Foreign Secretary finally summed up the British position:

> I presume a programme to which Russia, Prussia, Italy and Turkey and probably Austria and France would agree, would be the restoration to the Emperor of Russia of his sovereign rights in the Black Sea, ditto to the Sultan in the manner most agreeable to him — and a reaffirmation of all the remainder of the Treaty.[4]

VI

On 17 January, the conference at last assembled for its first plenary session. On the proposal of Granville, the plenipotentiaries agreed to embody in a protocol *ad hoc*, to be annexed to the general protocol of the sitting, a declaration 'that the Powers recognize that it is an essential principle of the law of nations that none of them can liberate itself from the engagements of a treaty nor modify the stipulations thereof, unless with the consent of the contracting parties by means of an amicable understanding'.

Brunnow then raised the question of substance which Musurus agreed to discuss 'in principle' whilst reserving his views as to details. A Prussian declaration of support for the Russian request completed the day's proceedings.[5]

---

[1] Granville to Gladstone, 5 Dec. 1871, ibid., pp. 172 f.

[2] Granville relied much on the opinions formerly held by Clarendon. Brunnow had told him unofficially that 'there appeared to him to be only one [possible equivalent]—that to which Clarendon had given the preference, and which has been raised in some of our newspapers—viz. the opening instead of the shutting of the Black Sea, with a reservation of the Sultan's Sovereign power' (ibid., p. 175). Granville believed that Clarendon 'was for opening the Black Sea, but he had another and in my opinion an objectionable plan—that the Porte should allow *us* to make a Malta or Sebastopol of Trezibond' (the same to the same, confidential, 6 Dec. 1870, ibid., p. 176). Curiously, a similar plan seems to have developed in Bismarck's fertile brain. At any rate, he asked Odo Russell whether England wished to acquire a naval station in the Black Sea—to which he saw no objection (Odo Russell to Granville, private, 18 Dec. 1870, R.A. I 67/104, copy). Gladstone adhered to his opinion. 'In the "Pontus" question I should say that a part of the Sultan's rights is more than the whole; as Elliot seems to think. He has a title to the whole: but if he cannot use them entire, and can use a portion, he may prefer the latter' (Gladstone to Granville, 6 Dec. 1870, Ramm, loc. cit., pp. 176 f.).

[3] 'Our colleagues seem to prefer the simple restoration to the Sultan of his Sovereign power as to the passage into the Black Sea' (Granville to Gladstone, 8 Dec. 1870, ibid., pp. 179 f.).

[4] Granville to Gladstone, 10 Dec. 1870, ibid., pp. 181 f.

[5] *Protocols of Conferences respecting the Treaty of March 30, 1856*, Parl. papers, C. 267 (1871), hereafter quoted as *Prot.*

The main problem now was to find an arrangement acceptable to the Porte as compensation for the de-neutralization of the Black Sea. The Austrian government proposed a complicated scheme under which Russian naval forces in the Black Sea would be balanced automatically by those of other powers. The Turkish government, on the other hand, made it clear that it wished simply to resume its sovereign rights.[1] A second meeting of the conference on 24 January proved inconclusive.[2] Finally, after further discussion 'in an unofficial and friendly manner', agreement was thought to have been reached on four articles, the most important of which recognized the Sultan's right of opening the Straits in time of peace 'by way of temporary exception' 'in case only that the interests of the security of his Empire should cause him to recognize the necessity of the presence of the vessels of war of the non-Riverain Powers'. However, at the plenary session of 3 February, Musurus unexpectedly proposed to substitute the term 'friendly Powers' for 'non-Riverain Powers' on the grounds that the latter restricted the rights of sovereignty and independence of the Ottoman Empire and had, moreover, the appearance of being directed against Russia. The proposed change aroused bitter opposition from the representatives of England and Austria, supported by that of Italy. Even Brunnow announced his support for the original draft. Musurus, in reply, declared that his instructions were 'very peremptory as regarded the proposed amendment' but finally agreed to refer the matter back to his government.[3]

The deadlock continued. No plenary meeting of the conference was held until 13 March. By this time, a French representative, the duc de Broglie, had made his belated appearance. The problem of the disputed clause was solved at last, thanks mainly to the diplomatic skill of the Italian representative. Under the terms of the convention finally accepted by all the plenipotentiaries, Russia was permitted to resume her sovereign rights in the Black Sea. The Sultan in exchange, was authorized, 'to open the said Straits in time of Peace to the Vessels of War of friendly and allied Powers, in case the Sublime Porte should judge it necessary in order to secure the execution of the stipula-

---

[1] Aali Pasha to Musurus, communicated to Granville on 9 Jan. 1871, P.R.O., G.D. 29/91.
[2] *Prot.*
[3] Ibid.

tions of the Treaty of Paris of the 30th March 1856.'[1] Russia's long struggle for the abrogation of the Black Sea clauses was over.

Alexander II was delighted.

> The Emperor is said to be personally overjoyed at the success of his policy and is reported to have ordered a 'Te Deum' to be sung in the chapel of the Winter Palace in honour of the conclusion of the Treaty, after which he publicly embraced the Chancellor of the Empire. — I cannot vouch for the accuracy of this report, but I learn from a thoroughly trustworthy source that His Majesty went to the Cathedral of St Peter and St Paul in the fortress, which contains the tombs of the Emperors, and there prayed for some time with signs of deep emotion at the grave of His Father, saying to his attendants as he left, that he trusted the shade of the Emperor Nicholas would now be appeased.[2]

VII

For the British government, one final hurdle remained to be surmounted. When Parliament reassembled for the new session,[3] Disraeli, in the debate on the Address, had criticized the policy of the government in a flamboyant and demagogic speech. There were, he declared, gentlemen on both sides of the House who considered the Crimean War to have been a great mistake. He was not one of them. By firmness, that war might have been prevented. However, once war had been declared, it had been a just and necessary war. The treaty by which it was concluded was admirable, because it had devised a plan for neutralizing the Black Sea 'which absolutely, as far as human arrangements could control affairs, really prevented that part of the world again disturbing the general peace'. It was deplorable that this safeguard, the only tangible outcome of the war, should now be thrown away. If this mockery were to occur, the mothers of England would feel 'very differently in future' and the sons too would 'not be so lavish of their lives'.[4]

Gladstone replied to this demagogy in a speech which did him little credit. After claiming that Granville's note had been

---

[1] Ibid.
[2] Rumbold to Granville, 19 Mar. 1871, F.O. 65/820, no. 28.
[3] On 9 Feb.
[4] *Parl. Debates*, CCLIV, cc. 83 ff.

'a becoming, adequate and manly answer', he tried to refute his opponent's assertion about the supreme value of neutralization.

That was never, so far as I know, the view of the British Government. In this House, in the year 1856, I[1] declared my confident conviction that it was impossible to maintain the neutralization of the Black Sea.[2] I do not speak from direct communication with Lord Clarendon, but I have been told since his death that he never attached value to that neutralization.[3] Again, I do not speak from direct communication, but I have been told that Lord Palmerston always looked upon the neutralization as an arrangement which might be maintained and held together for a limited number of years, but which, from its character, it was impossible to maintain as a permanent condition of a great settlement of Europe.

Disraeli had argued that ministers should have refused to enter a conference and should 'at all hazards and all extremities' have 'staked themselves' upon the neutralization of the Black Sea.

Now I come to the ground of positive fact when I say that if we had been prepared for that most chivalrous resolution, we should have adopted it with our eyes open to the fact that no one Power in Europe shared our opinion, or would be in the slightest degree responsible for our acts.[4]

---

[1] As Lord Cairns pointed out in the House of Lords five days later, Gladstone, contrary to the impression conveyed in his speech, was not, at the time, a member of the government. On the contrary, his attitude 'if not one of opposition, was one of very careful, and frequently hostile, criticism of the Government of the day' (ibid., c. 242).

[2] What Gladstone did in fact say in the House of Commons on 6 May 1856 was somewhat different and shrouded in ambiguity: 'I believe no part of the treaty is more popular in this House and in the country, and many look upon this arrangement as the principal glory of the treaty of peace. For my own part, I confess I view it with far different feelings, independent of the question that neutralization appears to be welcomed in terms not altogether justified by the facts of the case. Where ships of war are allowed to a certain extent to be kept up, and, as far as I can understand, available for war purposes, I can find no one to tell me what would be the application of that system of neutralization in time of war. In a state of peace no doubt the arrangement would work well, and so would all systems, but when we come to times of difficulty, when Russia may again be at war, when she may unhappily have resumed her supposed scheme of aggression upon Turkey, or when the Porte may be at war with any Power, then I believe you will find that neutralization means nothing more than a series of pitfalls, which, when you come to test them, you will find to be deeper than you expected' (ibid., CXLII, cc. 97 f.). This was somewhat different from what Gladstone now wished the House to believe.

[3] An assertion which Gladstone was soon obliged to retract.

[4] This was nothing less than an attempt deliberately to mislead the House. In fact, Austria, Turkey, France and Italy had, for different reasons, expressed their

France by official acts expressed her readiness to give up the neutrality of the Black Sea; Austria-Hungary 'several years ago proposed to Russia that the Treaty should be altered, and that the neutrality of the Black Sea should be abandoned';

> and it is in this state of things that the right hon. Gentleman finds it necessary to introduce to-night the polemics of the case before the House of Commons, and to show how wrong we were not to go to war single-handed in order to force on Russia the permanent contraction of her sovereignty over a portion of her territory. I am perfectly content to leave to the House and to the country the judgment on that portion of the question.[1]

Some weeks after this clash, the House of Commons held a final inquest on the recent proceedings on a motion by Sir Charles Dilke regretting 'that Her Majesty's Government accepted a proposition for the assembling of a Conference under the circumstances disclosed in the Papers relating to Prince Gortchakoff's Circular Note, which had been laid before Parliament'. In the ensuing debate, the government more than held its own and Dilke finally withdrew his motion. Gladstone and Granville had scored a signal victory.[2]

---

readiness to follow *any* British lead. The element of truth behind Gladstone's assertion is that, with the possible exception of Austria, no power *desired* war. The Turkish government was satisfied that war had been averted. 'Aali speaks with the most lively gratitude of the line you have followed throughout the whole proceeding and if, when Parliament meets, you should be reproached with not having broken with Russia, or, which would have come to the same thing, insisted upon a retraction of the Gorchakov declaration, you may feel that Turkey at least would not have thanked you for taking such a course, which would have been very ruinous to her' (Elliot to Granville, private, 27 Jan. 1871, P.R.O., G.D. 29/102).

The accuracy of Gladstone's statement was challenged privately by Otway—a 'Palmerstonian' Under-Secretary at the Foreign Office, who subsequently resigned (Gladstone to Granville, 14 Feb. 1871, Ramm, loc. cit., p. 219).

[1] *Parl. Debates*, CCLV, cc. 98 ff. Some days later, commenting on Gladstone's speech in the House of Lords, Lord Cairns challenged the accuracy of the Prime Minister's remarks with regard to Clarendon and Palmerston (ibid., cc. 240 ff.). Granville in reply was forced to admit that in 1855 Clarendon had strongly favoured neutralization and that there was 'no evidence whatever that Lord Clarendon changed his opinions'. At the same time, Granville was able to adduce some evidence to suggest that Palmerston from the first had regarded neutralization as only a temporary expedient (ibid., cc. 247 f.).

[2] This victory, however, may well have been bought at a price. It has been claimed that, from his handling of the Black Sea crisis was born 'a popular distrust of Gladstone's leadership in foreign affairs, a seed of grumbling that he had let the country down, which later events sprouted and Disraeli's dexterity watered, till it cast a shadow at the polls in 1874' (R. C. K. Ensor, *England, 1870–1914* (Oxford, 1936), p. 5).

VIII

Gorchakov's challenge had raised in an acute form the question of the sanctions on which the Crimean system rested, and the methods by which its remnants could be defended. With regard to the use of force there appeared, as the Turkish government noted, little alternative to an immediate offensive war against Russia. This was a course of action favoured by no one except, apparently, a section of the British press. The Austrian government called for a joint protest of the signatories, the strongest possible form of diplomatic action. This policy was rejected by England, as there seemed no likelihood of obtaining the support of all the signatories. Bismarck, Musurus and some British papers advocated a protest coupled with a warning that any practical implementation of Gorchakov's circular would lead to counter-action. This, the most logical and consistent rejoinder appears, for a moment, to have been favoured by Gladstone; it was also in the mind of the Austrian government. Granville, however, was averse to a policy which seemed likely to store up trouble for the future.

In the circumstances, the rejection of the different forms of 'counter-action' left only the possibility of a negotiated compromise. The first reaction of the British and Austrian governments had been to take their stand on the principles of international law which, in logic, involved the impossibility of a solution without the prior withdrawal of Gorchakov's circular. This, however, the Russian chancellor neither would nor could concede. To break the deadlock and open for England and Russia alike a convenient line of retreat, Bismarck, Granville, and Gorchakov agreed to assemble a conference. Although Gorchakov's circular remained formally unwithdrawn, the Russian government did, in fact, agree to submit its claim to its fellow-signatories as prescribed by international law. It could therefore later be argued that such naval armaments as Russia might one day undertake in the Black Sea derived their international sanction not from Gorchakov's controversial circular but from the decision of the London conference. In this manner the circular, without being formally withdrawn was neatly and effectively by-passed. The point, moreover, was reinforced by the British government when it secured general acceptance of the proposition that the conference would meet without preconceived notion as to its result. This fiction would make it possible to argue — at least formally — that the effective abrogation of the Black Sea clauses was in no way connected with the Russian circular.

In addition, the British government secured the signature of the London protocol reaffirming the principles of international law. Apart from constituting at least an implied condemnation of Gorchakov's circular, the protocol had little practical significance. It was, however, an additional sop to the British public in exchange for the abandonment of the Black Sea clauses.

With regard to the question of substance, the negotiation finally resolved itself into a search for 'compensations'. Somewhat ironically, the compensation demanded and finally secured by Turkey consisted — apart from the restoration of the Sultan's sovereign rights — of the abrogation of *Western* tutelage. This change in Turkish policy came as an unpleasant surprise to the British government. It accelerated the retreat from 'Palmerstonianism' and the policy of protecting the Ottoman Empire. Before long, Gladstone would be campaigning against the Bulgarian atrocities.

With the union of the Danubian Principalities under a foreign prince and the de-neutralization of the Black Sea, Palmerston's Crimean system had become an empty shell. Only a few sorry remnants like the Russian cession of southern Bessarabia survived, awaiting the final act of the drama which had opened with the Tsar's acceptance of the Austrian ultimatum in December 1855. Among these remnants was the Triple Treaty, designed to buttress the Crimean structure: it still remained to support the ruined building. Indeed the signatories, from time to time, were reminded of its existence. The British government, in particular, was made uncomfortably aware of obligations undertaken in different times and circumstances. The Triple Treaty had embodied the very spirit of the

Palmerstonian settlement: it had been left as a legacy to Palmerston's successors. Its later history forms a comment not only on the Crimean system but on treaties of guarantee in general and on the problem of the obsolescence of treaties which have lost their *raison d'être*.

Epilogue: The Faith of Treaties

England and the Triple Treaty of 15 April 1856

A guarantee is one of the most onerous obligations which one State can contract towards another. . . . A guaranty [*sic*], strictly construed, knows no limit either of time or of degree . . . and the integrity of that Power (to whom the guarantee is given) must be maintained, at whatever cost the effort to maintain it is prolonged; nay, though the guaranteed Power should contribute almost nothing to the maintaining it.

GEORGE CANNING in a memorandum of 18 September 1823

What is the nature and force of these guarantees in general? Are they to be understood as an abstract literal declaration, wholly irrespective of all the circumstances which may intervene before the possibility of being called to act upon them arises?

GLADSTONE in House of Commons, 1877

The Triple Treaty of 15 April 1856, by which England, France and Austria bound themselves to protect the independence and integrity of the Ottoman Empire and to enforce, if necessary, the observance of the recently concluded peace treaty, had formed a keystone of the Crimean system. Its signature had been hailed by Palmerston in the House of Commons as a major diplomatic achievement. Indeed, at least symbolically, the treaty of 15 April might be considered the climax of Palmerston's Eastern policy. It formed an integral part of what he described as 'one of the most important settlements during many ages of history'.[1]

Yet rarely did a treaty have a more undistinguished career. Some doubts of its effectiveness had been raised right at the start when Napoleon, in the interest of his *rapprochement* with Russia had tried to belittle French obligations. Austria, whose government had pressed vigorously for the conclusion of the treaty, within three years was to adopt a purely opportunist attitude towards it. There remained, however, England who not only prided herself on the faithful execution of her engagements, but who also had a direct interest at stake in the preservation of

---

[1] Palmerston in the House of Commons, 6 May 1856, *Parl. Debates*, CXLII, c. 127.

N

Palmerston's handiwork. She, at least, would surely honour her obligations and try to induce her partners to do the same. How, in fact, did she acquit herself when the question of 'honouring' the treaty did eventually arise?

I

The emergency with which the Triple Treaty was intended to deal — a direct challenge to the order established by the Treaty of Paris — was first seen to be approaching after the outbreak of the Franco-Prussian war.[1] More than once, the British ambassador in St Petersburg warned the Foreign Office that Russia would seek an early opportunity to upset the Crimean settlement. Ignat'yev, in Constantinople was throwing out broad hints to the same effect. All this convinced Gladstone that a Russian move was impending. The *casus foederis* of the Triple Treaty, therefore, might arise at any moment.

It was in these circumstances that the Turkish government — party to the general but not the triple treaty — made enquiry in London about the help it could count on in the event of Russian aggression. The Grand-Vizier, in conversation with the British ambassador, expressed particular anxiety with regard to finance and arms and wished to know whether, in the event of a Russian attack, he could look to the British government 'for assistance with reference to them'. Elliot, the ambassador, returned a cool reply. He explained to Aali that the available supply of breach-loaders was severely limited. Moreover, should England adopt a policy of neutrality,[2] arms could not be supplied without departing from it. Aali, finding this cold comfort indeed retorted with some warmth that England being 'a party to a solemn guarantee of Turkey, the case was very different from what it would otherwise be'. He could understand that circumstances might prevent a country from fulfilling its engagements to the

---

[1] Strictly speaking, the first open challenge to the Treaty of Paris had been the election of a foreign prince by the United Principalities in 1866. However the challenge, in this instance, had come not from the expected quarter but from the Roumanian national movement (supported by Napoleon III). The Roumanian provisional government was not among the signatories of the Treaty of Paris. Moreover, the infringement of the treaty resulting from the Roumanian action was, in the end, condoned by all the signatories.

[2] The mere fact that Elliot could use such language shows how far things had moved since the days of Palmerston. Ten years earlier, British neutrality in the event of a Russian attack on Turkey would have been unthinkable.

letter, 'but it would continue to be bound to render any assistance in its power and he hoped that the sympathies of Great
Britain, which had never been wanting to Turkey, might again
be calculated upon if the occasion called for it'.[1]

The Turkish appeal was unlikely to meet with a sympathetic
reception. Before sending an official reply, Gladstone, in a
memorandum, was reckoning up the chances of outside support
for Turkey in the event of a Russian attack. His conclusions
were wholly negative. Even England, 'whether sole or with
allies,' could no longer consider an intervention which public
opinion would not countenance. Turkey, in the past, had been
'habituated to look to external aid'. Of this, there was now 'no
prospect on which any sane man can rely'.[2] Whilst this was undoubtedly a realistic appreciation of the international scene, it
is at least remarkable that Gladstone, in his memorandum, did
not so much as consider the question of treaty obligations.

In any case, before the Anglo-Turkish exchanges were completed, the Russian government had sprung its expected mine:
on 9 November Gorchakov's circular denouncing the Black
Sea clauses was delivered at the Foreign Office. It could be
held that the contingency envisaged by the Triple Treaty of 15
April had thus, in fact, arisen. The signatories would have to
define their attitudes towards their obligations.

The French government, being 'otherwise engaged', was unlikely to take the initiative. In Vienna, Beust informed the
imperial council, that the neutralization of the Black Sea must,
in the long run, have proved intolerable to a great power like
Russia. Austria, recognizing this fact, had, even before the war,
reconciled herself to its abrogation:

> Dies erkennend habe man noch vor dem deutsch-französischen
> Kriege die Frage aufgeworfen was geschehen werde wenn
> Russland im Pontus eine Flotte bauen sollte, und wenn auch
> förmliche Verhandlungen über diesen Gegenstand nicht stattge-
> funden hätten, so habe doch die allgemeine Ansicht durchge-
> leuchtet, dass es deshalb zum Kriege nicht kommen müsse.

There remained the question of the Triple Treaty, which, however, in the circumstances of the moment, was unlikely to
operate:

[1] Elliot to Granville, 17 Oct. 1870, F.O. 78/2125, no. 242, confidential.
[2] Gladstone to Hammond, 28 Oct. 1870, P.R.O., G.D. 59/58.

Nach der heutigen Lage Europas werde sich mit diesem Vertrage gegenüber Russland wohl nicht viel ausrichten lassen, aber Oesterreich-Ungarn müsse zu der Frage doch immerhin Stellung nehmen.

In the end, after considerable discussion, Francis-Joseph who presided, summed up the sense of the meeting, that Austria should not venture further than Britain was willing to go.[1] Since Gladstone and Granville however, were resolved, if possible, to settle the dispute by peaceful means, they in their turn saw no occasion either to apply or appeal to the treaty of 15 April. It might appear that, by force of circumstances, the treaty had thus become a dead letter.

II

Fate decreed otherwise. The Turkish ambassador in Vienna, exasperated at the attitude adopted by Turkey's allies and 'guarantors', took it upon himself[2] to warn Beust that, unless Austria gave full support to Turkey, the latter would be obliged to seek a separate understanding with Russia. This was a spectre designed to daunt any Austrian statesman. It did not fail to alarm Beust. The Triple Treaty now suggested itself to his mind as a suitable instrument for preventing the 'defection' of Turkey. Apponyi (the Austrian ambassador), therefore, called at the Foreign Office with a note stating that Austria

se considère comme liée par le traité spécial du 15 avril 1856 et est prête à remplir les engagements qu'il lui impose vis-à-vis de la Turquie. En revanche, l'Autriche demande que les Puissances signataires de ce traité munissent leurs Représentants[3] d'instructions identiques et que l'Angleterre unisse ses efforts aux nôtres pour empêcher à Constantinople des velléités d'entente directe avec la Russie.[4]

Granville, who found the appeal to the Triple Treaty embarrassing, tried to side-step Apponyi. He was ready, he answered, to

[1] Minutes of the Austro-Hungarian Council of Ministers of 14 Nov. 1870, in H.H.S.A., Ministerrath für gemeinsame Angelegenheiten, Präsid. Sektion Dep. I, xxxx, p. 275.
[2] In making his communication to Beust, Musurus was exceeding his instructions (cf. Elliot to Granville, private, 9 Dec. 1870, P.R.O., G.D. 29/102).
[3] To the impending conference on Gochakov's circular.
[4] Apponyi to Granville, private, 29 Nov. 1870, P.R.O., G.D. 29/82.

concert with Austria the instructions to be given to the representatives of the two powers, but could not pledge beforehand
that they would be identical. He would be happy to join Beust
in preventing a secret Russo-Turkish understanding 'but was
not aware of the necessity for such an effort at present'.

Beust, however, was determined to establish his point that
the triple guarantee was still in force. Apponyi, therefore, once
more drew the Foreign Secretary's attention to the treaty.
Granville, acutely embarrassed, was forced to reply that he was
aware of its stipulations. However, in his view, the *casus foederis*
had not as yet arisen. The case the Triple Treaty was framed to
provide against, he argued, was an infraction of the Treaty of
Paris. None had, as yet, occurred.

> Although Russia had done that which had made a painful im-
> pression upon both Austria and England, there had as yet been
> no infraction of the Treaty. — This being the case, and one of the
> three co-signatories being in a position in which it might be
> difficult to require an exact execution of the stipulations of the
> second Treaty[1] it was better to postpone the discussion of it for
> the present.[2]

With that, for the time being, the Austrian government had to
content itself.

However, the Austrian appeal to the Triple Treaty had
thoroughly alarmed Granville, who had been brought to
realize that Britain, at the discretion of Austria, might get
drawn into a war which he was doing his best to avoid. He
privately told Gladstone:

> But what sticks in my gizzard is the Tripartite Treaty. How very
> foolish it was of us to have concocted it. But there it is with
> obligations as binding as were ever contracted.[3]

Granville, therefore, wished to cancel or at least attenuate
British obligations under the treaty. He had already suggested
that the 'best but most unlikely' compensation for the abrogation of the Black Sea clauses would be Prussia's adhesion to
the tripartite treaty.[4] He now repeated the suggestion, adding

---

[1] The implications of this argument will be examined below.
[2] Granville to Bloomfield, 1 Dec. 1870, F.O. 120/481, no. 137.
[3] Granville to Gladstone, 10 Dec. 1870, Ramm, loc. cit., pp. 181 f.
[4] The same to the same, 5 Dec. 1870, ibid., pp. 172 f.

that the Prussian signature 'would rather weaken than strengthen the obligations of England and would act as a powerful check against Russia trying to put them into force . . .'.[1] Indeed Odo Russell, then on his special mission to Prussian military headquarters in Versailles, had already been instructed to sound Bismarck privately on Prussia's willingness to accede to the treaty.[2]

Gladstone, whilst in full agreement with his colleague's desire to minimize British obligations under the treaty, did not share his views as to its binding force. As matters stood at present, he argued, the treaty was of little practical significance:

> Stringent as it is in its terms, it does not appear to me to have much force as a covenant at present, when Turkey declares her own incapacity to fight except with (virtually) our money. Guarantees as such seem to me to presuppose the capacity of any guaranteed State to fight for herself and then to supply a further auxiliary defence. At least I think it must be so in the case where nothing is expressed to give a different construction to the guarantee.

He was, moreover, of the opinion that any action with regard to the treaty, such as inviting Prussia to accede to it, 'would tend to rivet it upon us and enhance our obligation'.[3]

Gladstone's remarkable doctrine failed to allay Granville's disquiet. Bismarck, indeed, replied as expected that the German parliament would refuse to ratify 'an engagement of this kind which, in the present temper of the people of Germany, would be very unpopular'. Germans would resist 'any engagement to fight for other nations abroad . . . the conquests made by others will be indifferent to them'.[4]

Granville, however, had another string to his bow. Aali, the Grand-Vizier had put forward the suggestion that all the powers who had signed the Treaty of Paris should adhere to the Triple Treaty.[5] The British cabinet, in its reply, agreed to abandon the Triple Treaty if requested to do so by the Porte.[6]

---

[1] The same to the same, 10 Dec. 1870, ibid., pp. 181 f.
[2] Granville to Russell, 7 Dec. 1870, F.O. 64/737, no. 35, most confidential, reporting telegram.
[3] Gladstone to Granville, 12 Dec. 1870, Ramm, loc. cit., p. 185.
[4] Odo Russell to Granville private, 18 Dec. 1870, R.A. I 67/104, copy.
[5] Elliot to Granville, 13 Dec. 1870, ibid., H 5/53, reporting telegram.
[6] Ramm, loc. cit., p. 188, n. 6.

Aali, on being informed of this, expressed his pleasure at the proposal 'to cancel the Tripartite Treaty and to embody its provisions in the general Treaty'.[1] This, however, was not what the British government had intended. Granville spoke of 'a misunderstanding between the Turks and us about the cancelling of the Tripartite Treaty'.[2] Turkish objections to the British scheme were, in fact, insuperable:

> Aali's opinion ... is ... that if the Treaty of April were now to be cancelled, we should be regarded, in the East at least, as turning the left cheek to Russia after having received her slap on the right one. ...[3]

As a last resort, Granville then suggested the straightforward procedure, of cancelling the treaty, by the agreement of the signatories.[4] But Gladstone, by this time, was getting impatient with these diplomatic efforts. He himself had, from the start, relied on 'interpretation' rather than diplomatic action to attenuate the British obligation. He now told Granville:

> If you cannot merge the Tripartite Treaty by reason of the Turk's disliking such a measure, he will still more dislike any attempt to abate it by an agreement of the Three Powers. I should incline to let it alone, particularly as I feel that through the state of facts announced by the Turk himself, its inconvenient stringency is, in great measure, in abeyance.[5]

With that, Granville had to content himself.

The Triple Treaty, therefore, survived. Indeed the London conference, which freed Russia from the Black Sea clauses, distinctly affirmed in a special protocol (due to British initiative)

> that the Powers recognize that it is an essential principle of the law of nations that none of them can liberate itself from the engagements of a treaty or modify the stipulations thereof, unless with the consent of the contracting parties by means of an amicable understanding.[6]

In fact, at this very moment, whilst the British government was trying to teach that of Russia the rudiments of international law,

---

[1] Elliot to Granville, telegram, 20 Dec. 1870, R.A. H 5/58, copy.
[2] Granville to Gladstone, 23 Dec. 1870, Ramm, loc. cit., pp. 189 f.
[3] Elliot to Granville, private, 30 Dec. 1870, P.R.O., G.D. 29/102.
[4] Granville to Gladstone, 23 Dec. 1870, Ramm, loc. cit., pp. 189 f.
[5] Gladstone to Granville, 25 Dec. 1870, ibid., pp. 191 f.
[6] For the protocol of 17 Jan. 1871, cf. *Prot.*

it was itself attempting to default. A Blue Book of 1871 enumerating 'treaties of guarantee under which this country is engaged to interfere by force of arms . . . to attack or defend any government or nation' made no mention of the Triple Treaty.[1] Only Article VII of the Treaty of Paris was listed.

III

But the Triple Treaty was not dead. When, during 1876 Austria and Russia opened negotiations about a joint policy in the Eastern question, it re-appeared upon the scene. Article III of the main Austro-Russian Convention signed on 15 January 1877 laid down that

> Si le gouvernement de l'empereur [of Austria-Hungary] est invité à concourir à la mise en exécution du traité du 15 avril 1856, il déclinera son co-opération pour le cas prévu dans la présente convention[2] et, sans contester la validité du dit traité, proclamera sa neutralité.[3]

Cynicism could hardly go further, but it is significant that both the Austrian and Russian governments regarded the Triple Treaty as still in operation.

The British government too was soon to be reminded of its continued existence. At the end of February, Lord Campbell explained in the House of Lords that, during the previous fortnight, it had become fashionable to argue that the tripartite treaty of 1856 had become inoperative. It was claimed that Britain was under no obligation to intervene unless invited by her co-signatories and that, since such an invitation was unlikely, the treaty had become null and of no effect. He himself disagreed with this view, being convinced 'that the Treaties of the 30th March and 15th April, as they were modified by the Conference of the Powers of 1871, were still binding'. He based this opinion on the doctrine of Vattel, who had expressly denied the assertion that, unless the other contracting parties called upon a third party to it to act, a treaty was void and of no effect.[4] According to

---

[1] *Accounts and papers* (1871), LXXII, 275, p. 542.
[2] I.e. if Russia felt obliged to declare war on Turkey.
[3] Printed in B. H. Sumner, *Russia and the Balkans, 1870–80* (Oxford, 1937), pp. 597 f.
[4] The classic exposition of the doctrine here criticized was, of course, Stanley's celebrated 'interpretation' of the Luxembourg guarantee of 1867:

Vattel, no single contracting party had the right to interpret a treaty at its own pleasure. Moreover, any interpretation which led to an absurdity, and one which would render a treaty null and void was inadmissible. A treaty must be so interpreted as to give it its effect. If either of the contracting parties could or ought to have explained itself and had failed to do so, it must be to its own damage. Basing himself on these principles of Vattel's, he, Campbell, was of the opinion that the Triple Treaty had lost none of its binding force.[1]

Derby, the Stanley of the ill-fated Luxembourg guarantee and now Foreign Secretary, was placed in a predicament. He replied that the Triple Treaty had not been invalid when signed. It had, however, become so since, owing to the change of circumstances.

> My answer is [he replied] that, although the changed circumstances at the present time have made the Treaty of far less importance that it originally was[2] it does not at all follow that because you may choose to consider it for practical purposes as null and void, therefore it was so at the time when it was entered into.

Campbell had argued that the failure of Austria and France to call upon England did not extinguish her obligation to act.

> But as our obligations are only to them, if they do not choose to call upon us to fulfil what we have undertaken to do under certain circumstances, I do not see that it is for us to enter into the question of what may be their motives.[3] . . . That is their affair, not ours.[4]

The guarantee now given is collective only. . . . It means this, that in the event of a violation of neutrality, all the powers who have signed the treaty may be called upon [by whom? W.M.] for their collective action. No one of these powers is liable to be called upon to act singly or separately. It is a case, so to speak, of 'limited liability'. We are bound in honour — you cannot put a legal construction upon it — to see in concert with others that these arrangements are maintained. But if the other powers join with us, it is certain that there will be no violation of neutrality. If they, situated as we are, decline to join, we are not bound to make good single-handed the deficiencies of the rest. Such a guarantee has obviously rather the character of a moral sanction to the arrangements which it defends than that of a contingent liability to make war. It would, no doubt, give a right to make war, but it would not necessarily impose the obligation (*Parl. Debates*, CLVII, cc. 1922 f.).

[1] Ibid., CCXXXII, cc. 982 f.
[2] This was hardly the point at issue.
[3] Again, this appears completely irrelevant.
[4] Ibid., c. 1005.

With this doctrine, Campbell had to be satisfied at the time, but more was to be heard of the matter.

On 19 April, five days before Russia's declaration of war on Turkey, Rosebery re-opened the question in the House of Lords. Had the government, the noble Lord enquired, entered into any arrangements with the other signatories of the Triple Treaty, by which they had mutually released themselves from their engagements? Unless they had done this, he did not see how the binding force of that instrument could be disputed.

> The language of that Treaty was so strict that it left no loophole — it guaranteed in the most absolute form the integrity and independence of the Ottoman Empire.

How could any of the three powers, parties to the treaty, escape from its engagements? The declaration of the London protocol had made those obligations still more binding. England often boasted that she alone among the nations maintained her treaties 'with rigid and scrupulous fidelity'. Were they to disregard the validity of this treaty, assuredly 'a fatal blow would be struck at the validity of all Treaties'. One day, he feared, they might be placed in the position

> that we should either have to fight for Turkey, a war which the conscience of this country would refuse, or to draw back from our pledged word.[1]

Derby in reply no longer denied, as he had tried to do in his exchanges with Campbell, England's obligation under the Triple Treaty. Instead, he repeated his conviction that neither France nor Austria intended to call on England 'to fulfil what we are bound to under the Treaty of April, 1856'. It was for this reason that he had considered it unnecessary to take any steps with regard to that treaty 'or to free ourselves from the obligations which it involves'.

Turning from the practical to the theoretical side of the question, he agreed with Rosebery that treaties must be maintained, but added that no treaties

> can or are intended to be eternal. They are framed with reference to existing circumstances, and though I do not say whether that is so or is not the case in regard to the treaty of 1856, yet nothing

[1] Ibid., ccxxxiii, cc. 1427 ff.

has been more common in European diplomacy than the recognition of the fact that treaties do by the lapse of time and the force of events become obsolete.[1] I do not think it would be a fair or satisfactory conclusion to come to either that you must be eternally bound by a Treaty, made long ago[2] under conditions wholly different from those now existing, or that you are to be held guilty of a breach of faith because you consider it no longer binding.[3]

This first exchange between Rosebery and Derby did not dispose of the vexed question of the unwanted Triple Treaty. Before long, it became apparent that Derby's complacent assertion that the treaty would in no circumstances be invoked, rested on shaky foundations. It suddenly began to appear that Austria might be drawn into the Russo-Turkish conflict. On 14 May, therefore, Rosebery raised the matter once again. No man of ordinary sense, he claimed,

> could cast his eye on the map of Eastern Europe without perceiving that it was very difficult for Russia to strike a blow at Turkey without touching one of those numerous interests of Austria, interference with which might make it necessary for the latter Power to interfere in the contest.

Had Austria, in that event, the right under the Triple Treaty to compel England to go to war? The treaty of 15 April contained two distinct provisions. By the first, the three signatories undertook to guarantee jointly, severally and, as far as he could see, unreservedly the integrity and independence of the Ottoman Empire. By the second, they agreed to regard as a *casus belli* any infringement of the treaty of 30 March 1856. What, in this respect, was the position at the present moment?

> The Russian Army was marching into the Provinces of the Ottoman Empire. How, then, could it be maintained that the integrity and independence of the Ottoman Empire had not been interfered with?

[1] When Gorchakov had tried to act on this same doctrine, stated in far less uncompromising terms, Gladstone had observed in a memorandum:
'It is quite evident that the effect of such doctrine and of such proceeding which with or without avowal is founded upon it is to bring the entire authority and efficacy of all Treaties whatever under the discretionary control of each one of the Powers who may have signed them' (quoted in H. Temperley and L. M. Penson, loc. cit., pp. 332 f.).
[2] Even Derby must have known that the treaties in question had been signed in 1856 and solemnly reaffirmed as recently as 1871.
[3] *Parl. Debates*, ccxxxiii, cc. 1434 ff.

It was true that no power had as yet thought fit to treat this infringement as a *casus belli*, but was there any security that, during the progress of the Russo-Turkish war, none would decide to do so? If, however, one of the other signatories did at any time see fit to treat the infringement of the treaty of 30 March as a *casus belli*, England might be called on to intervene. It was his opinion, therefore, that as far as the Eastern question was concerned, there existed at present no graver matter than the point whether the Triple Treaty was or was not at this moment in operation. If it was inoperative, let the government declare that this was so; but, if it was operative, he held that it was a source of serious danger.

The argument about 'obsolescence' was unconvincing.

> The noble Earl said the other day that in his opinion Treaties were not eternal. Well, he supposed that was true. Treaties were not eternal any more than Protocols; but he would like to know from the noble Earl what period of existence he assigned to Treaties. Would he give them the average life of man? If that was to be their term, let them be decently buried and consigned to the sepulchre of archives when they reached it; but let them not sneak out of existence under the impression that nobody was to act upon them.

In the present instance, it would not be difficult to make arrangements to free England from the tripartite treaty. If that was not done, the day would come

> when that Treaty would involve us in the alternative of a war on the one hand, or — he would not say dishonour, but a very disagreeable proceeding — on the other.

He would therefore beg the Government to consider whether the time had not come for entering into an amicable arrangement with France and Austria by which England would be released from the engagements of the Triple Treaty.[1]

Derby, in declining the suggestion, admitted that Austria was 'not free from the possible danger of being embroiled in the war'. In such an event, moreover, it would obviously be to her advantage to fight with England as an ally rather than alone. As to whether she would, in fact, have a claim under the treaty

[1] Ibid., ccxxxiv, cc. 830 ff.

to call on England to join her, this involved various considerations 'difficult to discuss in a merely speculative manner'.

> The Treaty having been framed to preserve the integrity and inde-
> pendence of the Turkish Empire, the question might not unfairly
> be raised whether, if the contracting Powers had allowed that in-
> tegrity or that independence to be violated, and war having
> broken out between Russia and Turkey, one of those contracting
> Powers, at a later period of the war would have the right to call
> upon the others, not on the ground that the interests originally
> defined had been attacked, but on the ground that other interests
> had come to be involved.

It might, therefore, become a question of whether 'having
allowed the time of action to pass', Austria would be entitled to
call upon England later on the plea that her own interests were
concerned.

In fact, neither France nor Austria were likely to invoke the
treaty. They had been in very confidential communication
with the government of Austria — there had been a confidential
exchange of ideas between them — and he had not, for his part,
the slightest idea that Austria would call on England to act on
the conditions of the Triple Treaty in a manner which might be
a cause of embarrassment to them.[1]

At the same time, an attempt to terminate the treaty might
be misinterpreted.

> I do not think this would be the moment to take that step. You
> have to consider in dealing with these international engagements,
> not only what will be the actual effect of the thing you do, but
> what will be the interpretation put upon your acts and what will
> be the conclusions drawn from them. It is one thing to say that
> we are not going to war to maintain the Ottoman Empire, and
> another to take a step which might be understood by Europe —
> and not unreasonably — as a formal announcement of our in-
> difference to what might occur.

The matter, therefore, might well be left in abeyance until the
peace, when it would be a fair question to consider whether the

---

[1] What Derby did not, of course, know was that the reference to the Triple
Treaty in the Austro-Russian Convention of 15 Jan. 1877, virtually precluded the
Austrian government from appealing to it now.

engagements of the treaty of 1856 should be any longer continued.[1]

With this, the matter was allowed to rest until the congress of Berlin. There is no evidence to suggest that at that congress the Triple Treaty ever became a subject of discussion. Article LXIII of the Treaty of Berlin however, declared:

> Le Traité de Paris du 30 Mars 1856, ainsi que le Traité de Londres du 13 Mars 1871, sont maintenus dans toutes celles de leurs dispositions qui ne sont pas abrogées ou modifiées par les stipulations qui précèdent.[2]

When, in 1898, the British government published a further Blue Book containing 'copies of such parts of all treaties etc., now existing and still obligatory as contain an undertaking entered into by Her Majesty with reference to the territory or government of any other Power',[3] the Triple Treaty was once again omitted. On the other hand, rather incongruously, Article VII of the Treaty of Paris was still deemed to be in force — the last sad remnant of Palmerston's once proud Crimean system.

And yet even now, the ghost of the ill-fated Triple Treaty had still not been finally laid to rest. In 1902, when pleading against the extension of British treaty obligations, the third Marquis of Salisbury quoted the treaty of 1856 as a warning example. 'Remember', he concluded a minute on a War Office memorandum, 'the fall in 1877 of the tripartite guarantee of Turkey signed in 1856 by Austria, France and England.'[4] Finally, according to Professor Lilian Penson, the Triple Treaty was formally annulled in 1914.[5]

---

[1] Ibid., cc. 838 ff. Posterity must regret that Derby, in his reply, did not see fit to answer Rosebery's enquiry about the proper duration of treaties. The answer, undoubtedly, would have been illuminating.

[2] The Treaty of Berlin is printed in W. N. Medlicott, *The Congress of Berlin and after* (London, 1938), p. 419.

[3] *Accounts and Papers* (1899), CIX, C. 9088, Misc., no. 2 (1898), p. 98.

[4] Undated minute by Salisbury on War Office memorandum of 30.1.02, W.O. 106/44 E 1/6, quoted in L. Penson, *Foreign Affairs under the Third Marquis of Salisbury* (London, 1962), p. 20. I am obliged to Dr. John Grenville of the University of Nottingham for drawing my attention to this reference.

[5] Cf. L. Penson, 'Obligation by Treaty' in *Studies in Diplomatic History and Historiography*, ed. A. O. Sarkissian (London, 1961), p. 80. It is, however, impossible to discover the instrument of cancellation. The Librarian of the Foreign Office, after considerable research, 'can find no evidence that this treaty was formally annulled, or declared to have become annulled' (Librarian of Foreign Office to W. E. Mosse, 31 Jan., 1963).

IV

The fate of the treaty of 15 April reveals a curious paradox. British statesmen, Palmerston and Clarendon, had been largely instrumental in bringing it into existence: yet, as soon as the possibility of its application began to appear, however distantly, on the horizon other British statesmen, Gladstone, Granville, Derby, strained their ingenuity to 'wriggle out of it'. In this respect, there was little to choose between Liberal Gladstone and Conservative Derby: all that differed was the nature of their arguments. Whilst Gladstone contended that 'guarantees as such' presupposed 'the capacity of any guaranteed State to fight for herself', Derby, faithful to his Luxembourg doctrine, argued that British obligations were to France and Austria only. These, however, were to some extent secondary considerations. The real ground on which both Gladstone and Derby took their stand was that, since the conclusion of the treaty, circumstances had changed. In Gladstone's case, this argument was supported by empirical considerations: Derby, true to his pedantic nature, developed a whole theory of treaty obligations. At first, indeed, he contented himself with the simple doctrine that 'the changed circumstances of the present time' had made the Triple Treaty 'of far less importance than it originally was', but in his subsequent reply to Rosebery he generalized the case. Treaties, he now asserted, were 'framed with reference to existing circumstances' and European diplomacy had repeatedly recognized that they did 'by the lapse of time and the force of events become obsolete'.

This was doctrine more consonant with the realistic views of a Bismarck[1] or *horribile dictu*, the thesis of Gorchakov's circular, than with the commonly moralizing tone of British diplomacy,[2] journalism and public opinion. Clearly, circumstances altered

---

[1] Bismarck's views, it appears, completely coincided with those expressed by Stanley. He was later to write in his reminiscences:
'Die internationale Politik ist ein flüssiges Element, das unter Umständen zeitweilig fest wird, aber bei Veränderungen der Atmosphäre in seinen ursprünglichen Aggregatzustand zurückfällt. Die *clausula rebus sic stantibus* wird bei Staatsverträgen, die Leistungen bedingen, stillschweigend angenommen' (*Gedanken und Erinnerungen*, Volksausgabe, [Berlin, 1913], II, p. 287).
[2] As expressed in its purest form in the British reply to Gorchakov's Black Sea circular (Granville to Buchanan, 10 Nov. 1870, *Corr.*, no. 4), and in the British-inspired London protocol of 17 Jan. 1871 (*Prot.*).

cases. Whilst every British journalist felt impelled to bewail the disastrous effect of Gorchakov's doctrine on the 'sanctity' of treaties, few appear to have considered the practical implications of the Gladstone-Derby view. What value could be attached to an engagement framed only in relation to 'existing circumstances'? When did these circumstances cease? Who was to judge whether they had done so? Was every signatory to be the judge in his own cause? Derby, normally a model of logical exposition forbore to answer Rosebery's pertinent enquiries on these points. The only reply open to him would have been to repeat his doctrine in connection with the Luxembourg guarantee:

> Such a guarantee has obviously rather the character of a moral sanction to the arrangements which it defends than that of a contingent liability to make war. It would, no doubt, give a right to make war, but it would not necessarily impose the obligation.

That, certainly, would have been a realistic view of the case, but it is impossible not to wonder how doctrine such as this would have commended itself to Palmerston and Clarendon. As to the manner in which the Triple Treaty finally disappeared, was there not much to be said in favour of Mill's controversial plea that treaties should be concluded only for a stated number of years?

In fact, it is evident that the framers of the Triple Treaty of 1856 were careless in their drafting. They should clearly have written into the treaty that the guarantee of the Ottoman Empire was valid only so long as Turkey was capable of defending herself single-handed. They should have added that the treaty would operate only if one of the signatories called upon the others to act the moment the *casus foederis* arose and provided all the signatories were in a position to honour their obligations. Last but not least, they should of course have incorporated a clause stating that the treaty would remain in force only so long as there was no change in circumstances. It may be doubted whether a treaty conceived in terms such as these would have appealed to Palmerston and Buol.

The ambiguous attitude of *all three* signatories towards the Triple Treaty illustrates, of course, a major diplomatic 'fact of life'. If the Triple Treaty proved, from the moment of its signature, a useless 'scrap of paper', this was because, unlike treaties designed to achieve a specific offensive or defensive object, it was based on no long-term interest common to all the signatories. It was, on the contrary, the expression of a temporary mood,[1] a mood, moreover, which was already passing at the time of signature. When has a treaty of this kind — from the ill-fated Danish guarantee of 1852 to the Treaty of Locarno — ever achieved its purpose? Who still holds the view that Britain went to war in 1914 solely or even principally to honour her Belgian guarantee of 1839? And, one is tempted to ask, would possible future European treaties guaranteeing frontiers meet with a happier fate?

There is, as the fate of the Triple Treaty shows, little value in diplomatic engagements not based on a lasting community of interests; yet where such a community of interest exists, written agreements, as a rule, would seem hardly necessary. The Triple Treaty designed to buttress the Crimean settlement was shown in the event to have embodied the permanent interests of not one of the three signatories. It was this which spelt its doom. Unwanted, ignored, broken in the spirit if not the letter, it dragged out its undistinguished existence. It did not achieve even decent burial and consignment to the 'sepulchre of archives'. Unwept, unhonoured and unsung, it had, in fact, ignominiously 'sneaked out of existence' years before the British government posthumously proclaimed its demise. Like other carefully negotiated instruments both before and since, it had failed signally to achieve its object or, in fact, to serve any useful purpose whatever.

---

[1] Bismarck, speaking of the treaty of the triple alliance was to write in his memoirs:

'Er hat die Bedeutung einer strategischen Stellungnahme in der europäischen Politik nach Massgabe ihrer Lage zur Zeit des Abschlusses' (Bismarck, op. cit., p. 287).

Conclusion

I

The history of the Crimean system affords a striking example of the disintegration of a peace settlement as the result of changes in the 'balance of power'. Almost from the start, the system was weakened by the increasingly ambiguous attitude of Napoleon III towards it. Similarly, once Buol had disappeared from the scene, Austria by repeated offers to Russia showed how little intrinsic value she, in her turn, had come to attach to certain parts of the settlement. Moreover France and Austria — partners in the Crimean system — went to war with each other within little more than three years of the signing of the treaty. At the same time the Anglo-French alliance, keystone of the system, showed signs of steady disintegration. England, left (together with Turkey) the principal defender of the existing order in 'the East', began to change the basis of her Eastern policy. Gladstone clearly indicated that she would on no account re-fight the Crimean war. The rising power of Prussia, about to replace Austria as the leading 'Germanic' state, had proclaimed from an early moment its complete lack of interest in the Crimean settlement. Finally even Turkey herself began to show resentment at the European tutelage imposed on her by the Treaty of Paris. All this time, Russia was recovering from the effects of the Crimean war and gaining in strength and prestige. These changes in policies and power relations in their cumulative effect undermined the foundations of the Crimean system.

This gradual disintegration of the Crimean system posed in an increasingly acute form the problem of treaty revision. The arrangements made in Paris, whilst ceasing more and more to reflect the true distribution of power and interests, were challenged with growing determination by peoples as well as governments. There thus arose the problem of reconciling a variety of national demands with existing international instruments and obligations.

The first major challenge came from Roumanian nationalism supported by Napoleon. Repeated *faits accomplis* created by Roumanian nationalists were reluctantly accepted by the suzerain and the powers. Nor did the arrangements concerning the neutralization of the Black Sea effectively stand the test of time. The Russians, indeed, except for the 'harmless' subterfuge of the Odessa Steam Navigation Company, seem on the whole to have abided by the terms of the treaty. On the other hand, between 1866 and 1869 alone, there were no fewer than nine (relatively unimportant) infractions of the Straits Convention, giving rise to one collective and three individual protests to the Porte.[1] It is difficult not to accept Gorchakov's contention that, by 1870, the Treaty of Paris had lost much of its moral validity.

Moreover, the moral foundations of the Black Sea clauses had been undermined in a different sense. Austria, France and Prussia had, at different times tried to buy Russian support against each other by promises of diplomatic assistance in the abolition of the clauses. England and Turkey alone had never joined in the bidding. It would be difficult, in the circumstances, to maintain that the neutralization of the Black Sea represented the unanimous and strongly felt desire of the powers who had signed the Treaty of Paris.

The Russian government, therefore, had some excuse and much temptation for trying to free itself from the irksome restrictions of the treaty. To do this, it tried a number of expedients. The most satisfactory way of raising the matter appeared to be in a European congress. Not only was this the 'correct' procedure but with the promises and half-promises secured from France, Austria and Prussia, Russia would find herself in a strong bargaining position. However, in spite of Russian hopes, no congress assembled either in 1859 or 1866. Again in 1870, hopes of a new international settlement were cut short by the Prussian triumph at Sedan. There was now little prospect of Russia being able to raise the issue before an international forum.

Hopes of privately winning over England, the principal defender of the Black Sea clauses, were negligible. A confidential approach to the Russophile Russell in 1866 revealed that British

---

[1] These figures are taken from a detailed list compiled by the Foreign Office, printed in *Corr.*, no. 5.

opinion would not tolerate any major concession to Russia. Four years later, the British public's reaction to Gorchakov's circular would fully confirm this view.

This left only the policy of the *fait accompli* practised successfully in 1866 by Bismarck with regard to the treaties of Vienna and by Prince Charles and the Roumanian nationalists in regard to the convention of 1858. The Russian plan to follow a similar course in 1866 had been abandoned on account of misgivings about its possible consequences. But, when it was revived four years later, Gorchakov could, with some justification, point to the precedents of 1866, when the powers had acquiesced in *faits accomplis* both in Germany and the Principalities. He could also argue that other methods of freeing Russia from the shackles of the Black Sea clauses held out little hope of success.

II

A study of the Crimean system and its history produces the inescapable conclusion that the value of certain types of international engagement is — to say the least — highly problematical. A Draconic peace treaty imposed on a defeated enemy in the moment of victory appears — almost of necessity — of little practical value. It may, indeed, have a limited use as long as the preponderance of force remains on the side of the treaty-makers; the moment the balance shifts to the 'treaty-breakers', it is likely to become a dead letter. At best, a treaty imposed by force may have some slight effect on the course of events in the twilight period between the first state and the second. Treaties of guarantee, entered into freely by the partners in the victorious coalition, seem in hardly a better case. Such treaties, in the words of Stanley's notorious explanation 'would, no doubt, give the right to make war, but . . . would not necessarily impose the obligation'. What, it may be asked, can be the value of an engagement so interpreted? Surely several powers could hardly confer on themselves jointly and separately, the *right* to make war on a third party. That right, it would appear, must be inalienable unless specifically renounced. Yet even disregarding Stanley's interpretation, the fate of the Triple Treaty shows all too clearly the variety of arguments by which signatories, at different times, justified their determination not to act under the guarantee unless it suited the purpose of their national policies. And if it did suit them to go to war surely no prior treaty was needed.

In fact, it may be asked whether any *diktat* or any treaty of guarantee ever induced any power to do that which it would not in any case have done, let alone act in a manner considered contrary to the national interest. Where the first type of treaty has been observed by the vanquished party, the sanction, invariably, has been force or the threat of force. Nor would it be easy to find instances when a treaty of this kind has effectively bound the victors to one-another. As regards treaties of guarantee, these almost invariably have been 'honoured' when it suited the guarantors for their own purposes to do so, not otherwise. These conclusions, difficult to escape on the ground of general historical experience, are amply confirmed by the fate of the two treaties which formed the basis of the Crimean settlement.

III

The Crimean coalition was the outcome of a common struggle against Russia, waged avowedly in defence of the Ottoman Empire. The Crimean system constructed by Buol and Palmerston was an attempt to provide for that defence in the future by perpetuating the anti-Russian grouping. Its success, therefore, depended on a common policy of the partners in the 'Eastern question' and on their continued willingness to defend the integrity of Turkey. In fact, events soon showed that neither of these assumptions could be relied on with confidence. Almost from the start, the policy of France diverged significantly from that of her partners of 15 April. At least down to 1863, Napoleon showed himself not unwilling to weaken the Palmerstonian system for Russia's benefit. Less consistently, the Austrian government also showed its readiness to jettison part of the Crimean system. The determination to defend the settlement grew weaker even in England. After the Schleswig-Holstein crisis, the general British policy became one of abstention. Military action would be contemplated only in defence of Belgian independence and of Turkish control of the Straits. Palmerston, the inspirer of the anti-Russian coalition, died in 1865. Stanley, who eventually took his place, was a convinced 'isolationist'. In the circumstances, it may seem surprising that the Crimean system survived the crisis of 1866. Four factors account for its survival. The confidential sounding in London in May revealed to the Russian government that there was no hope of British acquiescence in any major change. The settlements first of the Roumanian and then of the German question offered Russia no opportunity to lay her demands before a European congress. In the autumn, Gorchakov's plan of unilateral action was abandoned because the Russian government, in the last resort, still felt too weak to face international complications. Finally, Beust's soundings in Paris early in 1867 revealed that Napoleon, in the interest of good relations with England, continued to stand by the settlement of 1856. There clearly remained in spite of everything sufficient sanction behind the Crimean system.

By 1870, the situation had changed. It was now assumed with some justification that Gladstone's government would be unwilling to take up arms in defence of the Treaty of Paris. It became clear, moreover, after the outbreak of the Franco-Prussian war, that France would be unable to do so. On the other hand, the prestige of Prussia and Bismarck, 'revisionist' as far as the settlement of 1856 was concerned, stood higher than ever before. If, during 1866, the forces defending the *status quo* had still been sufficient to hold Russian revisionism in check, this was no longer the case in the crisis of 1870.

Russia's determination to modify the Treaty of Paris never varied for one moment. At any time between 1856 and 1870 she was ready to seize with alacrity any favourable opportunity which might offer for regaining her sovereignty in the Black Sea. If the opportunity proved slow in coming, the general situation yet evolved in a direction increasingly favourable to the accomplishment of Russian designs. The odds, still considered too great in 1866, were regarded as promising four years later. Even so, the Tsar and Gorchakov, in counting on the 'pacifism' of Gladstone and his cabinet, very nearly miscalculated. British opinion proved more bellicose than had been (or could reasonably have been) foreseen. On the other hand, the Turkish government showed an unexpected moderation. Had the Porte refused to agree to the change, no settlement in the sense desired by Russia would have been possible. Once

Turkey indicated a willingness to acquiesce in a revision of the treaty, the other powers were likely to follow suit. The readiness of the Sultan to fall in with Russian wishes was, perhaps, the element which finally turned the scales against the defenders of the Crimean system.

IV

The fate of the Crimean system would seem to confirm the thesis that no peace treaty, guarantee, protocol or solemn affirmation can, in the long run, protect stipulations, arrangements or groupings which have ceased to correspond to international realities. It might, therefore, be asked whether, apart from recording a given situation or arrangement, they serve any useful purpose. Would it, for example, have made any significant difference to the subsequent course of events if the Black Sea had never been neutralized or if the Triple Treaty had never seen the light of day? Apart from the temporary weakening of Russia caused by the war itself, did the Crimean settlement and the political system it sought to perpetuate have any lasting effect? Did it prolong by a single day the life of the Ottoman Empire or exercise, in any important respect, a restraining influence on Russia? Did it not, on the contrary, from an early moment, become a near-anachronism and a source of embarrassment to the powers committed to its defence?

The creation of the Crimean system ranks high among the achievements of Palmerstonian diplomacy. It was England's 'reward' for the sacrifices of the Crimean War. To some extent, therefore, the statesmanship of Palmerston's later years must be judged by the subsequent fate of his system. The conclusion seems clear: the arrangements of 1856 — though perhaps the best attainable in the circumstances — did not stand the test of time. Palmerston himself hardly considered they would. The Crimean system was built on sand: it offered no prospect whatever of a lasting solution of the 'Eastern question'.

Index

PRINTED IN GREAT BRITAIN BY ROBERT MACLEHOSE AND CO. LTD
THE UNIVERSITY PRESS, GLASGOW